HELP, I'M DYING OF THIRST

A DAILY DRINK FROM THE WELL

BY: LAURA LEA SISNEY

PRESS

All poetry in this book is credited to William Cowper, (pronounced Cooper). Born: November 15, 1731 in Hertfordshire, England. Died: April 25, 1800 in East Dereham, Norfolk, England. Cowper's father was chaplain to King George II. He lived near Olney, Buckinghamshire, the namesake town of the Olney Hymns, which he co-wrote with John Newton, author of Amazing Grace. It is because his poetry touched my heart that I am including it in this book. I pray that it will touch your heart also.

www.xulonpress.com

To Tom,
With Love & Blessings!

Laura

John 4:14

INTRODUCTION

John 7:37-38 "On the last and greatest day of the Feast, Jesus stood and said in a loud voice, 'If anyone is thirsty, let him come to me and drink. Whoever believes in me as the Scripture has said, streams of living water will flow from within him.'"

There are so many times when we feel a gnawing in our spirits for something that will make us happy; for anything that will satisfy our longing; for that one thing that will give us peace and contentment. We look for fulfillment in many ways. The truth is there is nothing that will satisfy that emptiness within us except drinking from the well of Living Water: The well that never runs dry. Jesus is that Living Water.

We all have problems in this world; but there is good news. God is on His throne and He has the answer for our every need. There is no mountain so tall that we cannot climb, there is no river so wide that we cannot cross; there is absolutely nothing that we cannot handle with Jesus by our side. It is in His Word that we find the answers for all of our needs to be victorious in this world. Do you have a problem? Jesus is the answer.

My purpose for writing these devotionals is to encourage those reading them; and that through them God's word would give hope to those who have no hope: To give strength to those who are weak in spirit: To give peace to those who long for peace: To comfort those in despair, and Love to those who feel unloved. My prayer is that through God's Spirit, The Living Water, every need will be met. It is from His well that our thirst is quenched.

DEDICATIONS

꧁꧂

This book is dedicated to all of those who have been a part of my life. Each one of you has impacted my life in one way or another. I want to thank you for the lessons that each one of you have taught me on this journey of life.

Thanks to all of the 'Women at the Well' girls who have inspired me in so many ways.

Thanks to Kelly Jones for giving me computer help when I needed it.

Thanks to Brenda Black for giving me literary advice.

Thanks to Ginni Hawley for allowing me to quote her.

Thanks to Tahlia, my eight year old granddaughter who has been my biggest encourager during the entire time I have been writing this book.

An extra special thanks to Bill, my wonderful husband, who has been so patient with me while I was hidden away for hours reading and writing.

Thanks to Beth Moore (whom I have never met) for teaching me 5 very influential points for my life:

1. GOD IS WHO HE SAYS HE IS
2. GOD WILL DO WHAT HE SAYS HE WILL DO
3. I AM WHO GOD SAYS I AM
4. I CAN DO ALL THINGS THROUGH CHRIST
5. HIS WORD IS ALIVE AND ACTIVE IN ME

Most of all I want to thank and praise my Lord for giving me everything that I needed to write this book. I could never have done this in my own power and strength. I thank Him for giving me so many encouragers to continue writing these devotionals and to have them published.

GOD BLESS YOU ALL.

WATER FOR THE WEEKEND

My Soul Thirsteth for God
by William Cowper

I thirst, but not as once I did,
The vain delights of earth to share;
Thy wounds, Emmanuel, all forbid
That I should seek my pleasures there.

It was the sight of Thy dear cross
First weaned my soul from earthly things;
And taught me to esteem as dross
The mirth of fools and pomp of kings.

I want that grace that springs from Thee,
That quickens all things where it flows,
And makes a wretched thorn like me
Bloom as the myrtle, or the rose.

Dear fountain of delight unknown!
No longer sink below the brim;
But overflow, and pour me down
A living and life-giving stream!

For sure of all the plants that share
The notice of thy Father's eye,
None proves less grateful to His care,
Or yields him meaner fruit than I.

January 3

RESOLUTIONS

Psalms 147:10-11 His pleasure is not in the strength of the horse, nor his delight in the legs of a man; the Lord delights in those who fear him, who put their hope in his unfailing love.

I was watching a video of a most amazing young man. He is an accomplished pianist and trumpet player. He plays in the marching band at Louisville University. He is different than most young men; he was born without eyes, and with a tightening of the joints that prevented his limbs from ever straightening. But none of this has slowed him down from using the gifts that God gave him. When asked how he would describe his disabilities, he replied; "Not dis-abilities at all, more abilities. God made me blind and unable to walk—big deal, He gave me the musical gifts I have and the great opportunity to meet new people."

He told the story of how his father had helped him attain his goals. His father spoke of how pleased he was with the relation-ship that they had developed over the years since his birth. This young man did not see his affliction as a deterrent to the gifts and abilities God gave him. He pursued the gifts with eagerness and determination to be the person that God created him to be. Through that determination and the help of his earthly and Spiritual father, he was able to accomplish great things. He resolved to be all that God wanted him to be. This young man has put his hope in God's unfailing love.

Hearing the story of this young man, makes me ashamed of how I take for granted all of the wonderful gifts and blessings that my Heavenly father has given me. As we think about the resolutions for this New Year, let's resolve to use the gifts and the abilities that God has given us. Let's resolve to develop that relationship with our Heavenly Father that comes from seeking Him and His help. He wants to use us to make a difference in the world around us, and we cannot do it without His help. Let's put our hope in God's unfailing love.

January 4

HEARING THE BRIDEGROOM'S VOICE

John 3:29 The bride belongs to the bridegroom. The friend who attends the bridegroom waits and listens for him, and is full of joy when he hears the bridegroom's voice. That joy is mine, and it is now complete.

Do you remember when you were a new bride? Wasn't it exciting each day when you heard the sound of your husband's voice when he arrived home. You were eager to see him and to spend time with him. You wanted to share what had gone on that day in both of your lives. You tried to please him in every way just because you loved him. He was your best friend and you spent many hours planning your life together.

That's the kind of relationship that Jesus wants to have with us. Are you listening for the bridegroom's voice? The only way we can hear His voice, is if we are spending time communicating with Him in prayer and in His Word. It is impossible to develop a relationship with someone if we don't spend time in their presence. We should be excited about developing a relationship with the Lord. If we aren't, we must ask ourselves why, who, and what is keeping us from listening for His voice. Sometimes we take our relationships for granted, even those with our husbands. We go about our own way and neglect precious time with them. If that goes on for very long, it is difficult to renew that closeness that we once had with them. We must return to the excitement that we felt when our love was new. *Deuteronomy 6:5 Love the Lord your God with all your heart and with all your soul and with all your strength.* That's the kind of love that God wants us to experience.

Listen for His voice, He wants to come in and fellowship with you. *Revelation 3:20 Here I am! I stand at the door and knock. If anyone hears my voice and opens the door, I will come in and eat with him and he with me.* Even when we are Christians, we lock Him out at times. Let's eagerly open the door and let Him in. He is our bridegroom.

January 5

LIVING THE GOOD LIFE IN CHRIST

Matthew 19:16-17Now a man came up to Jesus and asked, "Teacher, what good thing must I do to get eternal life?" "Why do you ask me about what is good?" Jesus replied. "There is only One who is good. If you want to enter life, obey the commandments."

Have you ever heard someone say, "I try to live a good life"? When I hear a person make that statement, it always raises a flag in my mind, that says they are most likely not a Christian. There is only one way we can live a good life, and that is by the grace of God. We can never do enough to earn our salvation; that was provided to us through the blood of Jesus.

There are those who think because they do good things, that they will be able to enter heavens gates. But our eternal destination does not depend on what we do or think. It is only the Grace of God and our relationship with Jesus that counts. It is our choice to accept Him and follow Him that gives us entrance into Heaven. He provided us eternal life on The Cross.

Some believe that because they go to church and they are good people, they are Christians. But as I heard a speaker once say, "Going to church doesn't make you a Christian any more than standing in a garage makes you a car."

Some call themselves Christians because they believe God exists. We must not only believe that God exists (even Satan admits that); we must receive Jesus as our personal Savior. We must confess our sins and invite Him to come in to our hearts. He has paid the price on The Cross for our sins and so by His Grace we are saved. Our goodness lies only in Christ.

Do you consider yourself a good person? You might be according to the world's standards. But the truth is, there is only one way to claim the goodness of God and that is through the blood of Jesus. If you have not accepted Jesus as your personal Savior, don't let another day go by without asking His forgiveness for your sins. *For all have sinned and fall short of the glory of God. Romans 3:23 —* Acknowledge Him, confess your sin, believe and receive what He has for you. *The wages of sin is death; but the gift of God is eternal life through Jesus Christ, Our Lord. Romans 6:23*

January 6

GRACE REVEALED

1 Corinthians 2:9-10 However, as it is written: "No eye has seen, no ear has heard, no mind has conceived what God has prepared for those who love him" —but God has revealed it to us by his Spirit. The Spirit searches all things, even the deep things of God.

I have been a Christian for 28 years, but it has only been in the past few years that I have come to realize just how powerful the Holy Spirit is. It has been the most amazing and thrilling ride of my life. I have no doubt that I was truly saved when I came to Christ in 1982, but I had no idea what surrendering my all to the Lord was all about until a few short years ago. It was at a women's conference that I heard God speaking loud and clear, that I must surrender everything to Him. Until that time, I struggled in my quest for the answer to "What does God have for me to do"? I loved the Lord and had a desire to serve Him, but I wonder today if I truly was IN LOVE with Him. I thought I was, and if anyone would have asked me I would have said yes, however when I chose to surrender my all to Him, I suddenly experienced what the above passage of scripture is saying. My mind could not conceive what God had prepared for me. Today I can honestly say I not only love the Lord, I am IN LOVE with Him.

God has led me into a ministry that I would have thought was the last thing He would have called me to; that of being an encourager and a mentor to young Christian women. I had not raised my children in church on a regular basis. How could I possibly have anything to offer young mothers? It is because of my weakness that God has given me the strength, the desire, and the determination to follow Him in this amazing journey. He has given me a love for these young women that could only come from Him. He has opened doors that I would have never thought possible. Hear me when I say I could never do anything on my own—but because of God's amazing grace, I can do all things through Him.

Are you struggling with what God has for you to do, as I was? Perhaps like me, you hesitate on surrendering your all to Jesus. I ask myself why it took me so long to trust Him completely. Looking back on it, I believe that I was afraid to let Him have the controls, because I feared what He might require of me. It saddens me to think that I wasted so much time, when I could have been experiencing much sooner, the joy that He has given me the past few years. Don't let Satan rob you of the joy that God has for you. Let go of whatever it is that you are afraid to surrender to God. He has something wonderful prepared for you. I urge you to let Him have His way in your life. The grace of God far exceeds anything we can possibly imagine.

January 7

GIVING IN TO TEMPTATION

When tempted, no one should say "God is tempting me." For God cannot be tempted by evil, nor does he tempt anyone; but each one is tempted when, by his own evil desire, he is dragged away and enticed. Then, after desire has conceived, it gives birth to sin; and sin when it is full-grown, gives birth to death. James 1:13-15

How many times have we been tempted to do things that we know are contrary to God's word? I think we can all say that at one time or another we have faced temptations. Jesus himself was tempted by the devil. *Luke 4:1-2 Jesus, full of the Holy Spirit, returned from the Jordan and was led by the Spirit in the desert, where for forty days he was tempted by the devil.* It is not the temptation that is sin, it is what we do when tempted that matters. We must never give in to temptation. We must go to the Lord in prayer. *Mark 14:38 Watch and pray so that you will not fall into temptation. The spirit is willing, but the body is weak.* And Luke *22:40 On reaching the place, he said to them, "Pray that you will not fall into temptation."*

Always be on the alert for temptation. I can guarantee you that if you haven't already faced temptations, at some point in your life you will. Satan is always more than willing to poison our minds through temptation. If we are not alert and willing to submit the temptations to the Lord in prayer, we will not overcome it.

Giving in to temptation comes from our evil desires, it leads to destruction. We have a choice to make. Do we give in to those desires or do we rebuke Satan and in the name of Jesus and let God fight the battle for us. *1 Corinthians 10:13 No temptation has seized you except what is common to man. And God is faithful; he will not let you be tempted beyond what you can bear. But when you are tempted, he will also provide a way out so that you can stand up under it.*

If you are being tempted, don't think you are alone. All of us face temptations. Run to Jesus and tell Him all about it; He knows anyway, but He can't help you through it, if you don't open the door and let him in.

January 8-9

WATER FOR THE WEEKEND

Ephraim Repenting
by William Cowper

My God, till I received Thy stroke,
How like a beast was I!
So unaccustom'd to the yoke,
So backward to comply.

With grief my just reproach I hear;
Shame fills me at the thought,
How frequent my rebellions were,
What wickedness I wrought.

Thy merciful restraint I scorn'd,
And left the pleasant road;
Yet turn me, and I shall be turn'd;
Thou art the Lord my God.

"Is Ephraim banish'd from my thoughts,
Or vile in my esteem?
No," saith the Lord, "with all his faults,
I still remember him.

"Is he a dear and pleasant child?
Yes, dear and pleasant still;
Though sin his foolish heart beguiled,
And he withstood my will.

"My sharp rebuke has laid him low,
He seeks my face again;
My pity kindles at his woe,
He shall not seek in vain."

January 10

A HEAVENLY CROWN

1 Corinthians 9:25 Everyone who competes in the games goes into strict training, they do it to get a crown that will not last; but we do it to get a crown that will last forever.

Irena Sendler was a woman who spent her life helping others. She was responsible for saving 2,500 Jewish children by smuggling them out of the Warsaw Ghetto providing them false documents, and sheltering them in individual and group children's homes outside the Ghetto: A feat that she knew was extremely dangerous, so dangerous, that if caught would certainly have resulted in her life in prison or her death. In 1943 she was arrested by the Gestapo, severely tortured, and sentenced to death. Żegota (the counsel to aid Jews) saved her by bribing German guards on the way to her execution. She was left in the woods, unconscious and with broken arms and legs. She was listed on public bulletin boards as among those executed. For the remainder of the war, she lived in hiding, but continued her work for the Jewish children.

Although Irena was nominated for the coveted Nobel Peace Prize in 2007, she didn't get it. I was appalled, when I heard this news. I wondered how on earth she could have lost this award to something that didn't even compare to the wonderful things that she had done. And then I reasoned that she was the kind of woman who did not concern herself with awards on this earth. She was concerned about her fellowman, and how she could help them survive in a cruel world full of people that treated others like animals. She did not do it for recognition; she did it because she cared. She did it because God had given her a mission and a purpose, and she obeyed.

Irena Sendler may not have received an award here on this earth, but will most certainly receive her reward in heaven. What about us? Are we concerned about receiving recognition and glory for the things we have done here on earth, or are we looking for our reward in Heaven? *He regarded disgrace for the sake of Christ as a greater value than the treasures of Egypt, because he was looking ahead to his reward. Hebrews 11:26*

January 11

CIRCUMSTANTIAL CHANGES

Hebrews 13:8 Jesus Christ is the same yesterday and today and forever.

It seems like things in our lives are always changing. Sometimes it is difficult to make plans because of the things that we can't foresee. We get married and have plans to work, save money, and buy a house before we start a family; then that unexpected baby comes along and changes our plans. We buy houses and expect to live there for a long period of time; and then our plans are interrupted because of a change in our job situation. We save money for the future; then unexpected things happen that strip us of our savings. We plan to travel when we retire; then bad health comes and our plans are changed once again. We build relationships with others, and circumstances along the way break those relationships.

There is a song that says "Praise the Lord, He never changes, I go to Him, He's always there." God is the only thing; THE ONLY ONE that never changes. We can always depend on Him. He is there through every circumstance in our lives; through every change that life takes us through. We can be joyful in every circumstance. *Be joyful always; pray continually, give thanks in all circumstances, for this is God's will for you in Christ Jesus. 1 Thessalonians 5:16-18.*

When life gets difficult and times get rough; when we go through changes that are unpleasant, and we feel there is no hope for a secure future — remember that our God is always there. Look to Him for a stable presence and a love that never changes.

January 12

REJOICE EACH DAY

Psalms 118:24 This is the day the Lord has made; let us rejoice and be glad in it.

Consider this scenario—It is 5:00 in the morning and the alarm goes off. You reluctantly open your eyes and think 'It's too early to get up, I would just like to turn over and go back to sleep, but I have all of these things that I have to do, so I might just as well drag myself out of bed and get started.' You grudgingly give in to what your whole body and brain is rebelling against.

But wait a minute—let's think about this. Instead of rebelling against meeting the day with dread—what if you chose to rejoice for waking up to a new day with thoughts like these?—My eyes are open and I can see—I have ears and I can hear—I have feet and I can walk—I have hands that can function with no problem—I have a mouth and I can speak—I have a mind and I can think. I have been blessed with so many things. I thank the Lord for a new day to enjoy the beauty of God's creation and the blessings He has given me.

Now I know that there are people who function better at night than they do in the morning, but we can make a choice about the attitude that we have toward the day that the Lord has made. Do you think it might make a huge difference if we chose to greet the day joyously because God made the day just for us? And what if we choose to awaken each morning with thanksgiving for all parts of our bodies that are functioning well? We can count our blessings each day for the things that God has given us—things that we take for granted. Let's rejoice in the blessings of each day!

January 13

DON'T HIDE IN THE DARK

Genesis 3:8-9 Then the man and his wife heard the sound of the Lord God as he was walking in the garden in the cool of the day, and they hid from the Lord God among the trees of the garden. But the Lord God called to the man, "Where are you?"

Why do we try to hide our sin?—because we know when we are doing wrong, and we don't want others to see. We may be able to hide our sin from others, but we can never hide it from God.

Just as God was calling Adam and Eve in the garden, He will call our name when we are hiding in our sin. Will we listen for His call and repent? Or will we continue hiding in the dark? It is our choice. If we want to continue in the dark, He will let us. He did not make us robots, but people who are free to choose right from wrong. If we are looking for the light, we will find it. God's word will teach us and lead us to the light. *Psalm 119:105 Your word is a lamp to my feet and a light for my path.*

I will quote a minister I once heard; he said "Light increases light and darkness increases darkness. When we get spiritual light we want more light. When we live in darkness we gravitate toward more darkness." Do you hunger for light or are you bound on living in darkness? Light comes from Jesus our Lord and Savior. Darkness comes from the evil one. *John 1:4-5 In him was life, and that life was the light of men. The light shines in the darkness, but the darkness has not understood it.* Don't hide in the darkness of your sin, turn to the light and allow Jesus to restore you. Ask Jesus to shine His light on the sin that you are trying to hide. He is calling you. Listen and respond to His call.

January 14

A BEAUTIFUL WOMAN

Ezekiel 16:14 And your fame spread among the nations on account of your beauty, because the splendor I had given you made your beauty perfect, declares the Sovereign Lord.

Women spend thousands of dollars on products to make them selves beautiful. The cosmetic industry is cashing in on the insecurities of our outward appearance. There are products that are touted to make our skin look younger, dye to cover the natural color of our hair, clothes and jewelry to adorn our bodies, exercise equipment and hours spent on it to make our bodies more beautiful, etc. The list goes on.

How many outwardly beautiful women have you seen in the entertainment field that you would care to emulate? I don't know about you, but I don't know any that I would want to look like. In most of them, their inner beauty has been so neglected that it destroys their outward beauty. We could learn a lesson from them — their beauty is truly only skin deep.

Now I am not saying that we shouldn't do our best to enhance our looks, but not at the expense of neglecting our inward beauty. Are we concentrating so much on the outward appearance, that we are ignoring our spiritual appearance? What makes us beautiful? It is not found on the outside, but on the inside. How do we develop that beauty? We develop it by pursuing a relationship with our Lord. How do we establish that relationship? We establish it by spending time in His word and by talking to Him.

Real beauty can't be seen from the outside, it comes from the Lord's spirit in us. Our inward beauty shines through when we are allowing Jesus to be our light. The fruit of His Spirit can be seen by others making us beautiful in the sight of God.

Don't be consumed by outward appearance; rather be consumed with the desire to be beautiful in God's sight. *Charm is deceptive, and beauty is fleeting; but a woman who fears the Lord is to be praised. Proverbs 31:30*

January 15-16

WATER FOR THE WEEKEND

Afflictions Sanctified
by William Cowper

Oh how I love Thy holy Word,
Thy gracious covenant, O Lord!
It guides me in the peaceful way;
I think upon it all the day.

What are the mines of shining wealth,
The strength of youth, the bloom of health!
What are all joys compared with those
Thine everlasting Word bestows!

Long unafflicted, undismay'd,
In pleasure's path secure I stray'd;
Thou mad'st me feel thy chast'ning rod,
And straight I turned unto my God.

What though it pierced my fainting heart,
I bless'd Thine hand that caused the smart:
It taught my tears awhile to flow,
But saved me from eternal woe.

Oh! hadst Thou left me unchastised,
Thy precepts I had still despised;
And still the snare in secret laid
Had my unwary feet betray'd.

I love Thee, therefore, O my God,
And breathe towards Thy dear abode;
Where, in Thy presence fully blest,
Thy chosen saints for ever rest.

January 17

BE AN EXAMPLE

John 13:15 I have set you an example that you should do as I have done for you.

Jesus had just washed the feet of His disciples. He was their Lord and Teacher, yet he had humbled himself and washed their feet. He didn't feel like He was too good to serve them. He was a servant.

Do we consider ourselves too big to serve those around us? Are we willing to serve others in whatever way we can? If Jesus was willing to serve others, how can we refuse to do the same? Are we too good, too busy, or so unconcerned that we don't take the time to help others? As Christians we should be the examples of Christ.

Christ spent His 33 years on earth teaching His truth and serving others. He is still teaching us everyday. Are we listening? Are we being the example that He wants us to be? Let's not miss the opportunity to be the example of Christ in every area of our lives, especially in the area of serving others.

January 18

BOASTING IN THE LORD

2 Corinthians 10:15-18 Neither do we go beyond our limits by boasting of work done by others. Our hope is that, as your faith continues to grow, our area of activity among you will greatly expand, so that we can preach the gospel in the regions beyond you. For we do not want to boast about work, already done in another man's territory. But, "Let him who boasts, boast in the Lord." For it is not the one who commends himself who is approved, but the one whom the Lord commends.

Sometimes we see others doing a mighty work in the Lord's service, and envy them. Some are tempted to copy their ministry, and some actually do. But God's word tells us to recognize our limits. God has called each one of us to the place where He wants us to serve. And He has called us to the job that He wants us to do.

We should never try to emulate another. There is no service bigger than another's. *We have different gifts, according to the grace given us. If a man's gift is prophesying, let him use it in prophesying to his faith. If it is serving, let him serve; if it is teaching, let him teach; if it is encouraging, let him encourage, if it is contributing to the needs of others, let him give generously; if it is leadership, let him govern diligently; if it is showing mercy, let him do it cheerfully. Romans 12:6.* There is an entire world out there that needs to be ministered to; many different people and personalities; many different areas to spread the word. Let's each find our place and our gift, so that many souls will be led to Christ.

It is because of the grace of God that we can boast in anything that we are doing to further the kingdom of God. Let us never boast of anything that does not come from God: But we can boast in the Lord for the things that he has called us to do.

January 19

A HEART PREPARED TO HEAR

John 5:39 "You diligently study the Scriptures because you think that by them you possess eternal life. These are the Scriptures that testify about me, yet you refuse to come to me to have life.

The bible is the word of God written by those who God inspired. One would think that as we read the word, we would grasp the depth of our Father's love. But alas, many tines that is not the case. There is no amount of time spent in His Word that will bring us to His saving grace, unless we allow the Holy Spirit in. It is by the Spirit that we shall hear, believe and receive the word that God is speaking to us.

I have set in churches where the Word of God is read, and yet get the feeling that the one preaching it is not filled with God's Spirit. There have been times that I wonder if the one speaking, really understands what he is reading. I believe that there is no way one can discern The Word of God without His Spirit filling them with the truth.

I can remember a time when I would try to read God's Word and it didn't make any sense at all. It was after God's Spirit revealed my need for the Savior that the scriptures meant something to me. He is still teaching me today through His Word. If we are reading the bible and expect to hear the truth of His Word, we must be led by the Spirit. We receive the Spirit when we receive Christ as our personal Savior. Then and only then will He prepare our hearts to hear from Him. Then and only then can we testify of His amazing grace. His Word will light our way. *Your word is a lamp for my feet and a light for my path. Psalms 119:105*

January 20

CASTING YOUR NET

Luke 5:1-4 One day as Jesus was standing by the Lake of Gennasaret with the people crowding around him and listening to the word of God, he saw at the water's edge two boats, left there by the fishermen, who were washing their nets. He got into one of the boats, the one belonging to Simon, and asked him to put out a little from shore. Then he sat down and taught the people from the boat. When he had finished speaking he said to Simon, "Put out into deep water, and let down the nets for a catch."

Simon and his partners, James, John and Zebedee had been fishing all night and had caught nothing: But because they listened to Jesus and obeyed what He told them to do, they caught so many fish, that they had to call upon another boat to help them bring them in. As we see further along in the scripture, Simon reveals his fear of Jesus. He was afraid because he recognized his sinfulness. He also recognized the power of this man Jesus. But Jesus said to him, "Don't be afraid, from now on you will catch men."

When we listen to the words of Jesus, and we believe and receive the power that He has given us through the Holy Spirit, we too can be fisher's of men. Let's not be afraid to do what Jesus commanded us to do. One thing that stands out to me in this passage of scripture is the fact that Jesus told them to go out into deep water. Sometimes I think we are afraid to go into those areas that might be out of our comfort zone. Let's not be afraid to cast our nets in the unfamiliar areas. We must remember that God is with us wherever we go and He will prepare the way.

January 21

A PITY PARTY

Philippians 1:21-24 For to me, to live is Christ and to die is gain. If I am to go on living in the body, this will mean fruitful labor for me. Yet what shall I choose? I do not know! I am torn between the two: I desire to depart and be with Christ, which is better by far; but it is more necessary for you that I remain in the body.

Can you identify with what Paul is saying? I sure can. There are days when I become so heavy in spirit that I want to go on to be with the Lord; times when it seems like nothing is going right, times when I think that nobody understands who I am, and worse, it seems as though they don't even care. I call that my 'pity party'. Now I understand that Paul wasn't having a 'pity party', he had good reason to feel the way he did, after all, he was in prison for his passion for the Lord. Being human however, he must have pondered the whole picture, and compared to his struggles, he realized how happy he would be when the battle was over and he would be in the presence of his Lord.

We can't let our 'pity parties' take our eyes off of what God wants us to do. Our joy is made complete in Him. Paul's purpose in life was to preach the word. There were many times, I believe, that Paul experienced discouragement and thought he would rather die than go on, but he knew that he should remain and continue his work, because he wanted others to grow in their faith. No matter how discouraged we become; when others just don't understand our purpose, we must go on pursuing the life that God has called us to.

January 22-23

WATER FOR THE WEEKEND

Dependence
By William Cowper

To keep the lamp alive,
With oil we fill the bowl;
'Tis water makes the willow thrive,
And grace that feeds the soul.

The Lord's unsparing hand
Supplies the living stream;
It is not at our own command,
But still derived from Him.

Beware of Peter's word,
Nor confidently say,
"I never will deny Thee, Lord," —
But, "Grant I never may."

Man's wisdom is to seek
His strength in God alone;
And e'en an angel would be weak,
Who trusted in his own.

Retreat beneath his wings,
And in His grace confide!
This more exalts the King of kings
Than all your works beside.

In Jesus is our store,
Grace issues from His throne;
Whoever says, "I want no more,"
Confesses he has done.

January 24

DOING THE IMPOSSIBLE

Nehemiah 6:15 -16 So the wall was completed on the twenty-fifth of Elul, in fifty-two days. When all our enemies heard about this, all the surrounding nations were afraid and lost their self-confidence, because they realized that this work had been done with the help of our God.

Wow, just look what God's people had accomplished. They had re-built the walls around Jerusalem in just fifty-two days. Do you think they could have done this without the help of God? I don't; I believe that because of one man's faith in God and his fervent prayers, God gave them all the help they needed.

And look what happened when the job was completed. Their enemies were afraid and lost their self-confidence. Notice it says self-confidence. These were people who did not put their confidence in the Lord. They were people who tried to win battles on their own steam. Their hearts were not right with God and they were trying to undermine what God was doing for the Jews. When they saw that the Jews had accomplished the unbelievable task, they realized it was because of God's help.

How about you? Has God asked you to do something that seems utterly impossible? God would never ask us to do anything and then leave us to do it alone. All we have to do is have faith, pray and allow Him to direct our way. When we try to do the impossible on our own self-confidence, we will surely fail. With God all things are possible. *Jesus looked at them and said, "With man this is impossible, but with God all things are possible. Matthew 19:26*

January 25

A SERVANT'S HEART

Mark 10:42-43 Jesus called them together and said, "You know that those who are regarded as rulers of the Gentiles lord it over them, and their high officials exercise authority over them. Not so with you. Instead whoever wants to become great among you must be your servant and whoever wants to be first must be slave to all.

James and John the sons of Zebedee had asked Jesus if they could have the position of sitting next to Him in glory. What had made them think they should be more privileged than anyone else? I believe that there are some who have up front leading roles, and see themselves as special and therefore should be recognized with special favor.

I am reminded of a wonderful woman in our church who serves the Lord in one of the most important positions there is—that of running the nursery. I doubt that she gets a lot of thanks for it. But if you asked Mary if she cared, she would tell you no. She is not doing it for the accolades of the people; she is doing it for the Lord. The ones who serve the Lord in unrecognized positions are just as important as those who serve in the limelight. Sometimes we put those who seem to have a higher calling (there is no such thing), in higher regard than others. But God does not rate us on what we do but how we do it. God says that we must be a servant to all. Those who serve others may not receive awards and recognition in this life, but they will certainly receive their reward in heaven.

January 26

LADEN WITH A LOAD

1 Peter 5:6-7 Humble yourselves, therefore, under God's mighty hand, that he may lift you up in due time. Cast all your anxiety on him because he cares for you.

Are you struggling with anxiety right now? Do you feel as if there is nowhere or no one to turn to? Do you feel like you can't go on in your present circumstances? Well stop-look-and listen as you read God's word. His word says to cast all of your worries and concerns on Him because He cares for you.

Our God isn't someone that is a figment of our imagination. He is the God who loved us so much that He came as a man called Jesus, to walk among us, He died on the cross so that we might have eternal life—He rose again and when he ascended into Heaven, He sent His Holy Spirit to live in us to give us peace and joy. Do you think after doing all of this for us that He would abandon us to hopelessness and helplessness? Never would He do that. His love and mercy far exceeds any problem or concern that you have. He wants you to humble yourself to Him and let Him lift you up in His time and in His way. Run to Jesus with all of your cares and receive the help that only He can give you. He is there for you anytime you call on His Name.

January 27

ALIVE IN CHRIST

Matthew 10:40 "Anyone who loves his father or mother more than me is not worthy of me, anyone who loves his son or daughter more than me is not worthy of me, and anyone who does not take his cross and follow me is not worthy of me. Whoever finds his life will lose it, and whoever loses his life for my sake will find it."

There was a time in my life when I would have read this scripture, and believed that it was impossible to love anyone more that my mother, father, husband and children. That was of course when I was blinded by the truth of God's Word. That was when my life evolved around 'me' and the things that were important to 'me'. I was so wrapped up in myself and my own life that I couldn't see anything else. It was when my eyes were opened and I finally saw my need for Jesus; it was when I gave my life to Him; it was when I fell in love with him, that I discovered that my love for my family and for everyone else increased. When I died to self, I found that my life truly began. I never knew what love really meant up to the point of salvation.

Only through giving up our selfish pursuit of happiness; only by dying to self and accepting Jesus as our personal Savior, will we ever find everlasting life. When we put Jesus first in our life, our life truly begins: The meaning of love becomes clear. Then we are alive in Christ. *For as in Adam all die, so in Christ all will be made alive. 1Corinthians 15:22*

January 28

BELIEVE AND ACCOMPLISH

Luke 1:45 Blessed is she who has believed that what the Lord has said to her will be accomplished.

The dialogue that Mary and Elizabeth had during the time that they were awaiting the birth of the miracle babies that they were carrying is more than revealing. We can truly see that they were women of faith: A faith so strong that they believed the impossible: Impossible through human means; but not impossible with God.

Have you ever heard God's call in your heart and thought that it could not be accomplished? Has your faith ever been tested by being called to something that you thought you were not capable of doing? The truth of the matter is, we can do nothing without God. But when he calls us to do the impossible, we can depend on the fact that He will see to it that it will be accomplished. *I can do everything through Him, who gives me strength. Philippians 4:1*

Surely if Mary and Elizabeth could have faith in their circumstances, we can have faith in what God calls us to do. When we have the kind of faith that Mary and Elizabeth had, we can know for certain that whatever God calls us to do, we cannot fail. He would never call us out and then abandon us. He is the one who will give us the strength to carry out His call on our lives.

January 29-30

WATER FOR THE WEEKEND

FOR THE POOR
by William Cowper

When Hagar found the bottle spent
And wept o'er Ishmael,
A message from the Lord was sent
To guide her to a well.

Should not Elijah's cake and cruse
Convince us at this day,
A gracious God will not refuse
Provisions by the way?

His saints and servants shall be fed,
The promise is secure;
"Bread shall be given them," as He said,
"Their water shall be sure."

Repasts far richer they shall prove,
Than all earth's dainties are;
'Tis sweet to taste a Saviour's love,
Though in the meanest fare.

To Jesus then your trouble bring,
Nor murmur at your lot;
While you are poor and He is King,
You shall not be forgot.

January 31

FAITH IN DIFFICULT CIRCUMSTANCES

Daniel 2:16 Then Daniel went in, and desired of the king that he would give him time, and that he would show the king the interpretation. KJV

Our minister was leading us in a study on Daniel. As we read the above scripture, I sat there thinking about how much faith Daniel had. Daniel did not falter in his faith at all, even though he was in a difficult place. Because King Nebuchadnezzar couldn't find anyone who could interpret a dream he had, he ordered the execution of all the wise men of Babylon which included Daniel and his friends. When Daniel heard of this, he approached the King. He didn't say he thought he could interpret it; he didn't doubt that God had the answer for him; he just asked that the king would give him some time. Then he engaged the help of his friends to pray for God's mercy in revealing the mystery to him.

Daniel had faith that God would provide all that he needed to understand precisely what the dream meant. He knew that God would hear and answer the prayers that were poured out to Him. Oh what faith. As I thought about it, I realized that I wanted that kind of faith: Faith that would never doubt; faith that would never falter; faith that knows that God is in control.

Sometimes we face situations in life that seem absolutely hopeless, and our faith falters. But God hears and answers every prayer according to His will. Since His will is perfect, why can't we expect Him to do what He says He will do? *Now faith is being sure of what we hope for and certain of what we do not see. Hebrews 11:1*

We can learn so much about what faith is in the book of Hebrews chapter 11. *And without faith it is impossible to please God, because anyone who comes to him must believe that he exists and that he rewards those who earnestly seek him. Hebrews 11:6* It seems to me that if we fix our eyes on Jesus and seek Him in all things, He will hear from us and strengthen our faith as He answers our prayers according to His will.

LOOKING UP

Hebrews 12:2 Let us fix our eyes on Jesus, the author and perfector of our faith, who for the joy set before him endured the cross, scorning its shame, and sat down at the right hand of the throne of God.

Adrian Rogers, one of my most favorite ministers, told this story—A boy was having difficulty living the Christian life. He went to his pastor who told him to go see a painting. The caretaker at the gallery took him to a large room where the painting adorned an entire wall. The young man was repulsed at what he saw. It was a painting of Christ on the cross but the perspective from which the artist painted it was off balance. It looked grotesque. The caretaker said, "Son, you need to get closer." The young man came closer. "Son, you need to get lower." The young man got lower. "No, closer and lower." Before the young man knew what was happening, he was kneeling at the foot of the cross and when he looked up, he understood the entire painting.

Isn't that what we do as Christians? When we take our eyes off of the cross of Jesus, the whole picture of who He is, and who we are in Him becomes distorted. It is not a pretty picture. We lose all perspective of how beautiful our Savior is.

When we go through those times that we can not see the real picture of Jesus, like this young man, we need to get on our knees and look up to the cross of Jesus. When we get to that surrendered position, then the picture will come into focus and we can see Christ in all of His Glory. Let's humble ourselves and bow down and look up to the CROSS OF JESUS.

February 2

HEARING GOD'S VOICE

John 10:27 My sheep listen to my voice; I know them, and they follow me.

I have a friend who is going through some difficulties in a personal relationship.

He asked me for my advice. I advised him to seek out a Christian counselor such as a minister who has qualifications in such matters and to choose one that he knows is grounded in God's word; because I believe, if they are giving advice outside of God's Word, their advice will be wrong. I also advised him to seek God's wisdom first.

He asked me how you know when God is speaking to you. The answer is in *John 10:1-4 I tell you the truth, the man who does not enter the sheep pen by the gate, but climbs in by some other way, is a thief and a robber. The man who enters by the gate is the shepherd of his sheep. The watchman opens the gate for him, and the sheep listen to his voice. He calls his own sheep by name and leads them out. When he has brought out all his own, he goes on ahead of them, and his sheep follow him because they know his voice. But they will never follow a stranger; in fact, they will run away from him because they do not recognize a stranger's voice.* So in simple terms; we must have a right relationship with God. We must look and listen for His voice. If we do not have a right relationship with our Lord, I don't believe that we can truly hear what He is saying to us. If we are not seeking His Word, we will not hear from Him. I also believe that if we don't have a right relationship with God; we will not have a right relationship with anyone else.

THE LORD IS MY SHEPHERD, I SHALL NOT WANT—Read Psalms 23 and be blessed as you allow it to speak to your heart.

February 3

TELLING THE STORY OF JESUS

2 Timothy 1:8-9 So do not be ashamed to testify about our Lord, or ashamed of me his prisoner. But join with me in suffering for the gospel the power of God, who has saved us and called us to a holy life-not because of anything we have done but because of his own purpose and grace.

As I listened while a young Christian woman was giving her testimony, I was touched by what she had to say. She told of changes that had come about in her life by our Lord and Savior. It is an awesome thing to see what God can do in one's life. In spite of the terrible things in our past that could have destroyed us, Jesus can deliver us and use it for His glory and His purpose.

It is important to share the stories of God's grace. It not only inspires those who need to hear the story: It inspires and encourages others to testify of the changes in their life through Jesus. The miracle that comes through Jesus healing power is more than we can ever fully understand. *2 Corinthians 5:17 Therefore, if anyone is in Christ, he is a new creation the old has gone, the new has come!* Only through the blood of Jesus can we be forgiven of our sins. Only through Him can we overcome past hurts. Only through Him can we forgive those who have hurt us. Only through Him can we be victorious Christians. Only through Him can we become the people that God wants us to be.

When we open ourselves up to tell of the amazing love of Jesus and what He has done in our lives, others will be blessed. If we are Christians, we have a story to tell about the grace of God. When the Pharisees told Jesus to rebuke His disciples for speaking about the Lord, Jesus said *"I tell you, if they keep quiet, the stones will cry out. Luke 19:40*

I would encourage you to tell the wonderful story of your salvation experience. Some of you may think your past is too ugly. Some of you may think your testimony wouldn't be inspiring because you don't have such a dramatic testimony. It doesn't matter what your testimony is. All sin is ugly and it's only by God's grace that we are saved. He doesn't rate our sins and neither should we. We are all victors through our Savior.

There's a song that says it all, YOUR LOVE FOR ME COULD ONLY BE WHAT HELD YOU ON THE CROSS. Let's tell the world our story—Christians are inspired and it points non-believers to The Cross.

February 4

OUR ADOPTION

Ephesians 1:4-5 For he chose us in him before the creation of the world to be holy and blameless in his sight. In love he predestined us to be adopted as his sons through Jesus Christ, in accordance with his pleasure and will.

It is difficult for us to comprehend how a mother can give her child up for adoption. Thank the Lord for every woman who has the courage to give life to their child instead of a death sentence. Our daughter-in-law is adopted. It was because of her biological mother's decision to give her life that she was adopted into a Christian home. It was there that she was taught Christian values. It was there that she found love and security that she may never have had if not for her biological mother's decision to put her child's needs before her own. She is now the wife of our son and the mother of two of our precious granddaughters. She is an intricate member of our family and we love her as if she were our own. Who knows what direction her life would have taken had it not been for her mother's decision to put her up for adoption.

There are some people born into this world who were either unwanted by their parents, or their mother was not in a position to care for them. I have heard it said that when one is adopted, they are special indeed because the adoptive parents truly wanted them. And they paid a large price for them. God paid the ultimate price for us.

As Christians we have been adopted into the family of God and He paid the ultimate price for us.

I am so thankful that I am a part of the family of God. I shudder to think what my life may have been like if it weren't for the grace of God. When we were adopted into His family through the blood of Jesus, the entire direction of our lives was changed. He has given us eternal life; he has given us freedom from sin and shame. He has made a way for us to live abundant lives. We have a choice as to whether of not we want to be adopted into God's family. Why would one choose to be orphans in this world of sin and strife when they could be a child of the King who supplies all of our needs? What a shame that there are those who will never know the security of His love because they have refused to be His adopted child.

February 5-6

WATER FOR THE WEEKEND

EXHORTATION TO PRAYER
by William Cowper

What various hindrances we meet
In coming to a mercy seat!
Yet who that knows the worth of prayer,
But wishes to be often there?

Prayer makes the darken'd cloud withdraw,
Prayer climbs the ladder Jacob saw,
Gives exercise to faith and love,
Brings every blessing from above.

Restraining prayer, we cease to fight;
Prayer makes the Christian's armour bright;
And Satan trembles when he sees
The weakest saint upon his knees.

While Moses stood with arms spread wide,
Success was found on Israel's side;
But when through weariness they failed,
That moment Amalek prevailed.

Have you no words? Ah, think again,
Words flow apace when you complain,
And fill your fellow-creature's ear
With the sad tale of all your care.

Were half the breath thus vainly spent
To heaven in supplication sent,
Your cheerful song would more often be,
"Hear what the Lord has done for me."

February 7

SLOW LEARNER

Numbers 24:15-16 Then he uttered his oracle: "The oracle of Balaam son of Beor, the oracle of one whose eye sees clearly, the oracle of one who hears the words of God, who has knowledge from the Most High, who sees a vision from the Almighty, who falls prostrate, and whose eyes are opened.

Three times Balak's men approached Balaam and asked him to curse the Israelites, and every time he would tell them to stay the night. I find it interesting that scripture each time says that God approached Balaam; it didn't say that Balaam sought His council. God allowed Balaam to go with them but to say only what He told him to say. It also says that God was angry. Why wouldn't He be? He had told Balaam the same thing every time he met with him. He must have been weary of the tenacity of Balaam. Could it be that Balaam was hoping each time that there would be a loop hole that would allow him to collect the reward that Balak offered him? Balaam finally opened his eyes to see the truth. I would say he was a mighty slow learner, wouldn't you?

How many times are we tempted to do something that we already know is wrong, but we keep trying to wiggle our way around it to satisfy our own desires? It is so easy to see the mistakes of those we read about in the bible, but oh so difficult to see our own faults. We too are mighty slow learners. Why can't we just take God at His Word the first time He tells us something? Why do we procrastinate hoping God will change His mind?

February 8

OVERCOMING THE WORLD

1 John 5:5 Who is it that overcomes the world? Only he that believes that Jesus is the Son of God.

I have been reading one of Barbara Johnson's books: In it she tells how she lost two of her sons in death, and how she suffered through another son's confession of being gay. I have a Christian sister that has three sons that had fallen into drugs. Two of them are still battling their addictions and one of the two is gay. Another of my Christian sisters has a son in prison because of drugs. And another mother has a son who is in prison for life for murder. We hear testimonies from those who have been raised by parents of drug addicts, and abusers. The stories just go on and on. We have all had heartaches in our lives in one way or another. Even though some of them are worse than others, they are all heartbreaking and hurtful to those going through them.

It seems impossible that anyone could find peace in the midst of these trials. If we were of the world, that would be true, but because of Jesus Christ, we have overcome the world. Satan would love for us to succumb to our heartaches and keep us from receiving the peace that God offers us through the blood of Jesus, but praise God, He is all powerful and Satan cannot win over Him. *You dear children are from God and have overcome them, because the one who is in you is greater than the one who is in the world. 1 John 4:4.* What an amazing Father we have who can give us the peace that passes all understanding (Philippians 4:7) *You will keep in perfect peace him whose mind is steadfast, because he trusts in you. Isaiah 26:3.* When we are children of God we have already overcome the world.

47

February 9

PRAISING GOD IN AFFLICTIONS
AND DISCIPLINE

1 Thessalonians 4:18 Give thanks in all circumstances, for this is God's will for you in Christ Jesus.

How can we praise God through afflictions and discipline? We won't unless we are His children and understand that we <u>will</u> have them in our lives and why? *Acts 20:23 I only know that in every city the Holy Spirit warns me that prison and hardships are facing me.* Paul understood and was prepared for it. There are many times in all of our lives that we have troubles, through no fault of our own. God allows them for a reason. Through them all He is teaching us in one way or another. It is for our benefit that He allows them. *Romans 5:3 Not only so, but we also rejoice in our sufferings, because we know that suffering produces perseverance; perseverance, character; and character, hope.*

There are times when we are afflicted because of disobedience. Sometimes we wander away from the path that God wants us to walk and often times it results in sin. And God may afflict us in one way or another to bring us back. God disciplines those He loves. *And you have forgotten that word of encouragement that addresses you as sons: "My son, do not make light of the Lord's discipline, and do not lose heart when he rebukes you, because the Lord disciplines those he loves, and he punishes everyone he accepts as a son." Hebrews 12:5-6*

I once was afflicted after I had wandered from the path of God. Looking back on it I see that it was the most wonderful thing that could have happened to me. For it provided me the time I needed with my Lord. I was brought back into a right relationship with Him. When we see the benefits that we attain from afflictions, then we can understand why God allows them in our lives. He punishes us because He loves us. We truly can praise God in all circumstances.

February 10

PRAYING IN TRUST AND FAITH

Jude 20 But you, dear friends build yourselves up in your most holy faith and pray in the Holy Spirit.

I have heard it said that if you pray with disbelief, you might just as well not pray at all. We must pray with faith that God hears and answers our prayers. He always answers them in His time and in His way. He might not answer them the way we want Him to, but He will answer. He never says maybe, He answers with a yes, no, or wait.

Matthew 26:39 Going a little farther, he fell with his face to the ground and prayed, "My Father, if it is possible, may this cup be taken from me. Yet not as I will, but as you will." Jesus knew what was going to happen to Him and He still prayed for His Father's will. When we pray we must always pray according to God's will. Can you put your trust in Him? Can you believe that God's will is best? Will you be satisfied with the way God answers your prayer? I can't see the future, and I certainly don't want to have my will over the one that holds the future. We may be praying for something that God knows will not be in our best interest.

My mother prayed for her children's salvation for 91 years before she saw her prayers answered. She never gave up; she had faith that God heard her prayers, and would answer them. *I prayed for this child, and the Lord has granted me what I asked of him. 1 Samuel 1:27.* Hannah had prayed for years for a child and because of her faith, he answered her prayer and gave her the child that she had prayed for.

We can trust God because He knows what's best for us. We can have faith because we have seen over and over again how He has been faithful to those who put their faith and trust in Him. So let's start praying with the assurance that God hears our prayers and will answer them in His time and in His way and of course according to His will.

49

February 11

PUT A SONG IN YOUR HEART

Psalm 69:30 I will praise God's name in song and glorify him with thanksgiving.

I don't remember for sure how old I was when my dad met the Lord, somewhere between 12 and 14, but I will never forget the night. It was, as they say, the proverbial red letter day. Mother had prayed for my dad's salvation since the day they married. My dad was one of those people that I'm sure others thought would never come to know the Lord. He would drive mother to church but he would not be moved by the Spirit; until one very special night. He had set in many services listening to the preachers sermons, but it was through a song one particular night that the Spirit of The Lord spoke to Him in a clear voice; the song was 'What Would You Give In Exchange For Your Soul?' The young man who sang it was a seminary student. He had a special place in my dad's heart from that moment on. Daddy had heard the same message being preached many times, but it was through the song being sung that his heart was stirred and he finally realized that he needed the Savior.

There are many times when God uses music to stir one's heart. I, like my dad, am moved by music. When God's word is set to music, there is something special about it. *Psalm 40:3 He put a new song in my mouth, a hymn of praise to our God. Many will see and fear and put their trust in the Lord.* The song that stirred my dad's heart that night was not a praise song; it was a song that asked a question that resonated in his heart. But after that night my dad sang a new song, a praise song that came from the heart. *Psalm 96:1-2 Sing to the Lord a new song; sing to the Lord, all the earth. Sing to the Lord, praise his name, proclaim his salvation day after day.* There is just nothing like singing the praises of God.

February 12-13

WATER FOR THE WEEKEND

I WILL PRAISE THE LORD AT ALL TIMES
by William Cowper

Winter has a joy for me,
While the Saviour's charms I read,
Lowly, meek, from blemish free,
In the snowdrop's pensive head.

Spring returns, and brings along
Life-invigorating suns:
Hark! The turtle's plaintive song
Seems to speak His dying groans!

Summer has a thousand charms,
All expressive of His worth;
'Tis His sun that lights and warms,
His the air the cools the earth.

What! has autumn left to say
Nothing of a Saviour's grace?
Yes, the beams of milder day
Tell me of his smiling face.

Light appears with early dawn,
While the sun makes haste to rise;
See His bleeding beauties drawn
On the blushes of the skies.

Evening with a silent pace,
Slowly moving in the west,
Shews an emblem of His grace,
Points to an eternal rest.

February 14

LOVING IN ACTION

"A new commandment I give you; Love one another. As I have loved you, so you must love one another. By this all men will know that you are my disciples, if you love one another." John 13:34-35

God has commanded us to love one another. Jesus set an example to show how to love one another——unconditionally. If we show that kind of love toward our brothers and sisters, people will be able to see that there is something different about us. When we came to Christ we made a choice to accept Him as our personal Savior. We made a choice to love Him and to serve Him.

Love is an action word. We can't just say that we love another and then not put that love in action, I don't think people would believe us if we saw a sister or a brother in need and did not offer to help them out.

Agape love is something that comes directly from the heart of God. Any other kind of love is a selfish love—a love that expects something in return. Agape love can only be displayed by those who know Christ. *This is how we know what love is; Jesus Christ laid down his life for us. And we ought to lay down our lives for our brothers. 1John 3:16*

As we celebrate Valentine's Day, let's stop and appreciate those we love and show them how much we love them through our actions—not just with our mouth.

February 15

THE POWER OF GOD'S WORD

Psalms 119:130 The unfolding of your words gives light; it gives understanding to the simple.

I was baptized in August of 1983. The night before that special occasion I wrestled with Satan. He tried to tell me that I wasn't worthy of being baptized. I lay in bed and wept and prayed. The Lord spoke to me by giving me the scripture *Psalm 119:105 Your word is a lamp to my feet and a light for my path.* I knew that He wanted me to open His Word. I got out of bed and obeyed His bidding. As I looked to the scriptures I was led to Psalm 116. The entire passage was illuminated in my heart but the verse that confirmed what God wanted me to do was *Psalm 116: 14 I will fulfill my vows to the Lord in the presence of all his people.* I suddenly knew that I was worthy to be baptized into the family of God because of the price Jesus paid for me. I felt like a ton of bricks had been lifted from me. Up to that point, I had been ready to back out of my baptism. God spoke to me so clearly that there was absolutely no way I could have doubted His desire for me to be baptized.

Our God is so gracious and so faithful. He will not allow one of His children to be oppressed by the lies of Satan when we cry out to Him in our distress. He hears our cry for help and He delivers us out of our troubles. *Psalm 18:6 In my distress I called to the Lord; I cried to my God for help. From his temple he heard my voice; my cry came before him, into his ears.* The power of God's word is totally amazing. It covers everything and anything that might concern us. We don't have to figure it out ourselves, God will show us the way if we let Him.

February 16

THE WEALTH OF THE LORD

1 Timothy 6:17-19 Command those who are rich in the present world not to be arrogant nor to put their hope in wealth, which is so uncertain, but to put their hope in God, who richly provides us with everything for our enjoyment. Command them to do good, to be rich in good deeds, and to be generous and willing to share. In this way they will lay up treasure for themselves as a firm foundation for the coming age, so that they may take hold of the life that is truly life.

Are you blessed with an abundant wealth? Is it more important to you than serving the Lord? Do you put more thought into trying to acquire more than you do in thoughts of what God has for you? Do you spend more time worshipping your things than you do worshipping God? Are you unwilling to share your wealth with others? If you can answer yes to any of these questions, you need to rethink your priorities.

This is not our eternal home. Nothing in this world should be as important as our relationship with our Heavenly Father. *But store up for you selves treasures in heaven, where moth and rust do not destroy, and where thieves do not break in and steal. For where your treasure is, there your heart will be also. Matthew 6:20-21.* Worldly wealth does not bring peace, worldly wealth does not bring happiness, and worldly wealth does not bring eternal security. Only our relationship to our Lord can bring all of the things that are essential to our spiritual life. Worldly wealth can be taken away from us at any time but the wealth that our Savior offers us is for eternity.

Let's praise the Lord for His provisions. You may not be rich as the world sees it but as children of God you are rich in the heavenly realm. True wealth comes from our relationship with the Lord. Let's use every gift that He has given us according to His will.

February 17

IMPRESSIONS

One of the definition's of <u>impress</u> according to Webster's dictionary is—a: to produce a vivid impression of b: to affect especially forcibly or deeply: gain the admiration or interest of— her honesty *impressed* us.

There was a time in my life when I was really impressed by people of <u>wealth,</u> <u>fame,</u> <u>position,</u> <u>power</u> and <u>education.</u> I thought that any or all of these things would be what a person would need to be happy. I admired people who had them and I felt inferior to them. I thought that these were the successful people in life. Today I know different and am now impressed with people entirely for a different reason. I now am impressed by those who know the Lord and are showing that love by their fruits. Why—because I know that success is knowing Jesus and following His desire for us.

<u>Wealth</u> does not bring happiness-*Matthew 10:20 At this the man's face fell. He went away sad, because he had great wealth.*

<u>Fame</u> may last for a while but not for eternity. Our identity should be in Christ. *Colossians 1:27 To them God has chosen to make known among the Gentiles the glorious riches of this mystery, which is Christ in you, the hope of glory.*

<u>Position and power </u>in this world can be taken away quickly. *Daniel 2:21a He changes times and seasons; he sets up kings and deposes them.*

<u>Education</u> does not give us Godly wisdom. *1 Corinthians 1:30 It is because of him that you are in Christ Jesus, who has become for us wisdom from God-that is, our righteousness, holiness and redemption.*

We are all impressionable. Let's pray that we are not being impressed by the wrong people and the wrong things. There is danger in it. The things in this world are all fleeting but the things of God are eternal.

February 18

WHAT IS YOUR WORTH

John 3:16 For God so loved the world that he gave his one and only Son, that whosoever believes in him shall not perish but have eternal life.

Do you feel worthless? What do you really believe your life is worth? According to God, because of His love for us, we are worth the death of His Son. What an awesome thought. We have a Savior who was willing to die on the cross for us; for you and for me. All God asks of us is to accept the gift of His Son. Worthy is the lamb that was slain; Slain for the entire world. And through the price that he paid for our sins we have been made worthy of calling ourselves children of God.

As I have been reading the gospels account of our Saviors crucifixion, I am more humbled each day by the truth of it all. *But God demonstrates his own love for us in this: While we were still sinners, Christ died for us. Romans 5:8* Yes, while we were still sinners, Jesus became the scapegoat for our sins. It is more than we can ever comprehend. How could anyone love a sinner so much that they would lay down their life for them? Only Jesus, the Lamb of God, would do such a thing. Only because of Him are we worthy. So when you start feeling worthless, remember the Cross.

February 19-20

WATER FOR THE WEEKEND

JEHOVAH-JIRAH THE LORD WILL PROVIDE
by William Cowper

The saints should never be dismayed,
Nor sink in hopeless fear;
For when they least expect His aid,
The Saviour will appear.

This Abraham found: he raised the knife;
God saw, and said, "Forbear!
Yon ram shall yield his meaner life;
Behold the victim there."

Once David seemed Saul's certain prey;
But hark! The foe's at hand;
Saul turns his arms another way,
To save the invaded land.

When Jonah sunk beneath the wave,
He thought to rise no more;
But God prepared a fish to save,
And bear him to the shore.

Blest proofs of power and grace divine,
That meet us in His word!
May every deep-felt care of mine
Be trusted with the Lord.

Wait for His seasonable aid,
And though it tarry, wait:
The promise may be long delayed,
But cannot come too late.

February 21

WHITER THAN SNOW

Luke 11:39 Then the Lord said to him, "Now then, you Pharisees clean the outside of the cup and dish but inside you are full of greed and wickedness."

I am an x-smoker. For years I had been very particular about the outside of my body being clean and well groomed, and then I would turn right around and pollute myself with the disgusting effects of smoke both outside and inside. Since becoming a Christian I see a far more important issue than being clean outwardly, it is that of being clean inside. I praise God for His willingness to make me clean from the inside out through His Son.

So many times we are consumed with those things that will make us look good outwardly but ignore those things that feed our spirits and make us clean inside. No matter how many times we wash and groom ourselves outwardly, it will not make us clean inwardly. Only Christ can do that. It is impossible to be clean in our spirit without the Spirit of the Lord. We are shallow people without the Holy Spirit leading us and directing us to be the person that He wants us to be.

2 Corinthian 5:17 Therefore, if anyone is in Christ, he is a new creation; the old has gone, the new has come! He can make us clean vessels to be used in His service. There's a song that says WASH ME AND I SHALL BE WHITER THAN SNOW. Praise His Holy Name.

February 22

PUT ON THE NEW

Isaiah 43:18-19 "Forget the former things; do not dwell on the past. See, I am doing a new thing! Now it springs up; do you not perceive it?

Are you still wearing the filthy rags that you wore when you were lost in sin? Satan would love for us to remain in the same dirt, but God has clothed us with His righteousness. When God rescued us from death into life through Jesus Christ, He gave us new life. The old person was buried, and we were born anew through the blood of Jesus, who gave us victory over our past sins. He gave us new garments of white. We need to throw those filthy rags away forever.

Don't let Satan bring back the memories of those past sins, he will try, but our God is a God who never remembers our past sins. *For I will forgive their wickedness and will remember their sins no more." Hebrews 8:12.* Once He has forgiven us, He will never bring them up again. If you are reminded of them, it does not come from our Heavenly Father, but from the father of lies. If Satan can't bring you back into sin in your present circumstances, then he will try defeating you, by reminding you of the sins you committed before you came to The Cross of Jesus.

BORN AGAIN, THERE'S REALLY BEEN A CHANGE IN ME, BORN AGAIN, JUST LIKE JESUS SAID. BORN AGAIN AND ALL BECAUSE OF CALVARY. I'M SO GLAD THAT I'VE BEEN BORN AGAIN. That song is just ringing in my heart and ears as I write this devotional. I am so glad that when I was born again, I was given a new life. A life in Christ: The one who clothed me with His righteousness. *2 Corinthians 5:17 Therefore, if anyone is in Christ, he is a new creation; the old has gone, the new has come!* Praise God!

February 23

AMBASSADORS FOR CHRIST

2 Corinthians 5:20-21 We are therefore Christ's ambassadors, as though God were making his appeal through us. We implore you on Christ's behalf: Be reconciled to God. God made him who had no sin to be sin for us, so that in him, we might become the righteousness of God.

Webster's dictionary defines ambassador in this way: I: an official envoy; especially: a diplomatic agent of the highest rank accredited to a foreign government or sovereign as the resident representative of his or her own government or sovereign or appointed for a special diplomatic assignment 2a: an authorized representative or messenger b: an unofficial representative, traveling abroad as ambassadors of goodwill

Christ died on the cross for all. Even if we had been the only person on earth, He would have died for each one of us. It is an amazing thing that God loved us so much that He sent His Son to die on the cross so that we might have eternal life. Why then, wouldn't we who have come to the cross and accepted God's forgiveness, not be willing to become ambassadors for Christ. We should be excited about sharing the good news to all around us. We would have been lost, had it not been for the Cross of Jesus.

We are special people—we are God's children—we have been appointed as ambassadors to the world around us. That is our great commission—*He said to them, "Go into all the world and preach the good news to all creation. Mark 16:15.* What better news in the entire world than this? We have eternal life through Jesus Christ. Let's get excited about what Jesus did for us, and recognize ourselves for who we are—appointed Ambassadors of Christ. There is no rank more important that that.

February 24

BE PREPARED

1 Thessalonians 5:1-4 Now, brothers, about times and dates we do not need to write to you, for you know very well that the day of the Lord will come like a thief in the night. While people are saying, "Peace and safety," destruction will come on them suddenly, as labor pains on a pregnant woman, and they will not escape. But you brothers are not in darkness so that this day should surprise you like a thief.

I believe that most of us go out of our way to secure our homes with safety locks, burglar alarms, etc. We warn our children about being lured away by strangers. We buy automobiles that offer safety features. We make it a priority to protect and ready ourselves for approaching danger of all kinds. I wonder how many however, prepare themselves for the coming of the Lord. Have we made our lives secure in Christ. We never know in what year, day, or hour that He will make His appearance. Yet seemingly there are many who are not concerned about their spiritual condition.

It seems to me that people are concerned only about their needs for today, not realizing that the world may end tomorrow. How said it is to think that they will be lost to an eternity in hell simply because they did not prepare for a future in Heaven with the Lord.

As brothers and sisters in Christ we need not fear at what hour or what day Jesus will come again, because we have prepared ourselves for His coming. My heart grieves, as I am sure yours does also, for those who will be lost. Let's make it a daily prayer to lift those who are not prepared to open their eyes and see their need for Christ.

February 25

GREATER THAN GOLD

Psalms 135:5, 15, 18. I know that the Lord is great, that our Lord is greater than all gods. The idols of the nations are silver and gold, made by the hands of men. Those who make them will be like them, and so will all who trust in them.

The Lord is greater than any other god. He is the maker of the heavens and the earth. He is our Hope, our Strength, our Provider, our Comforter, our Friend, our Redeemer. He supplies all of our needs.

Why then do we look to other gods for our happiness? Can we rely on them to supply all of our needs? They might temporarily make our lives more comfortable, but will they help us in times of distress? Can they give us hope when we are dying? Can they give us strength in times of weakness? Can they provide our spiritual needs? Can they comfort us when we have suffered great pain? Are they a friend that will walk beside us in life's storms? Can they redeem us from our sins?

The only god that we can put our trust in is the Lord. He is greater than anything this world has to offer. People have a tendency to run after other gods, thinking that they can make them happy and provide the things that they need. God's word says that those who make them will be like them and so will all who trust in them. What good will they do you when you really need a Holy God; none at all.

When the crippled man at the temple Beautiful asked for money, Peter *said "Silver or gold I do not have, but what I have I give you. In the name of Jesus Christ of Nazareth, walk." Taking him by the right hand, he helped him up, and instantly the man's feet and ankles became strong. He jumped to his feet and began to walk. Acts 3:6-8a.* Could silver and gold have done for him what God did? No— Our God is the only one who can give us what we need. He is far greater than all the silver and gold we can acquire.

Our first commandment is, "*You shall have no other gods before me.*" *Exodus 20:3*

What about you? Do you worship God before anything else? Or does He take back seat to another?

February 26-27

WATER FOR THE WEEKEND

JEHOVA-ROPHI., I AM THE LORD WHO HEALETH THEE
by William Cowper

Heal us, Emmanuel! Here we are,
Waiting to feel Thy touch:
Deep-wounded souls to Thee repair
And, Saviour, we are such.

Our faith is feeble, we confess,
We faintly trust Thy word;
But wilt Thou pity us the less?
Be that far from Thee, Lord!

Remember him who once applied,
With trembling, for relief;
"Lord, I believe," with tears he cried,
"Oh, help my unbelief!"

She too, who touch'd Thee in the press,
And healing virtue stole,
Was answer'd, "Daughter, go in peace,
Thy faith hath made thee whole."

Conceal'd amid the gathering throng,
She would have shunn'd Thy view;
And if her faith was firm and strong,
Had strong misgivings too.

Like her, with hopes and fears we come,
To touch Thee, if we may;
Oh! Send us not despairing home,
Send none unheal'd away!

February 28

YOU CAN'T HIDE

Numbers 32:23 "But if you fail to do this, you will be sinning against the Lord; and you may be sure that your sin will find you out."

Sunday, our minister was saying that this was one of his dad's favorite scriptures to share with his children. It brought back memories of my own mother. She was constantly using that same scripture when she suspected that I had done something wrong or that I had told an untruth. It didn't loom as large in my mind at that time, as it does today.

No matter what our sin is, it is a sin against our Father. There are so many times we have hidden sin in our lives. We may be hiding it from the world, but there is no way that we can hide it from our Lord. He sees everything we do, He hears every word we speak, and He knows our every thought. We may fool those around us, but never our Lord.

We should be most concerned about what our Father thinks of us. We grieve Him when we sin, and I believe He grieves even more when we try to hide it from Him. Let's just confess our sins and receive the forgiveness and blessing that He has for us when we are honest with Him. He is a great and forgiving God. *Who is a God like you, who pardons sin and forgives the transgression of the remnant of his inheritance? You do not stay angry forever but delight to show mercy. Micah 7:18*

March 1

OUR WEAKNESS—GOD'S STRENGTH

Judges 6:15:16 "But Lord," Gideon asked, "How can I save Israel? My clan is the weakest in Manasseh, and I am the least in my family." The Lord answered, "I will be with you, and you will strike down all the Midianites together."

Can you imagine all of the emotions that Gideon must have felt when God instructed him to go and save Israel out of Midean's hands? I think he must have experienced feelings of doubt, fear, shock, disbelief, inferiority, inadequacy and awe. Think about it; he was the weakest of men among the weakest clan.

Can you identify with Gideon? I sure can. Anything God has ever asked me to do; I have had the same emotions: Doubt as to whether or not I am really hearing from God: Fear of the unknown: Shock and disbelief that He would even consider me worthy: Inferiority and inadequacy to do the things that He has asked me to do. And awe when I finally understood that it was really from God. And I believe it is understandable when we consider our own weakness. But then there's God.

Our strength comes from the Lord. *I can to everything through, him who gives me strength. Philippians 4:13* When God asks us to do anything for Him, He will go with us. He will supply everything we need to accomplish what He has instructed us to do. If you are thinking that you are too weak to do the thing that God is asking you to do, think again. One thing we know for certain: Anything that God is in charge of will be carried out to completion and according to His will. Let's believe Him and understand that it is in His strength, not ours that all things will be accomplished.

66

March 2

EDUCATED BY THE SPIRIT

Acts 4: 13 When they saw the courage of Peter and John and realized that they were unschooled, ordinary men, they were astonished and they took note that these men had been with Jesus.

Wow! Just think of that. Peter and John in my eyes were giants in the spiritual aspect. To think of them as being uneducated men is difficult to wrap my mind around. How encouraging it is to know that God can and will use anyone He desires to carry out His work. If it were not so I would have no hope of ever being used by God. These men had been with Jesus. It occurs to me, that being with Him is the only qualification that we need to do the work that God has for us to do. How revealing the scriptures are that tells us *"Apart from me you can do nothing John 15:5* and *I can do all things through Christ who strengthens me. Philippians 4:13*

The truth is, if we don't rely on the Lord and His Word for all of our spiritual wisdom, we will never be educated in God's plan for us. We can go to the best schools in the world but if we don't have the relationship with the Lord that only comes through accepting His Son, we will never be called by Him to carry out His purpose in our lives.

Isn't it wonderful to know that we never have to feel inferior to anyone if we are children of God? How marvelous our Lord is that he can take the most unlikely people and educate them in His way according to His plan for each of us.

March 3

FATHER KNOWS BEST

2 Corinthians 1:8-10 We do not want you to be uninformed, brothers, about the hardships we suffered in the province of Asia. We were under great pressure, far beyond our ability to endure, so that we despaired even of life. Indeed, in our hearts we felt the sentence of death. But this happened that we might not rely on ourselves but on God, who raises the dead. He has delivered us from such a deadly peril and he will deliver us. On him we have set our hope that he will continue to deliver us, as you help us by your prayers.

The definition of despair according to Webster means: to lose all hope or confidence of winning. Have you ever been in such despair that you felt like you could not endure? If you have, you are not alone. Even Paul had those despairing thoughts and, I must admit, so have I.

Why do you suppose we have those times of despair in our life? Could it be that we try to control every situation and then we realize that nothing we are doing is affective? The above scripture says it happens so that we will learn not to rely on ourselves, but to trust in God; the God who raises the dead. Do you think He just might be a little better qualified than us to handle the battles? How audacious we are, to think we can change any circumstance. Yet we try to take it on ourselves to do a job that only our Heavenly Father can do.

He must watch us with sadness as we try to change circumstances around us to fit our interpretation of what we think they should be. If only we could allow Him to handle every circumstance first—not as a last resort. Until we learn to let go and let God have control, we will suffer those times of discouragement and despair. God's will is perfect, so is His timing. Let us wait with patience for His work to be done—in His time and according to His will, not ours.

He not only sees our circumstances, he supplies all of our needs. And notice the very last part of the scripture: He also puts in our lives those friends who love us and share our burdens, and lift us up in prayer. I thank Him for the gift of Godly friends who pray when I am going through difficult times, don't you? Our Heavenly Father truly does know best.

March 4

GOD'S CREATION

Genesis 1:1, 26 In the beginning God created the heavens and the earth. Then God said, "Let us make man in our image, in our likeness, and let them rule over the fish of the sea and the birds of the air, over the livestock, over all the earth, and over all the creatures that move along the ground.

As I was praying about the devotional that God wanted me to write this morning I came to my computer, turned it on, and behold, there was a beautiful power-point showing the beauty of the world. I knew immediately that it was the subject that God had put in front of me to write about

As I was watching this beautiful power point, I couldn't help but rejoice in the beauty of God's creation. I have a difficult time considering how some people deny the fact that God exists. I couldn't possibly think that this beautiful world just exploded into existence. The only way that a gorgeous place like this could ever be formed, is by a creator.

God created man in His own image. God has made each one of us individually. We each have our own DNA and our own set of fingerprints, none of which are alike. That thought alone should make people realize that there is a Creator. I am not an accident and neither are you. You and I are God's creation and he gave us dominion over the entire world.

He gave us a magnificent brain and the ability to use it. To some He gave the gift of creating beautiful things, like great gardens, out of what He has given us. We may not be one of those people who have a lot of creativity for design, but we each have a responsibility to take care of the things that God created. We have no right to abuse those things that He has so graciously given to us. Let's do our part to maintain God's beautiful creation. Most importantly, give Him the glory for His creation.

March 5-6

WATER FOR THE WEEKEND

JEHOVAH-SHAMMAH
by William Cowper

(Ezekiel, xlviii.35)

As birds their infant brood protect,
And spread their wings to shelter them,
Thus saith the Lord to His elect,
"So will I guard Jerusalem."

And what then is Jerusalem,
This darling object of His cares?
Where is its worth in God's esteem?
Who built it? who inhabits there?

Jehovah founded it in blood,
The blood of His incarnate Son;
There dwell the saints, once foes to God
The sinners whom He calls His own.

There, though besieged on every side,
Yet much beloved and guarded well,
From age to age they have defied
The utmost force of earth and hell.

Let earth repent, and hell despair,
This city has a sure defence;
Her name is call'd, "The Lord is there,"
And who has power to drive him hence?

March 7

HIDDEN TREASURE

Matthew 6:19-22 "Do not store up for yourselves treasures on earth, where moth and rust destroy, and where thieves break in and steal. But store up for yourselves treasures in heaven, where moth and rust do not destroy, and where thieves do not break in and steal. For where your treasure is, there your heart will be also.

Are we so busy trying to store up treasures here on earth, that we are neglecting the treasures that God wants us to store up in heaven? The treasures that we store up here will not last. And we certainly can't take them with us. Those material things that we have in this life will mean nothing when we meet our Savior face to face. We will have to answer to Him as to why we were so enthralled with acquiring worldly wealth, that we didn't have time for Him. I believe that wealth is a curse if it is robbing us of the treasures God offers us.

I know many Godly men and women who have nothing according to the world's standards, but oh what riches they are storing up in heaven. They may live their entire life on this earth with little or nothing, but they will receive a great reward in heaven. When their time on this earth is over, I can just see our Lord meeting them, embracing them, and leading them to their heavenly home filled with a treasure chest full of the wonderful treasures that they stored up while on this earth.

If we are blessed with wealth here in this life, God expects us to use it for His glory. He has given it to us to use wisely. If we are letting that wealth come between us and our Lord, we are pitiful beyond measure. If money and all that it can buy is our passion, we have missed it all. I would rather be a pauper serving my Lord, than a rich woman whose God is in her earthly treasures.

March 8

BITTER OR BETTER

Ruth 1:12, 13, 15, 20. Return home, my daughters; I am too old to have another husband. Even if I thought there was still hope for me— even if I had a husband tonight and then gave birth to sons—would you wait until they grew up? Would you remain unmarried for them? No, my daughters. It is more bitter for me than for you, because the Lord's hand has gone out against me!" "Look," said Naomi," your sister-in-law is going back to her people and her gods. Go back with her." "Don't call me Naomi, she told them. "Call me Mara, because the Almighty has made my life very bitter.

Naomi's husband, Elimelech, had moved her and their 2 sons to Moab because of a famine in Israel. Elimelech, it seems died shortly after they moved there. Their 2 sons Mahlon and Kilion married Moabite women and both sons died about 10 years later. After their deaths, Naomi left Moab to return to Judah and when her 2 daughters-in-law said they would go with her, she told them to go back. One chose to do so and the other (Ruth) chose to go with Naomi. But Naomi told her to go back with her sister-in-law to her people and to her gods.

Naomi was bitter at God for taking her husband and sons from her. I believe if she hadn't been so bitter, she would never have suggested that Ruth go back with her sister-in-law to their gods. She obviously was not putting her faith and trust in the Lord. She even told others to call her Mara (which means bitter) instead of Naomi (which means pleasant). She was so angry at God that she wanted everyone to know it, even to the point of changing her identity.

Naomi (or should I say Mara) was mad at God and blaming Him. Have you ever been so mad at God that you changed your identity? Probably not, but there are many times that people become so angry at God that their entire personality changes. Instead of being determined to walk in faith and trust that there will be a better tomorrow, they choose to be bitter people.

Are we prepared to allow diversity to make us better people, putting our faith, hope and trust in God, believing what God's word says; *And we know that in all things God works for the good of those who love him, who have been called according to his purpose. Romans 8:28.* Or will we become bitter which leaves us in misery?

March 9

LOVING—NOT LEAVING

Ruth 1:16-18 But Ruth replied, "Don't urge me to leave you or to turn back from you. Where you go I will go, and where you stay I will stay. Your people will be my people and your God my God. Where you die I will die, and there I will be buried. May the Lord deal with me, be it ever so severely, if anything but death separates you and me."

Yesterday I wrote about Naomi and her bitterness toward God. I believe that in the ten years that Ruth was married to Naomi's son, and before his death, Naomi loved the Lord and had taught Ruth to love Him also. I believe that Ruth loved Naomi so much that she never wanted to be separated from her. It certainly doesn't sound like a decision that she would have made if she hadn't had a tremendous love and respect for Naomi. I also believe that she made her decision because of her love for the Lord, and her willingness to go where He directed her to go.

As we read further along in the account of Ruth, she found herself gleaning grain from the fields of Boaz a relative on her husband's side and he took notice of her. *"I've been told all about what you have done for your mother-in-law since the death of your husband—how you left your father and mother and your homeland and came to live with a people you did not know before. May the Lord repay you for what you have done. May you be richly rewarded by the Lord, the God of Israel, under whose wings you have come to take refuge." Ruth 2:11-12.* Don't you think Naomi was the one who told others what Ruth had done for her? I do, because I don't think Ruth would have. I think she was far too humble a person to tell the good thing she had done.

Ruth was one of those rare women who was loving and faithful, and listened to her Lord in all things. What an inspiration to all women. Doesn't it inspire you to be like Ruth? It does me. I desire to have the kind of dedication to the Lord that Ruth had, and I want to show the kind of love to others that she demonstrated to Naomi.

March 10

WILLINGNESS FROM THE HEART

Ruth 2:22-23 Naomi said to Ruth her daughter-in-law, "It will be good for you, my daughter, to go with his girls, because in someone else's field you might be harmed." So Ruth stayed close to the servant girls of Boaz to glean until the barley and wheat harvests were finished. And she lived with her mother-in-law.

We have already seen the kind of love that Ruth had for her mother-in-law, Naomi. She was willing to follow her to a strange land, and she was willing to work for her well-being. She was a rare woman indeed, a priceless jewel to everyone, most especially Naomi.

Now we see how the love between Ruth and Naomi grows deeper each day to the point that Naomi now calls Ruth her daughter. It seems that Naomi has traded bitterness and disappointment for tremendous love and concern for Ruth. It would be difficult not to love someone like Ruth. When another person has showed you the kind of love that Ruth did to Naomi, you can't help but love them back. I think too, that it would be almost impossible to remain a bitter person when you were living with someone as positive and loving as Ruth.

Naomi has come a long way from the bitterness in her heart that she had when they left Moab. She no longer has the attitude of 'woe is me'. She has gone from feeling sorry for herself, to being concerned about Ruth's welfare. Further along in the story we see wonderful things happening as a result of a willing heart to love and serve another.

I can well imagine that in her bitterness Naomi was not a pleasant person to be around. But in spite of every obstacle that I feel sure Naomi put in Ruth's way at that time, Ruth was faithful to love and serve her. Are we always willing to love and serve those around us who are unpleasant? Or do we have an attitude of anger and think to ourselves that it just isn't worth it, and so give up on them?

Praise the Lord He didn't have that attitude toward us. He gave up His life for our sins. We are like filthy rags, but He loves us anyway. He doesn't turn His back on us and he doesn't give up on us, when we are going through the bitterness of life. He keeps loving and serving us, and waiting on us to turn away from the bitterness in our hearts to love Him.

March 11

BLESSINGS OF LOVE

Ruth 4:13-15. So Boaz took Ruth and she became his wife. Then he went to her, and the Lord enabled her to conceive, and she gave birth to a son. The women said to Naomi: "Praise be to the Lord, who this day has not left you without a kinsman-redeemer. May he become famous throughout Israel! He will renew your life and sustain you in your old age. For your daughter-in-law, who loves you and who is better to you than seven sons, has given him birth."

I have been meditating on the book of Ruth the past several days. If you have never read it, please, I urge you to treat yourself to one of the most beautiful love stories in the bible. I can guarantee that you will be blessed as this story of Ruth's love and kindness for others unfolds. Ruth was a Godly woman who loved The Lord and served Him and others well. God used her in a powerful way.

As we have already seen, she loved her mother-in-law unconditionally. And now we see the love that was shared between Ruth and her husband. As I read the account of how she and Boaz found each other, it is easy to see the plans of God being played out. After the kinsmen-redeemer first in line refused to redeem her, Boaz second in line as kinsmen-redeemer married her. God blessed their marriage with the birth of a son. The lineage of Jesus can be traced back to Boaz. Wow! Christ, our Redeemer, was from the same family as Ruth's husband. And now we are part of that same family. When we make the decision to accept Jesus as our Savior, we are His children.

What an amazing story, what an amazing life, what an amazing woman. Can you imagine being that kind of a Godly woman?—A woman who is willing to love and serve others regardless of the circumstances. Ruth was truly an example of a Godly woman. She should be an inspiration for us all to be more loving, kind, and serving to others.

March 12-13

JEHOVAH-SHALOM. THE LORD SEND PEACE
by William Cowper

Jesus! Whose blood so freely stream'd
To satisfy the law's demand;
By Thee from guilt and wrath redeem'd,
Before the Father's face I stand.

To reconcile offending man,
Make Justice drop her angry rod;
What creature could have form'd the plan,
Or who fulfil it but a God?

No drop remains of all the curse,
For wretches who deserved the whole;
No arrows dipt in wrath to pierce
The guilty, but returning soul.

Peace by such means so dearly bought,
What rebel could have hoped to see?
Peace by his injured Sovereign wrought,
His Sovereign fasten'd to a tree.

Now, Lord, Thy feeble worm prepare!
For strife with earth and hell begins;
Conform and gird me for the war;
They hate the soul that hates his sins.

Let them in horrid league agree!
They may assault, they may distress;
But cannot quench Thy love to me,
Nor rob me of the Lord my peace.

March 14

THE WORD

John 1:1-2 In the beginning was the Word, and the Word was with God, and the Word was God. He was with God in the beginning.

I had bibles in my home before I knew and understood who the Author was and never really had the desire to read them. When I gave my life to the Lord, I was presented a bible by a precious couple, who God used as instruments to turn my eyes upon Jesus. That book became dear to me and I was so hungry for The Word that within a couple of years that bible was falling apart. I knew that I had to get another one and I was devastated because I had marked, highlighted, and written something in it on many pages. I thought I could not possibly live my life without that particular bible.

This past week, I thought I had lost the bible that had replaced the one I have just referred to. Once again I was having a melt-down: I searched everywhere and I called several people to have them trace my steps in places that I had been. I called it my everyday bible, because it was my favorite and because it is the one that I had marked in over and over again. Thank God I found it because it is such a treasure.

But this morning as I was reading this particular bible, God reminded me that His Word will never be lost. It is not the book that is important; it is The Word in it. The above scripture says that The Word is God. No matter how many bibles we have, no matter how many translations, no matter how much they are marked in, no matter how many we have used until they are in shreds, no matter how many we have misplaced—His Word will never be lost. His Word will live on and on in our hearts. After all it is not the book that matters; it is the Author of the book that gives us life.

March 15

A BEAUTIFUL MODEL

1 Thessalonians 1:6-7 You became imitators of us and of the Lord; in spite of severe suffering, you welcomed the message with the joy given by the Holy Spirit. And so you became a model to all the believers in Macedonia and Achaia.

I want to be an imitator of the Lord, don't you? Wow, what a testimony of one's life that would be. God's Word even tells us how to attain it, by welcoming the message with joy given by the Holy Spirit.

As women, I believe that at sometime in our lives most of us have dreamed of being a beautiful model. On the physical side, that isn't possible for all of us. But because of our acceptance of Jesus and the Holy Spirit, we can be a perfect model of our Lord. I would rather be known for my inward beauty, than an outward beauty. It is only because of Christ that we have the appealing inward beauty that others see, a beauty that gives others hope. *To them God has chosen to make known among the Gentiles the glorious riches of the mystery, which is Christ in you, the hope of glory. Colossians 1:27*

Sometimes we get bogged down with discouragement over one thing or another, and we let the joy of our salvation wane. Our entire countenance changes to a look of sadness. Let's not let that happen. Let's dwell on the good things, so others can see Christ in us. Wouldn't it be wonderful if others could see us and say, "Look at that beautiful woman, she looks just like her Father"?

March 16

PEACE IN THE STORM

Psalm 107:28-30 Then they cried out to the Lord in their trouble, and he brought them out of their distress. He stilled the storm to a whisper; the waves of the sea were hushed. They were glad when it grew calm, and he guided them to their desired haven.

Our youngest granddaughter spent the night with us the other night. There was a thunderstorm and she was awakened with fear. She ran over to me crying, I grabbed her up and enfolded her in my arms. She immediately was consoled. I returned her to her bed, where she promptly went back to a peaceful nights sleep.

Consider how much better off we would be, if during the storms in our lives, we would run to our Father to let Him console us. His arms are always open, ready to embrace us with His peace and His love. So many times we are paralyzed with fear. We quake in our fears and retreat to our own areas that do not give us the peace we are looking for. If, like a child, we would immediately run to the one who can calm the storm, our fears would be stilled and He would console us and give us peace.

There are going to be many storms in our lives, but we don't have to fear them. We will find that peace when we put our faith and trust in Jesus. He is our Comforter, and He provides peace in the midst of all of our storms. *Psalm 91:4-6 He will cover you with his feathers, and under his wings you will find refuge; his faithfulness will be your shield and rampart. You will not fear the terror of night, nor the arrows that flies by day, not the pestilence that stalks in the darkness, nor the plague that destroys at midday.* When we are going through the storms, let's turn to Jesus and run into His arms and receive the peace that He has for us

March 17

WORSHIP IN HOLINES

Malachi 1:6-8 "A son honors his father and a servant his master. If I am a father, where is the honor due me? If I am a master, where is the respect due me?" says the Lord Almighty. "It is you, O priests, who show contempt for my name. But you ask, 'How have we shown contempt for your name?' You place defiled food on my altar. But you ask 'How have we defiled you?' By saying that the Lord's Table is contemptible. When you bring blind animals for sacrifice, is that not wrong? When you sacrifice crippled or diseased animals, is that not wrong? Try offering them to your governor! Would he be pleased with you? Would he accept you?" says the Lord Almighty.

The Old Testament talks about how displeased God was when people brought blemished sacrifices to His alter. When we read about them, we are appalled that they would offer them to God. Don't we do the same thing when we come to church to worship and then the entire time we are there, we are thinking about other things? Are we there because it's Sunday morning and it is the thing to do? Or are we there because we want to praise the Lord and worship Him with our whole heart? Are we thinking about everything else except what the preacher is saying? Or are we listening to every word that he is preaching? Are we singing the songs with joy and understanding or are we just singing empty words? Are we looking at our watches to see if the 'worship' service is almost over so that we can get out of there? Or are we so caught up in the Spirit that we hate to see the worship time end?

We no longer have to bring animal sacrifices into the sanctuary because Jesus was the supreme sacrifice for our sins. But we need to bring our sacrifices to the Lord, even though they aren't living sacrifices. We need to bring our sacrifice of praise to Him.

It is an insult to our Lord to come to His house to worship for any reason other than to honor and praise His name. If we are coming out of a feeling of obligation, and if we have our minds on everything except worshipping Him, then we are bringing blemished sacrifices into His house and to His alter. We may pay our tithes and say our empty prayers, and make our presence be known, but if we are not giving our best to Him with our undivided attention, and in the spirit of Holiness, we might just as well not be there. *"Oh, that one of you would shut the temple doors, so that you would not light useless fires on my altar! I am not pleased with you," says the Lord Almighty, "and I will accept no offering from your hands."* Malachi *1:10*—that makes a pretty clear statement about what God thinks of our 'empty worship'. GOD DESERVES OUR BEST!

March 18

WAIT AND SEE

Genesis 15:2-4 But Abram said, "O Sovereign Lord, what can you give me since I remain childless and the one who will inherit my estate is Eliezer of Damascus?" And Abram said, "You have given me no children; so a servant in my household will be my heir," Then the word of the Lord came to him: "This man will not be your heir, but a son coming from your own body will be your heir."

God had promised Abram that he would give him a son of his own. Scripture tells us that when he and Sarai didn't have that son in the time frame that they thought was reasonable; they took control of the situation and made their own plans to have an heir. We all know the disastrous results of that. Read all about it in Genesis 16 & 17. The results of that are being felt today.

Are we like Abram and Sarai? Do we take things in our own hands when we can't see God at work? Just because we can't see God's plan for our lives, doesn't mean that He isn't working in our lives. It must be in His time, not ours. If we run ahead of God and take control of our own lives, it could be a disaster. We need to trust in the Lord for His timing. *I am still confident of this: I will see the goodness of the Lord in the land of the living. Wait for the Lord; be strong and take heart and wait for the Lord. Psalms 27:13-14.* Let's just wait and see what marvelous things God has for us.

March 19-20

WATER FOR THE WEEKEND

JEHOVAH-SHAMMAH
by William Cowper

As birds their infant brood protect,
And spread their wings to shelter them,
Thus saith the Lord to His elect,
"So will I guard Jerusalem."

And what then is Jerusalem,
This darling object of His cares?
Where is its worth in God's esteem?
Who built it? who inhabits there?

Jehovah founded it in blood,
The blood of His incarnate Son;
There dwell the saints, once foes to God
The sinners whom He calls His own.

There, though besieged on every side,
Yet much beloved and guarded well,
From age to age they have defied
The utmost force of earth and hell.

Let earth repent, and hell despair,
This city has a sure defence;
Her name is call'd, "The Lord is there,"
And who has power to drive him hence?

March 21

THE MIRACLES OF GOD

Psalms 77:11:-12 I will remember the deeds of the Lord, yes, I will remember your miracles of long ago. I will meditate on all your work and consider all your mighty deeds.

Have you been crying out to God to rescue you from the sin of doubt and despair? Have you been praying for a situation that seems impossible? Have you been in doubt that the situation will ever change? I don't know about you, but I can answer yes to every one of these questions.

Let's consider all of the miracles that God has performed in many lives from the time of Adam to today. He has performed so many, that we could never count them. Why would we think He is through performing miracles? He is the same God who parted the sea for the Israelites. God's word says that He will never leave us nor forsake us. He hears our every prayer.

Don't give up, just remember the miracles of the past and meditate on them. Remember the miracles that He has performed in your own life. Put your faith and your trust in the Lord.

March 22

SPIRITUAL FRUITS

Galatians 5:22 But the fruit of the Spirit is love, joy, peace, patience, kindness, goodness, faithfulness.

Do you display every one of the fruits of the Spirit everyday? If you do, I commend you and admire you. As for me, I am sorry to say—I don't. Some days I believe I do, other days I will display one or maybe more of them: And some days I wonder if I display any of them. Why is it difficult to display the fruits of the Spirit on a daily basis?

Let's consider each fruit separately:

Love—*But I tell you: "Love your enemies and pray for those who persecute you, that you may be sons of your Father in heaven." Matthew 5:14*

Joy—*Out of the most severe trial, their overflowing joy and their extreme poverty welled up in rich generosity. 2Corinthians 8:2*

Peace—*"I have told you these things so that in me you may have peace. In this world you will have trouble. But take heart I have overcome the world." John 16:33*

Patience—*2 Corinthians 1:6 If we are distressed, it is for your comfort and salvation, if we are comforted, it is for your comfort, which produces in you patient endurance of the same sufferings we suffer.*

Kindness—*And the Lord's servant must not quarrel; instead, he must be kind to everyone, able to teach, not resentful.*

Goodness—*But I tell you who hear me: Love your enemies, do good to those who hate you, bless those who curse you, pray for those who mistreat you. Luke 6:27*

Faithfulness—*Let love and faithfulness never leave you; bind them around your neck, write them on the tablet of your heart.*

The above scripture's I believe give us knowledge in how we can display the fruits of the Spirit. We should think about these scriptures and pray that God would purge us of anything that would disable our ability to show the fruits of the Spirit.

March 23

PRESERVING THE RIGHT

Judges 2:10, 12b, 14a, 15 After that whole generation had been gathered to their fathers another generation grew up, who knew neither the Lord nor what he had done for Israel. They had brought them out of Egypt. They followed and worshiped various gods of the peoples around them. In his anger against Israel the Lord handed them over to raiders who plundered them. Whenever Israel went out to fight, the hand of the Lord was against them to defeat them, just as he had sworn to them. They were in great distress.

I don't know about you, but this is sounding all too familiar to me. We live in a country that was founded on Christian principles: But as we look around now, it is difficult to see that the people running our country are seeking God's wisdom. It is evident in fact that they are trying to kick God out and take over the control. As I see it, it has brought nothing but distress and insecurity to us all. We even see evidence that those who have been raised in our own country with Christian values are now being influenced by those religions that have been welcomed in to our Christian nation.

What are we to do? I believe that we are to stand firm in our Christian beliefs and fight for the freedom that we once knew here. Yes, we still have freedom to speak our hearts and our minds, and we must take advantage of it before it's too late. Those who are trying to drive the Christians in to hiding are certainly making their voices heard. How long will it be before the Christians become silenced? We not only have the right to speak our mind, we MUST. If we don't, we are going to be overcome by the evil that prevails.

There is one thing that is certain. If we are God's children and we are trusting in Him, we have absolutely nothing to fear. No matter what happens we are conquerors threw Christ. *In all these things we are more that conquerors through him who loved us. Romans 8:17*

March 24

DIFFERENT WORLD—SAME GOD

Proverbs 4:11-15 I guide you in the way of wisdom and lead you along straight paths. When you walk, your steps will not be hampered; when you run, you will not let it go; guard it well, for it is your life. Do not set foot on the path of the wicked or walk in the way of evil men. Avoid it, do not travel on it; turn from it and go on your way.

While conversing with a young man one day about the relevance of God's Word, he said that we lived in a different world than it was when I was growing up: He implied that we should not have the same standards of living today and that God was more lenient than He once was.

There are many people and churches today that have compromised God's Word. They try and fit it to the standard of living in today's world. Many young people have grown up with parents who have taught them the right way, but alas, they have been sidetracked by worldly ways, and it is more appealing to them than the truth that they were taught. They would rather listen to lies than the truth. *"When you tell them all this they will not listen to you; when you call to them, they will not answer. Therefore say to them, 'This is the nation that has not obeyed the Lord its God or responded to correction. Truth has perished; it has vanished from their lips. Jeremiah 7:28*

The world is constantly changing but God and His Word never changes. *The grass withers and the flowers fall, but the word of our God stands forever. Isaiah 40:8.*

March 25

A CHILD'S HEART

Matthew 19:13-14 Then little children were brought to Jesus for him to place his hands on them and pray for them. But the disciples rebuked those who brought them. Jesus said," let the little children come to me, and do not hinder them, for the kingdom of heaven belongs to such as these."

One day when my 3 year old granddaughter was staying with me, she asked if she could call her daddy. Her daddy was working and I hesitated to let her interrupt him: But decided it would be ok. When her daddy answered the phone and heard her voice, he was overjoyed that she had wanted to call him. She talked to him for a little while and then said to him, "I love you, daddy", to which he replied I love you too, honey."

I could have denied my son a blessing, had I not allowed Ellison to call him. Do we deny our children the privilege of worship when we fail to take them to church? Children seem always eager to attend church. They love to hear the stories of Jesus. Are we hindering them from that?

We could take a lesson from our children. Are we always as anxious as they are to be in the presence of Jesus? Do we run to Him with the eagerness of a child? If our earthly fathers are over-joyed when we call them, can you imagine how our Heavenly Father feels? He wants us to be as little children. He wants us to call to him with a heart like that of a child, who just simply wants to talk to their Father. He wants to hear us say, "I love you, Jesus."

March 26-27

WATER FOR THE WEEKEND

JEHOVAH JESUS
by William Cowper

My song shall bless the Lord of all,
My praise shall climb to His abode;
Thee, Saviour, by that name I call,
The great Supreme, the mighty God.

Without beginning or decline,
Object of faith and not of sense;
Eternal ages saw Him shine,
He shines eternal ages hence.

As much when in the manger laid,
Almighty Ruler of the sky,
As when the six days' work He made,
Fill'd all the morning stars with joy.

Of all the crowns Jehovah bears,
Salvation is His dearest claim;
That gracious sound well pleased He hears
And owns Emmanuel for His name.

A cheerful confidence I feel,
My well placed hopes with joy I see;
My bosom glows with heavenly zeal,
To worship Him who died for me.

As man He pities my complaint,
His power and truth are all divine;
He will not fail, He cannot faint;
Salvation's sure, and must be mine.

March 28

EMBRACING TRUTH

2 Corinthians 10:5-6 We demolish arguments and every pretension that sets itself up against the knowledge of God, and we take captive every thought to make it obedient to Christ. And we will be ready to punish every act of disobedience, once your obedience is complete.

I am involved in a bible study called 'Me Myself & Lies' and it is very enlightening as we find out how many times we buy in to the lies that Satan tells us. Satan wants to defeat us by planting seeds of doubt in our minds of who we are in Christ. If he can get us to believe his lies, it weakens us and paralyzes us to the point of discouragement.

I know what it is like to buy into the lies of Satan. And I believe that you at one time or another have fallen into his trap of lies also. But wait a minute; why on this earth would we be intimidated by the one who is trying to devour us. God tells us that Satan is the father of lies.

Jesus said, *"Yet because I tell the truth, you do not believe me! Can any of you prove me guilty of sin? If I am telling the truth, why don't you believe me?" John 8:45-46.* His word is truth. He empowers us to overcome all evil thoughts and lies. We serve The One who gives us wisdom, strength and power in His Name to overcome.

Who are you going to believe? I don't know about you but I believe God. Let's embrace His truth so that we will be ready to punish every act of disobedience.

March 29

FROM DEFEAT TO VICTORY

Psalm 22:1-5 My God, my God, why have you forsaken me? Why are you so far from saving me, so far from the words of my groaning? O my God, I cry out by day, but you do not answer, by night, and am not silent. Yet you are enthroned as the Holy One; you are the praise of Israel. In you our fathers put their trust; they trusted and you delivered them. They cried to you and were saved; in you they trusted and were not disappointed.

I had the pleasure of visiting with a young woman yesterday that I have known from a child, but had not seen for many years. I will call her Mercy (to protect her real identity) because that seems to be who she is now. Mercy was an unhappy child raised in the shadow of a sister who was her mother's favorite. She was constantly verbally abused and it took its toll in her ability to see herself as she truly was. We knew her as a precious child; quiet, timid, beautiful and loveable. I can remember wanting to take her in my arms and cuddle and protect her.

She has grown into a gorgeous Christian young woman who knows that she is loved by the Lord and she has finally found her true identity in Him. She was relating a story to me that brought her to this point. There was a period in her life when she had suffered so many battles and felt such defeat that she actually told God that she was giving up on Him.

It was just at that time when she was introduced to a young teenage boy who had been beaten by a gang, and it had left his teeth and mouth mangled drastically. Her job puts her in contact with many dentists. As a result of her concern for him and a dentist who gave his talent, his ability and his time, directed by the Lord, this young man was put back together, not only physically but spiritually. He like Mercy, also was about to give up on the Lord. They cried out to God and they both found the help they needed through God's amazing grace.

Sometimes it is in the most difficult and discouraging times in our life that we hear from God. We see His love and His power and His mercy revealed when we least expect it. When we put our faith and trust in God, we are never disappointed. Job was such a man, and his life was not only restored but it was restored with more blessings than before. What an awesome God we serve.

March 30

HIDE AND SEEK

Jeremiah 29:13 You will seek me and find me when you seek me with all your heart. I will be found by you, declares the Lord, and will bring you back from captivity. I will gather you from all the nations and places where I have banished you declares the Lord and will bring you back to the place from which I carried you into exile.

Have you been held captive by sin in your life? Have you broken fellowship with the Lord? Have you taken a path that has put you in exile? Do you feel like you have been banished by God? Perhaps you have found yourself in a place where you cannot hear from God. I have been there before. It is the loneliest place in the entire world. Nothing seems right when we are away from God; indeed, nothing is right. But look what God says. When we seek him with all our heart, we will find him. He promises to bring us back from the place where He has banished us.

We serve a gracious and forgiving God. No matter what circumstance has captured us and sent us into exile, we can find our way back. God is waiting with open arms when we seek Him. We don't have to live in that lonely place without Him; He desires to bring us back to that peaceful home with Him.

If you have been in that lonely place, seek the Lord with all of your heart. You will find Him and you will be brought back to the relationship that will bring you peace and contentment. When we are living in the place where God wants us, we will never be lonely again.

March 31

THE ANOINTED

1 John 2:27 As for you, the anointing you received from him remains in you, and you do not need anyone to teach you. But as his anointing teaches you about all things and as that anointing is real, not counterfeit—just as it has taught you, remain in him.

At a time when I was in a bible study called ANOINTED, TRANSFORMED, REDEEMED. We were discussing whether or not we are anointed. As I was studying in God's Word and searching for the truth on the matter, this is my conclusion. One of the definitions in Webster's dictionary for anointed is: to choose by or as if by divine election; *also*: to designate as if by a ritual anointment. I believe in the Holy Trinity. God's Word tells us that The Father, The Son, and The Holy Spirit is the three in one. Since the Word was ordained and anointed by God to those whom He empowered to write it, we can be certain of its truth and authority. I am convinced that everyone who receives the Holy Spirit is anointed by God. *But you have an anointing from the Holy One, and all of you know the truth. John 2:20*

God's Word says that when we accept Jesus as our personal Savior, we also receive the Spirit of the Lord: Therefore the Spirit lives in us. We are anointed people from that time on. It is the Spirit who empowers us to do marvelous things. He gives us wisdom, knowledge, power, and authority, to do the things that He calls us to do. Why then do we not believe it? If we don't accept the truth, we will not be able to carry out the plans that God has for us. We are paralyzed because of our failure to grasp the truth of the Holy Spirit living in us and the power that is ours through His Spirit.

We recognize God's anointing on other's lives, but often times we fail to see it in our own. Let's consider why we are reluctant to believe that we have been anointed. Are we letting Satan lie to us and tell us that if we believe it we are puffing ourselves up? Do we feel as if we are unqualified to do what God has asked us to do: We are, but God doesn't call the qualified, He qualifies the called and I might add the anointed? Are we afraid of the work that might be involved if we submit to His call in our lives? God wants us to believe and accept His anointing power. For it's through His anointing that we are able to do unimaginable things.

April 1

ARE YOUR BAGS PACKED?

Galatians 5:22 But the fruit of the Spirit is love, joy, peace, patience, kindness, goodness, faithfulness, gentleness and self-control.

Every time we go on a trip, I pack my bags so full, you can hardly carry them. I always take more than I need, and I am not willing to leave any of it at home just in case I might possibly need some of it. I mean, after all does it hurt to have extra baggage?

It might not hurt to carry extra baggage on a trip but when we carry extra baggage within our spirits it can be devastating. What baggage should we carry with Heaven as our final destination? What would they reveal about us?

Are they packed with un-forgiveness? Then we don't have room for *love.*

Are they packed with anger? Then we don't have room for joy.

Are they packed with worry, doubt, and fear? Then we don't have room for peace.

Are they packed with frustration? Then we don't have room for patience.

Are they packed with bad attitudes? Then we don't have room for kindness.

Are they packed with hate? Then we don't have room for goodness.

Are they packed with self-centeredness? Then we don't have room for faithfulness.

Are they packed with an un-kind spirit? Then we don't have room for gentleness.

Are they packed with evil desires? Then we don't have room for self-control.

As Christians how can we display the fruits of the Spirit which is *love, joy, peace, patience, kindness, goodness, faithfulness, gentleness and self-control Galatians 5:22*, if we carry bags full of sinful thoughts, it leaves no room for the fruit that the Holy Spirit wants to display in us on our journey? When we accepted Jesus as our personal Savior, he did not mean for us to carry a heavy load. His word *said "Come to me all you who are weary and burdened, and I will give you rest. Take my yoke upon you and learn from me, for I am gentle and humble in heart, and you will find rest for you souls. For my yoke is easy and my burden is light. Matthew 11:28-30.*

Jesus died on that cross so we don't have to carry those heavy loads. Let's unpack those bags with all of the garbage and fill them up with the fruits of the Spirit.

April 2-3

WATER FOR THE WEEKEND

JEHOVAH OUR RIGHTEOUSNESS
by William Cowper

My God, how perfect are Thy ways!
But mine polluted are;
Sin twines itself about my praise,
And slides into my prayer.

When I would speak what Thou hast done
To save me from my sin,
I cannot make Thy mercies known,
But self-applause creeps in.

Divine desire, that holy flame
Thy grace creates in me;
Alas! impatience is its name,
When it returns to Thee.

This heart, a fountain of vile thoughts.
How does it overflow,
While self upon the surface floats,
Still bubbling from below.

Let others in the gaudy dress
Of fancied merit shine;
The Lord shall be my righteousness,
The Lord forever mine.

April 4

DOES YOUR HUSBAND SEE JESUS IN YOU?

1Corinthians 7:14 For the unbelieving husband has been sancti-fied through his wife and the unbelieving wife has been sanctified through her believing husband. Otherwise your children would be unclean, but as it is, they are holy.

My husband must have had a difficult time seeing Jesus in me when I first became a Christian. I suddenly thought I had all of the answers for how he should act, how he should speak and what he should do. Not only did I think I had the answers, I was trying to control him and thought my mission in life was to change him. Even though he is a professing Christian, he wasn't living the life I had planned for him. I would become irritated and sullen when he didn't line up to my expectations. I prayed constantly, that God would change him. I was seeing his faults, but not my own. *Matthew 7:3 Why do you look at the speck of sawdust in your brother's eye and pay no attention to the plank in your own eye?* I needed to pray for God to change me and my attitude toward my husband. It was after I allowed God to change me that I started to see major growth in not only my husband's life but in my own. I began to see how I didn't show him the proper respect that he deserved.

Have you ever been guilty of the same thing? Are you constantly criticizing him?

How often do you tell him you love him for who he is? What if you started giving him praise for his good qualities instead of berating him for the faults that you see? What if you started seeing him through the eyes of Jesus instead of through your critical eyes? Many marriages are wrecked because we let Satan destroy the love that we have for one another. When we get in the habit of seeing only the bad qualities in our husbands, we are blinded to all of the good.

We took a vow to marry for better or for worse. If your husband is a Christian let God give him direction on how to live a fruitful life. If he isn't a Christian, pray for him and don't put yourself in the judge's seat. Let God do the work that only He can do. We can't change another, only God can do that. We need to forgive our husbands for there shortcomings (we all have them), and move on. Let's learn to love them the way God's word tells us to. If they aren't where they need to be with the Lord, maybe your commitment and patience will be a testimony to them. Let's show that agape love that a wife should have for her husband. Let them see that Jesus is Lord in our lives. They won't see it if we have a critical spirit. They will only see it if we let go and let God take control.

April 5

DOWNCAST EYES

Psalms 42:5 Why are you downcast, O my soul? Why so disturbed within me? Put your hope in God, for I will yet praise him, my savior and my God.

Psalms 121:1-2. I lift up my eyes to the hills—where does my help come from? My help comes from the Lord, the Maker of heaven and earth.

I have a friend who is very witty. She can make a joke out of everything. We were talking one day about what age does to our bodies. She said something like this, "I happened to look down into a mirror the other day and I was horrified at what I saw, everything just seemed to be drooping into a blob, so I made a decision: I will never look down into a mirror again: I will hold it up and look in to it, it makes an amazing difference." Of course it was very funny to me because I could certainly identify with what she was talking about because I have had the same experience.

We can't do anything about our aging bodies but we can certainly do something about our Spirits. We can keep them young, alive and active through God and His Word. As the psalmist says, we don't have to look down with downcast eyes; we can look up to God and praise Him for all things. He will make us radiant when we keep our eyes on Him. So if you are downcast with a heavy heart, look up to The One who will lift your spirit. Psalms 34:5. Those who look to him are radiant; their faces are never covered with shame.

April 6

WE ARE GOD'S CHILDREN

How great is the love the Father has lavished on us that we should be called children of God; and that is what we are. 1 John 3:1a.

While babysitting my youngest granddaughter one day, she was in my computer room with me, when her father entered our house. When she turned around to go into another room she saw him coming down the hall, she yelled, "Daddy, daddy, daddy" and threw her arms around his legs; he lifted her up and gave her a big hug. Her daddy was so thrilled when she ran to him and reached out for his hugs. If our earthly father is that happy when their child runs to them with outstretched arms, just think how happy our Heavenly Father is when we run to Him. His love for us is bigger than anything we can ever imagine.

If you are a parent, you know a little bit about the love that God has for us. When you are watching your child while awake or sleeping, working or playing, you look on with love at what you have created. Not always are we proud of the choices they make, but the love is always there. Nothing they do can ever take away that love. It is comforting to know that our Heavenly Father loves us in spite of our mistakes. Just like a parent praises their children for the good choices they make in their life, our Heavenly Father praises us when He sees us making good choices. And like a parent who grieves over the mistakes that our children make, our Heavenly Father grieves over the mistakes that we make. But he is always waiting with open arms to embrace us with His love.

Are we eager to run into His arms everyday? Do we have a desire to be in His presence at all times? It makes our Father sad when we choose to turn our backs on Him and walk away from the fellowship that He wants with us. It is in His arms that we find peace and comfort and strength. *Come unto me all you who are weary and burdened, and I will give you rest. Matthew 11:28* Let's run to Him with arms outstretched.

April 7

SOMETHING TO TALK ABOUT

1 John 4:5-6 They are from the world and therefore speak from the view point of the world and the world listens to them. We are from God, and whoever knows God listens to us, but whoever is not from God does not listen to us. This is how we recognize the Spirit of truth and the spirit of falsehood.

I was talking to some Christian friends yesterday about how difficult it is to carry on a conversation with people who do not know the Lord. Nothing is more difficult for me than to be in an atmosphere surrounded by people who expect me to speak their language. I truly do feel like a foreigner. When your favorite topic is the Lord and His children, it does not interest them at all. So what is left—idle and shallow talk in most cases? There are times when the conversation is intelligent and interesting, but usually it is something that does not hold my interest. There are times when the talk is rather offensive and I find myself wandering off.

It would be easy to stay in our comfort zones with our Christian brothers and sisters, but that is not what we are supposed to do. Otherwise how could we ever have the chance to point them to Jesus? *Mark 16: 15 He said to them, "Go into all the world and preach the good news to all creation."* This is the great commission Jesus gave to us as Christians.

I have many unsaved friends whom I love dearly. I consider it a privilege to pray for them. My desire for them is that one day they will come to know my Lord and Savior. It is no secret to them that I am a Christian. Even though they are not particularly interested in discussing spiritual things, I have noticed that they will ask me to pray for different people or situations in their lives.

Let's remember that we were once sinners, and there were Christians who had to listen to our mundane talk. They were people in our lives who prayed for us and witnessed to us. Let's go out into the world and mingle with those who do not know Jesus. Let's pray for them and love them into the kingdom of God.

April 8

RECOGNIZING YOUR TALENTS

Matthew 25:15 To one he gave five talents of money, to another two talents, and to another one talent, each according to his ability.

I have a sister that has many God given talents. She is the best cook in the world—she could stand up against any on the Cooking Channel. She is a wonderful decorator—her home could be in House Beautiful. Her gift of hospitality is beyond belief—she has been known to invite a total stranger to dinner. She gives 110 percent in helping others. She is one of the most generous people I know. God has blessed her with these talents and so much more. She is one of those people that you could be jealous of if you didn't feel secure in the talents that God has given you. She not only has these talents, she uses them. Yet with all of these, she doesn't recognize them. It is totally amazing to me, how she can not see the amazing person God created her to be.

Why are we reluctant to admit that God has given us our talents? He expects us to use them to and for His glory. It is not a prideful thing to recognize our talents when we give God the glory. We need to recognize them for what they are and where they come from. We are all given different talents according to the ability God has given us. We should not look at our sisters and our brothers talents and think that ours are inferior. Nobody should feel inferior to another. Let's thank God for the talents that He has given us.

There was a time when I was envious of others talents and wondered why I didn't have any. I realize today how insulting that was to the Lord. He has created each of us according to His plan for our lives. It took me many years to see God's plan for me. I didn't recognize my own talents. I was too busy looking at the talents of others. I am in awe of what God will do in our lives if we will surrender our all to Him. He will open our eyes to see what He wants us to do and how He wants us to use the talents that He has given us. Don't be ashamed to recognize them. With grateful hearts we can truly say, *I can do all things through Christ who strengthens me. Philippians 4:13* God will bless us abundantly when we use our talents.

April 9-10

WATER FOR THE WEEKEND

JEHOVAH-NISSI. THE LORD MY
by William Cowper

By whom was David taught
To aim the deadly blow,
When he Goliath fought,
And laid the Gittite low?
Nor sword nor spear the stripling took,
But chose a pebble from the brook.

'Twas Israel's God and King
Who sent him to the fight;
Who gave him strength to sling,
And skill to aim aright.
Ye feeble saints, your strength endures,
Because young David's God is yours.

Who order'd Gideon forth,
To storm the invaders' camp.
With arms of little worth,
A pitcher and a lamp?
The trumpets made his coming known
And all the host was overthrown.

Oh! I have seen the day,
When with a single word,
God helping me to say,
"My trust is in the Lord,"
My soul hath quell'd a thousand foes
Fearless of all that could oppose.

But unbelief, self-will,
Self-righteousness, and pride,
How often do they steal
My weapon from my side!
Yet David's Lord, and Gideon's friend,
Will help his servant to the end.

April 11

HOLDING EACH OTHER UP

Exodus 17:12 When Moses hands grew tired, they took a stone and put it under him and he sat on it. Aaron and Hur held his hands up—one on one side, one on the other—so that his hands remained steady till sunset.

There are many times in our life that we become weak, not just physically but spiritually. It is in our times of need that our Christian family can hold us up and help us out with our struggles. *If one falls down, his friend can help him up. But pity the man who falls and has no one to help him up! Ecclesiastes 4:10* Have you ever felt so down that you did not even know how to pray? I have. Sometimes we just need an encouraging word or a shoulder to cry on. There are times when we need physical help. There was a time in my life that I was unable to cook and the Lord would send someone to my door with food. Just when I thought we were going to run out, someone else would bring more. God provided what I needed through these precious people.

What a blessing God has given us in one another. He ministers to us through His children. Thank God for those who are willing to stand with us, holding us up when we are too weak to stand alone. When we love one another in the love of the Lord, we want to lift one another up whenever the need arises.

Serving one another is a privilege God has given us and it takes us away from a self-serving life. When we focus on the Lord, He will give us the desire to help our 'family' when they are in need.

April 12

FUN IN THE SON

Romans 15:13 May the God of hope fill you with all joy and peace as you trust in him, so that you may overflow with hope by the power of the Holy Spirit.

I read a story about a girl that had been to a youth rally and the director asked the group "How many of you came here to have a good time?" She was the only one that raised her hand; she suddenly knew that she had given the wrong response, or at least the response that was expected of her. The director said "We have not come here to have a good time."

What is it that makes people think that if we are Christians we should not have a good time? There was a period in my life that I thought it would not be possible to have a good time in the Lord. How wrong I was. Today the happiest times in my life is when I am with the Lord and His family praising God.

If we are Christians, we should be showing the world how happy we are. It can not be very enticing to those who don't know Jesus if we are walking around with a sad countenance. When we think about all that our Lord has done for us, how can we not be joyful? He has given us a Spirit of joy. I can hardly contain my joy in Him at times. Shouldn't we want people to see how much we love the Lord and that our joy comes directly from HIM?

There are people all over this world who believe that they have no hope in the struggles and trials of this world. They need to see that Christian's have overcome their problems through the blood of God's Son. They need to see the joy as a result of their decision to let God take control of their life. They can't help but be attracted to a person who displays freedom with joy from their past struggles, or when they see that they are joyful in their present trials. Let's show them that we can have FUN IN THE SON.

God's word is full of the joy that God provides us in Him. If you want to be revived in the Spirit, look up all of the scriptures that talks about the joy in our Lord. I would especially ask you to read 1 Chronicles 16:8-36—What a wonderful passage.

April 13

WASHED IN THE BLOOD

Exodus 30:10 "Once a year Aaron shall make atonement on its horns. This annual atonement must be made with the blood of the atoning sin offering for the generations to come. It is most holy to the Lord."

Have you ever heard someone say that they just didn't like to read the Old Testament? I have—to be perfectly honest, before I came to know the Lord; I was guilty of saying that same thing. I just didn't understand it. Isn't it wonderful how God opens the eyes of His children? It didn't take me long to learn to love The Word in it's entirety after coming to The Cross. Now it seems amazing to me how I could have been so blind.

All through the Old Testament it speaks of blood offerings being offered up to God for the atonement of sin. Without the Old Testament we can't begin to see what the precious blood of Christ means to us. *Romans 3:25a God presented him as a sacrifice of atonement, through faith in his blood.*

The Old Testament is full of wonderful stories to be passed down from generation to generation. And there is much to be learned from each one of those stories, but the greatest knowledge in it is the fact that all the sacrifices made for the atonement of sin was temporary until JESUS BLOOD was shed. It is because of God's great love for us that he sacrificed the blood of His Son to pay the penalty for our sins once and for all. There is no further sacrifice needed. How great is His love? *Romans 5:8 But God demonstrates his own love for us in this: While we were still sinners Christ died for us. Praise His Holy Name.*

April 14

BROKEN INTO BEAUTIFUL

Psalm 32:5 Then I acknowledged my sin to you and did not cover up my iniquity. I said "I will confess my transgressions to the Lord"- and you forgave the guilt of my sin.

I just read the testimony of a wonderful Christian woman. She had made the choice as a young girl to abort her unborn child. She was a Christian girl who bought into the lies of Satan because of the fear of others finding out her secret. She knew at the time that she was committing a great sin but did it anyway. She went through hell as a result of her choice. When she finally turned to Christ and received forgiveness. He turned her brokenness into something beautiful. She is now a wonderful example of what Christ can do. She shares her testimony with the world. She is a gifted worship leader, songwriter, speaker and author. She sings the song Broken Into Beautiful with a first hand knowledge.

Is there something in your past that you just do not think God will forgive? If there is, you are wrong to think that God will not forgive you. There is nothing that God will not forgive. Even David, a man after God's own heart committed murder. When we acknowledge our sins, God will forgive them. God is just waiting for us to come to Him so that He can heal our broken spirits. There is only one way to true and lasting peace. It is because of God's grace that we can attain it. It is because of God's mercy that we have been saved from a life of misery and shame. *The Lord your God is a merciful God. Deuteronomy 4:31a.*

We all have things in our past that come back to haunt us if we let them. God's desire for us is to seek His forgiveness and move on with Him. He wants to take our brokenness and make it into something beautiful.

April 15

KEEP YOUR EYES ON JESUS

Psalm 25:15 My eyes are ever on the Lord, for only He will release my feet from the snare.

When the Lord spoke to me about starting a ministry for young Christian Women, He, at that time, also gave me the name for it— Women at the Well. I never doubted it until somebody informed me that there was already a national group with that name. I immediately became concerned that I might be infringing on the name. I started questioning God about why He would tell me to give it that particular name if it was going to cause problems. I looked the group up online and found out that they did indeed exist. I contacted them and told them my story. They wrote back telling me that they were only in the state of California and there would be nothing wrong with me keeping the name. They were gracious enough to encourage me in this ministry.

Why had I become so discouraged and fearful? Because I hadn't trusted in the Lord. I should have called on Him immediately. *Psalm 24:17-21 The troubles of my heart have multiplied; free me from my anguish. Look upon my affliction and my distress and take away all my sins. See how my enemies have increased and how fiercely they hate me; let me not be put to shame, for I take refuge in you.*

It was very disconcerting when I realized that I had taken my eyes off of Jesus and the minute I did, I started feeling discouraged. I knew that what God had given me came from Him and yet I allowed Satan to try to destroy my joy and peace. We must not let Satan do that to us. It is when we are doing the work that God has called us to that the evil one comes in and tries to rob us of our peace. He wants us to become discouraged in the hope that we will give up doing the will of God. We must keep our eyes on Jesus. When he calls us to something, He will see us through. *1 Chronicles 28:20 David also said to Solomon his son, Be strong and courageous, and do the work, Do not be afraid or discouraged, for the Lord God, my God is with you. He will not fail you or forsake you until all the work for the service of the temple of the Lord is finished.*

April 16-17

WATER FOR THE WEEKEND

Grace and Providence
by William Cowper

Almighty King! Whose wondrous hand
Supports the weight of sea and land;
Whose grace is such a boundless store,
No heart shall break that sighs for more.

Thy providence supplies my food,
And 'tis Thy blessing makes it good;
My soul is nourish'd by Thy Word,
Let soul and body praise the Lord!

My streams of outward comfort came
From Him who built this earthly frame;
Whate'er I want His bounty gives,
By whom my soul forever lives.

Either His hand preserves from pain,
Or, if I feel it, heals again;
From Satan's malice shields my breast,
Or overrules it for the best.

Forgive the song that falls so low
Beneath the gratitude I owe!
It means Thy praise: however poor,
An angel's song can do no more.

April 18

RESTORED JOY

Isaiah 12:1-3 In that day you will say: "I will praise you, O Lord. Although you were angry with me, your anger has turned away and you have comforted me. Surely God is my salvation; I will trust and not be afraid. The Lord, the Lord, is my strength and my song; he has become my salvation. With joy you will draw water from the wells of salvation.

What a wonderful God we serve. He is always ready, willing and able to forgive us of all sin: Even when we have grieved Him; and, yes, angered Him by our sinful actions. He never holds grudges; He never refuses to hear our confession of sorrow, and our pleas for forgiveness. Because of our salvation provided us through His Son, we do not have anything to fear. We can praise His name in all circumstances.

Have you done something that you know was not pleasing to the Lord? Are you afraid to trust the Lord enough to ask Him for forgiveness, so that He can restore you to the joy of your salvation? Don't be—He is your strength and your song—He is your salvation, and He wants to restore your joy. Just return to Him, His arms are outstretched to you; He will put His arms of love around you, and He will forgive you and restore your peace and your joy.

April 19

SILENT SANCTUARY

Exodus 25:8 "Then have them make a sanctuary for me, and I will dwell among them."

Due to the nature of our business, my husband and I travel a great deal. Now I am not complaining; I know that we have been blessed in many ways by the opportunities God has given us. It seems, however, that at those times I find it most difficult to be alone with God. There are always distractions, which does not allow for total concentration and fellowship with the Lord. I miss those times of solitude and I get homesick for my time alone with Jesus.

I have a special place in my home that I have made as my own sanctuary. I can go in that silent sanctuary, shut the door, and commune with God like no other place in the world. It is there that He has my undivided attention. It is there that I can hear Him speak to me. I am always anxious to run to that sanctuary, knowing that He will meet me there.

Is it difficult for you to find a quiet place to meet with Jesus? If it is, find a place today; any place where you can be alone with Him. I heard a speaker (a mother with several children) say that her sanctuary is when she locks herself in the bathroom because there was no other room that had a lock. Find that special place where you can find silent solitude. Ask God to help you find that special place and that special time to be alone with Him.

April 20

THE LAST SUPPER

The last time that Jesus sat at the table with all of His disciples was the day before His crucifixion. We know it today as Maundy Thursday. As I was reading this morning about the last supper that Jesus had with His disciples, I was thinking about how Jesus heart must have hurt for these men. He knew that one of them (Judas) was going to betray Him, in fact he already had. *Then one of the Twelve—the one called Judas Iscariot—went to the chief priests and asked," What are you willing to give me if I hand him over to you?" So they counted out for him thirty silver coins. Matthew 26:14-15*

Jesus also knew that one of His beloved (Peter) would soon deny Him three times even though Peter vehemently denied it. *Peter asked, "Lord, why can't I follow you now? I will lay down my life for you." Then Jesus answered, "Will you really lay down your life for me? I tell you the truth, before the rooster crows, you will disown me three times.* I find this very disturbing because Peter was truly sincere when he said what he did. He thought his faith was so strong that he could withstand anything, but he soon found out that he would cave in to fear and he would deny Christ three times just as Jesus predicted.

What if the next time we take communion would be our last? Jesus still knows our hearts today. When we partake of His Supper, do we have pure hearts? Or are we taking communion knowing that we are not worthy because we have betrayed Him in our hearts?

Let's remember Peter, who at the time thought he would never betray Jesus. Let's pray as we partake at the Communion table, what portrays Christ's body and His blood that our hearts are right with God. And let's pray that we would always be willing to stand against anything that would take our eyes off of Jesus to the point of denying Him.

April 21

FROM DESPAIR TO JOY

John 3:16-18 "For God so loved the world that he gave his one and only Son, that whoever believes in him shall not perish but have eternal life. For God did not send his Son into the world to condemn the world, but to save the world through him. Whoever believes in him is not condemned, but whoever does not believe stands condemned already because he has not believed in the name of God's one and only Son.

Good Friday is the day that we remember the sacrifice that Jesus made for us: The day that He gave His life for the sins of all. We can call it Good Friday because we know the rest of the story. But at the time, those followers of Jesus must have thought of it as the worst day of their lives. Think of the sorrow that they must have felt when they witnessed their hope nailed to a cross. *A large number of people followed him, including women who mourned and wailed for him. Luke 23:27.* I can only imagine the despair that they felt. They had to watch the man whom they loved so much being tortured and crucified. They didn't understand what was happening.

But O what joy on the morning of the third day when the two Mary's went to look at the tomb and witnessed the miracle of His resurrection. *So the women hurried away from the tomb, afraid yet filled with joy, and ran to tell his disciples. Matthew 28:8* Don't you imagine that they were thrilled as they suddenly started to recall all that Jesus had said to them the previous days just before His crucifixion? What a happy day the first day of the Resurrection of Jesus, the day we now call Easter. Joy truly came in the morning.

They didn't really understand what happened on Good Friday because they couldn't see the future. We know the rest of the story. We know the hope that we have in Christ if we know Him as our personal Savior. He is our hope of glory. *To them God has chosen to make known among the Gentiles the glorious riches of this mystery, which is Christ in you, the hope of glory. Colossians 1:27*

We have heard the entire story. We have a choice to make. We can believe what we have heard or we can reject it. What about you? Do you believe in Him? Have you accepted Him as your personal Savior? He died on that Cross for you and for me—but we must believe it and receive it. If you haven't done that, please don't let another day go by without making that decision to believe, to receive and follow Jesus.

April 22

GRIEF TO JOY

John 16:20 I tell you the truth; you will weep and mourn while the world rejoices. You will grieve, but your grief will turn to joy.

The people, who were followers of Christ, were grieving, while the others around them were rejoicing as they witnessed His crucifixion. What a despairing day for them. They had believed that Jesus was the hope for their future and now they had to stand and watch Him die. Don't you imagine that they thought their hope was gone?

On that day when Mary went and saw the empty tomb, she quickly spread the word that Jesus wasn't there. The other followers ran to see that indeed the tomb was empty. While they went away with questions in their minds about where he was, Mary sat there at the empty tomb crying, until Jesus revealed himself to her. The joy she felt must have been all that she could ever have imagined.

On the evening of that first day of the week, when the disciples were together, with the doors locked for fear of the Jews, Jesus came and stood among them and said, "Peace be with you!" After he said this, he showed them his hands and side. The disciples were overjoyed when they saw the Lord. John 20:19-20. What joy must have filled their hearts, as they finally realized the truth of what Jesus had been telling them. Their joy was restored and they had hope once again.

It is because of Jesus death on that Cross, and His resurrection, that we can have joy and hope for our future. It is because of Him that we know we have eternal life. We need not be fearful about anything, because, as the song goes—'We know who holds the future, and life is worth the living just because HE LIVES!'

The grief of His death on the Cross for our sins was turned to joy the day Christ arose.

April 23-24

WATER FOR THE WEEKEND

JESUS HASTEN TO SUFFER
by William Cowper

The Saviour, what a noble flame
Was kindled in his breast,
When hasting to Jerusalem,
He march'd before the rest.

Good will to men, and zeal for God,
His every thought engross;
He longs to be baptized with blood,
He pants to reach the cross!

With all His suffering full in view,
And woes to us unknown,
Forth to the task His spirit flew,
'Twas love that urged Him on.

Lord, we return Thee what we can:
Our hearts shall sound abroad,
Salvation to the dying Man,
And to the rising God!

And while Thy bleeding glories here
Engage our wondering eyes,
We learn our lighter cross to bear,
And hasten to the skies.

April 25

A GODLESS NATION

Deuteronomy 32:5-6 They have acted corruptly toward him; to their shame they are no longer his children, but a warped and crooked generation. Is this the way you repay the Lord, O foolish and unwise people? Is he not your Father, your Creator, who made you and formed you?

If you are like me, you are very concerned about how our country is headed. As I was reading God's Word this morning in Deuteronomy 32, I couldn't help but see the similarities between the Israelites and what is happening in America now. Moses was speaking to the Israelites, but it is as if he were speaking to the American people today.

Our nation was founded on Christian principles, but to look at it today, you would never know it. We have been very successful in turning our backs on God and doing everything in our power to kick Him out of our nation. We have not remembered the days of old. *You deserted the Rock, who fathered you; you forgot the God who gave you birth. Deuteronomy 32:18.*

Just as God was not pleased with Israel when Moses spoke to them, He is not pleased with America today. I pray that the American people will wake up before it is too late. *"It is mine to avenge; I will repay. In due time their foot will slip; their day of disaster is near and their doom rushes upon them." Deuteronomy 32:35*

The good news for we Christians is; we have nothing to fear, no matter what comes. God has promised to deliver us. We can rejoice in the Lord Our God. *Rejoice, O nations, with his people, for he will avenge the blood of his servants; he will take vengeance on his enemies and make atonement for his land and people. Deuteronomy 32:43.*

April 26

ENDURING TRIALS

Psalm 34:19 A righteous man may have many troubles, but the Lord delivers him from them all.

As Christians, do we encounter trials? Of course we do. In fact God's Word tells us that we will go through times of trouble. This life has a way of rendering severe blows. It could be illness, the loss of a loved one, loss of a job, or a difficult person. At other times it might be a wayward child or a broken relationship. Are you going through some kind of trial right now? Don't be discouraged. We may face trials and troubles of all kinds in this world but God sees us through every one of them.

Isn't it wonderful that we have a God that knows all about our trials? Not only does He know about them, he walks with us through them all. There was a time in my life that I didn't walk with the Lord. I didn't have the knowledge that God would give me strength and would deliver me through them all. Now, I can't imagine going through difficult troubles and trials in life without Him. He is my help, my strength, my comfort and my hope in all things: And He is yours too. *Psalm 41:10 So do not fear, for I am with you; do not be dismayed for I am your God, I will strengthen you and help you; I will uphold you with my righteous right hand.*

Let us remember that God is with us. He is our Sustainer, our Comforter, our Peace, and our Strength. He is our All in All. We are more than conquerors through Christ. *No, in all these things we are more than conquerors through him who loved us. Romans 8:37*

April 27

BREAKING BONDAGE

Though we are slaves, our God has not deserted us in our bondage. He has shown us kindness in the sight of the kings of Persia; He has granted us new life to rebuild the house of our God and repair its ruins, and he has given us a wall of protection in Judah and Jerusalem. Ezra 9:9

I have been talking with someone who has been under bondage for a sin that she committed years ago, before she found the Lord. In all the years since then, she has allowed Satan to rob her of joy and peace, because she has never forgiven herself for her past sin. It is tragic to think that she and others like her, has the power to break the chains that bind them, but do not use it.

Just as God did not desert Israel in their sin, He will not desert us either. He is there to fight the battle for us as we put on His full armor. *Put on the full armor of God so that you can take your stand against the devil's schemes. For our struggle is not against flesh and blood, but against the rulers, against the authorities against the powers of the dark world and against the spiritual forces of evil in the heavenly realms. Ephesians 6:11*

Are you under bondage because of past sins? You need not be; you must understand that God does not bring our past sins up to us. That is the tool of Satan. You must rebuke him in the name of Jesus. When you came to the cross of Jesus, He forgave you of all sin. *Jeremiah 31:34* tells us He doesn't even remember them. Why then, should you?

If we continue to allow Satan to tell us lies, we will never enjoy the peace and joy that God intends for us to have. If you are struggling with a sin that you committed in the past, let it go; surrender it to the Lord and let Him fill you with every good thing that He has for you. Don't remain in the chains of bondage. Let Jesus break those chains and set you free.

April 28

A NURTURED GARDEN

Galatians 5:22-23 But the fruit of the Spirit is love, joy, peace, patience, kindness, goodness, faithfulness, gentleness and self-control.

My mother and dad both had what you would describe as a green thumb. Their vegetable and flower gardens were something to behold. They were absolutely beautiful and everyone admired them. They spent hours nurturing them so that they would produce the most beautiful, abundant gardens that they could possibly grow. It wasn't an easy task, there would be times I would see them working in extreme heat, and there were times that they were weak physically but would still be out working in their gardens. They didn't stop there either. Once those gardens produced the abundant crops, they would pick the harvest, they would preserve it and then they would give most of it away. We children especially benefited greatly from their labor of love.

Producing the fruit of the Spirit is like those gardens of my parents. We must work at it to produce beautiful fruit. Without spending time with our Lord and letting Him nurture us, we are not likely to become what God wants us to be. We need to develop a relationship with God so that He can prune us until we display the fruits of the Spirit. God will not force us to spend time with Him. We must have the desire to become what God wants us to be. We must desire the fruits of the Spirit. Just like a neglected earthly garden will not bear a beautiful crop, neither will our hearts develop beautiful fruits of the Spirit. We must spend time in His Word, and we must spend time in prayer. We must seek Him and allow Him to grow us into a beautiful flower that others will admire. When we are fully developed into the beautiful person that God desires for us to be, others will be blessed and they also will benefit from our beauty. Let us keep on keeping on until we have developed every fruit of the Spirit.

April 29

CHOSEN

Acts 9:15 But the Lord said to Ananias, "Go! This man is my chosen instrument to carry my name before the Gentiles and their kings and before the people of Israel. I will show him how much he must suffer for my name.

Wow this is Saul that God was talking about: The man that had spent his adult life persecuting the Lord's disciples. Yet God was choosing him to carry the message of His name to the Gentiles and their kings, and before the people of Israel. It is truly amazing that God would choose one like him.

Why do you suppose God chose him for such a tremendous job? Don't you think that people would be very impressed with the changes in his life? Most people knew him and knew how he had pursued God's people with murderous threats against them. I believe that they would have to think something miraculous had happened to him. What a testimony Paul had. He spent the rest of his life proclaiming God's word to the world around him.

Isn't it encouraging knowing that God will not only forgive those who have persecuted His name, but He will use them to reach others. Have you been praying for someone, thinking that they will never change their attitude toward God? We see only the present but God sees the future—He knows the changes that He can make in a life. He uses many people like Paul (Saul) to carry His message to the world. Be encouraged by Paul's testimony. God many times uses the most unlikely people to spread the word.

WATER FOR THE WEEKEND

LIVELY HOPE AND GRACIOUS
by William Cowper

I was a groveling creature once,
And basely cleaved to earth:
I wanted spirit to renounce
The clod that gave me birth.

But God hath breathed upon a worm,
And sent me from above
Wings such as clothe an angel's form,
The wings of joy and love.

With these to Pisgah's top I fly
And there delighted stand,
To view, beneath a shining sky,
The spacious promised land.

The Lord of all the vast domain
Has promised it to me,
The length and breadth of all the plain
As far as faith can see.

How glorious is my privilege!
To Thee for help I call;
I stand upon a mountain's edge,
O save me, lest I fall!

Though much exalted in the Lord,
My strength is not my own;
Then let me tremble at His word,
And none shall cast me down.

May 2

PLOWING GROUND

Hosea 10:12 Sow for yourselves righteousness, reap the fruit of unfailing love, and break up your unplowed ground; for it is time to seek the Lord, until he comes and showers righteousness on you.

I am not a gardener but my parents were. I watched them garden all of my life and saw the process they went through to reap a harvest of plenty. They would plow the ground, sow the seed, water it when the rain did not come; they pulled weeds and hoed around the plants as the ground became hard. It was a lot of hard work, but they were always willing to spend time in that garden nurturing it so that it would produce a great crop.

Do you know what happens to unplowed ground? Nothing but weeds grows, and at the time of harvest there will be nothing worth having. Our hearts are like unplowed ground. If we don't plow the ground with the word of God and seek Him, our hearts will become hard and will not reap the harvest of good fruit. God's word says it is time to seek the Lord until He comes. It is when we seek Him that we find Him. And when we find Him he showers us with righteousness.

If the seed has been planted in your heart, nurture it just like you would an earthly garden; pull out those ugly weeds of sin, water it with the Word of God and keep it plowed; so when the time for harvest comes you will reap a harvest of righteousness.

May 3

CALL OF LEVI

Luke 5:27-28 After this, Jesus went out and saw a tax collector by the name of Levi sitting at his tax booth. "Follow me," Jesus said to him, and Levi got up, left everything and followed him.

When Jesus said to Levi (Matthew) "Follow me," he immediately got up and followed Him, leaving everything behind. He did not hesitate, ask why, and take time to ponder the situation, or even consider what it would mean for his future. He just got up and followed Him. He had faith that this man, Jesus, was someone special. He instinctively knew that he could trust him with his life.

Have you left everything behind to follow Jesus? I think sometimes, we hesitate to walk the path that Jesus has called us to walk, because we don't want to give up everything. We are not sure just where God might lead us: So we lag behind, dragging our feet; or we just simply say no.

God would never lead us on a destructive path. We can be sure that wherever He leads us, it is going to be a place where blessings will abound. Since Jesus has a purpose for each one of us, He will lead each of us to a special place. Let's trust God and follow Him wherever He leads. Doesn't it excite you to see what He has in store for you? It does me.

May 4

CALL OF LEVI-PART 2

Luke 5:29 Then Levi held a great banquet for Jesus at his house, and a large crowd of tax collectors and others were eating with them.

A banquet is a lavish dinner where the best of everything is shared: Most of the time it is given to celebrate an occasion or a person. Levi was so excited about his new found friend, Jesus, that he held a great banquet in His honor. It seems as though he invited everyone he knew to celebrate and share in his excitement.

Are we that excited about introducing Jesus to everyone we know? Jesus is willing to come to our banquet table. He wants to meet every one of our acquaintances. He would love to be the guest of honor in our homes. Are we opening our hearts and our homes to allow Jesus to be our guest of honor? Or are we ashamed to introduce Him to every one we know? Think about it. God's word says, *"If anyone is ashamed of me and my words in this adulterous and sinful generation, the Son of Man will be ashamed of him when he comes in his Father's glory with the holy angels." Mark 8:38*

May 5

A PRAYING NATION

Deuteronomy 4:6-7 Observe them carefully, for this will show your wisdom and understanding to the nations, who will hear about all these decrees and say," Surely this great nation is a wise and understanding people." What other nation is so great as to have their gods near them the way the Lord our God is near us whenever we pray to him?

Today is the National Day of Prayer. As I was reading this passage of scripture this morning, it was difficult to pick just a couple of verses out and not write the entire chapter. I would encourage you to read it.

We have been so fortunate to live in a country that was founded on Christian values. We are fortunate enough even now, to proclaim a National Day of Prayer. I wonder however, how long we will be able to have the freedom to do so. We have been blessed in past years to have our leaders not only recognize it, but to take an active role in supporting it wholeheartedly. Will we continue along that line? Or will we see a subtle decline in the enthusiasm that we have had for the privilege of showing the world that we are a Christian nation?

Sometimes it seems like our prayers are not heard as we look around us and see the lack of interest in our Lord: But God hears every prayer. We can trust Him in whatever He decides. His plan will not be thwarted. We each have a responsibility to pray for our country.

If my people, who are called by my name, will humble themselves and pray and seek my face and turn from their wicked ways, then will I hear from heaven and will forgive their sin and will heal their land. 2 Chronicles 7:14 'If' is a very big word: Not only is it a big word, it is one of the most powerful. 'If' could be the catalyst that could change the whole direction of how our nation is headed. If it were not true, God wouldn't have said it. As we read this verse, let's realize the power behind it and PRAY, PRAY, PRAY.

May 6

A GODLY MOTHER

Proverbs 31:15a, 17, 20, 24a, 25a, 26, 27, 28a, 30. She gets up while it is still dark; she provides food for her family. She sets about her work vigorously; her arms are strong for her tasks. She opens her arms to the poor and extends her hands to the needy. She makes linen garments. She is clothed with strength and dignity. She speaks with wisdom, and faithful instruction is on her tongue. She watches over the affairs of her household and does not eat the bread of idleness. Her children arise and call her blessed. Charm is deceptive, and beauty is fleeting; but a woman who fears the Lord is to be praised.

We will be celebrating Mother's Day on Sunday and I can't help reflecting on what a wonderful mother I had. She was truly the pattern of a Godly Woman described in Proverbs 31. She filled that description as well as anyone I have ever known. She worked from sun up to sun down to provide all the things that is a mother's responsibility, and then some.

Proverbs 29:15 The rod of correction imparts wisdom, but a child left to himself disgraces his mother. Mother was a very kind woman and was demonstrative in her affection. But she was not a pushover for anything that undermined her authority as a mother. She had no problem correcting me when I needed it. She was adamant about my obedience to her. I never endured a punishment that I wasn't deserving of. Mother may have punished me for doing wrong, but I never once doubted that she loved me. In all honesty, I knew that her reason for correction was because of her love for me.

Proverbs 22:6 Train a child in the way he should go, and when he is old he will not turn from it. Of all the things my mother taught me, the most important thing of all was how to love the Lord. In all of her busyness, she never neglected my spiritual needs. My mother taught me all about Jesus from an early age on. As a little girl, she would tuck me in at night and always prayed with me. She took me to church every Sunday, even though a lot of the time we had to walk several blocks. We never sat down to a meal without saying grace. As busy as she was, I would see her reading her bible on a daily basis. She taught me the importance of having a relationship with the Lord.

Unfortunately, when I left the protection of my home, I decided I could live my life without the Lord. In all of those years in between, I never forgot what my mother taught me, and when I was 42 years old I finally gave my life to Jesus. I thank the Lord for the Godly mother that He gave me. I wonder if I would be a Christian today had it not been for her teaching me Godly wisdom. If you had a Godly mother, like me, you are so blessed. If you didn't have, you can take the initiative to be one yourself. The most important thing we can give our children is Godly wisdom.

May 7-8

WATER FOR THE WEEKEND

LIVING AND A DEAD FAITH
by William Cowper

The Lord receives his highest praise
From humble minds and hearts sincere;
While all the loud professor says
Offends the righteous Judge's ear.

To walk as children of the day,
To mark the precepts' holy light,
To wage the warfare, watch, and pray,
Show who are pleasing in His sight.

Not words alone it cost the Lord,
To purchase pardon for His own;
Nor will a soul by grace restored
Return the Saviour words alone.

With golden bells, the priestly vest,
And rich pomegranates border'd round,
The need of holiness expressed,
And called for fruit as well as sound.

Easy indeed it were to reach
A mansion in the courts above,
If swelling words and fluent speech
Might serve instead of faith and love.

But none shall gain the blissful place,
Or God's unclouded glory see,
Who talks of free and sovereign grace,
Unless that grace has made him free!

May 9

SHARING THE WORD

John 4:39 Many of the Samaritans from that town believed in him because of the woman's testimony.

Wow, wouldn't that be a wonderful thing. Just to know that many believed because of what we have told them about Jesus? There are many people in this world today who have never heard the wonderful stories of Jesus. I believe we always think in terms of foreign countries when we consider those who have never heard the word. But there are so many all around us in our own country, in our own community, who have never heard the good news. Many have never been in a church or around Christian people on a day-to-day basis. They are starving for The Word.

Are we telling the people around us about Jesus? Or are we keeping it to ourselves. *"My food,"* said Jesus *"is to do the will of him who sent me and to finish his work. Do you not say, 'Four months more and then the harvest'? I tell you, open your eyes and look at the fields! They are ripe for harvest. John 4:34-35* We must not wait; there are many who may die before they hear the word. It is up to us to tell them about Jesus. Many may never enter the doors of a church, and the only word they will ever hear may come from us. Are we willing to take the message to them? Let's step out of our comfort zones and reach out to those around us and share the good news of Jesus with them. When God opens the door for us to share our testimony with those who do not know Christ, enter in and give them the food for which they are starving.

May 10

THE PURSUIT OF HAPPINESS

Ezekiel 7:19 They will throw their silver into the streets and their gold will be an unclean thing. Their silver and gold will not be able to save them in the day of the Lord's wrath. They will not satisfy their hunger or fill their stomachs with it, for it has made them stumble into sin.

It seems as if the whole world is on a fast track toward a pot of gold. For some reason, they think that wealth is going to provide them with all they need. Many are in pursuit of it at the expense of their health, their family, their friends, and their soul.

Wealth may give you all of the material things that you desire; but it cannot buy your health back when it's gone: It cannot provide companionship when you are lonely: It cannot bring happiness when you're sad: It cannot buy love: And most importantly it cannot buy eternal life.

When all is said and done, the only thing that provides all that we need is Jesus. Without Him we are lost. We must seek Jesus and not silver and gold. He is the only one who can provide eternal life.

May 11

THE REFLECTION OF CHRIST

2 Corinthians 3:18 And we, who with unveiled faces all reflect the Lord's glory, are being transformed into his likeness with ever increasing glory, which comes from the Lord, who is the Spirit

We are always talking about how we want people to see Jesus in us, and of course we do; but I wonder if we use that phrase out of a prideful attitude. Do we leave the impression to others that what we are saying is 'Look at me—I am holier than you?'

Our hope is built on nothing less than Jesus Christ. That is the reason that we should desire to look like Jesus—He is the hope of glory. Our testimony should be that because of the cross, we are special people. And it is because of the salvation that Christ obtained for us through His death and resurrection, that we are His children. It is because we have chosen to accept Him and His sacrifice for our sins, that others can see His reflection in us. Not because of anything we have done, but because of what He did for us. We can do nothing outside of Christ living in us, to show others a picture of Him.

Our prayer should be that others will see a difference in our life, because of what Christ did for us, not because of a 'holier than though' attitude. Our lives should point others to the hope that they can have through Him. *To them God has chosen to make known among the Gentiles the glorious riches of this mystery, which is Christ in you, the hope of glory. Colossians 1:27*

May 12

STANDING FIRM

1 Corinthians 16:13 Be on your guard; stand firm in the faith; be men of courage; be strong.

In a recent beauty pageant, the contestant from California was asked how she felt about same sex marriage. Now I have no doubt but what every judge there, knew that this girl was a Christian because they have many opportunities to interview them before the pageant. He was trying to make her look bad in the eyes of the world. My first impression was one of pure anger, but after thinking it over, I realized that God allowed him to ask that for a reason. I was reminded of the scripture in *Genesis 50:20 You intended to harm me, but God intended it for good to accomplish what is now being done, the saving of many lives.*

When the girl was asked the question, her reply was that she thought it was a great thing to live in a country that has free choice, but that she personally felt that marriage was between a woman and a man only, because that is what God's Word proclaims.

There were millions of people watching that night and they heard the truth from a young beautiful Christian girl who was standing up for what she believed in, even though she probably realized that it might cost her the crown. She was more concerned about her faith than she was an earthly crown. She was most definitely standing firm in her faith.

When interviewed the next day on national television, she explained that it was more important to her to stand on her Christian principles, than to win a crown. She said the reason she didn't win was because it was not God's desire for her to. *Romans 8:28 And we know that in all things God works for the good of those who love him, who have been called according to his purpose.*

What a testimony to the whole world. Would we, under the same circumstance, be willing to stand firm in front of the entire world and proclaim such faith, even though it might mean the loss of a crown? I pray that each one of us would have the courage to stand firm in our faith just as this girl did. She may not wear a crown on this earth, but she certainly will in heaven. She will have her reward there, and in the meantime, God has used her in a powerful way, simply because of her faith in Him.

May 13

FAITH BUILDER

Colossians 2:6 So then, just as you received Christ Jesus as Lord, continue to live in him, rooted and built up in him, strengthened in the faith as you were taught, and overflowing with thankfulness.

As I write this devotional I am overflowing with such thankfulness and joy that I can hardly contain myself. Why? Because one I love and have been praying for has surrendered his heart to the Lord.

This man has spent his life as an agnostic bordering on atheist. He couldn't understand why a loving God would allow his young brother to drown at the age of four in his presence. Satan has tortured him with this all of his life. But praise God, He is bigger than Satan. *You dear children are from God and have overcome them, because the one who is in you is greater than the one who is in the world. 1 John 4:4*

Satan roams around looking to devour, but our Lord is wooing us to Him, so that we might gain eternal life. When we become a child of God we suddenly understand that we will see our brothers and sisters once again and will with them, spend eternity in the presence of Jesus.

Sometimes we pray so long for something to happen and when it doesn't happen quickly, our faith falters and we start doubting that our prayers will ever be answered. I humbly and ashamedly admit that I have been guilty of this so many times. It truly boosts our faith 100% when we see someone we have prayed for so long come to Christ.

If you, like me doubt at times and almost lose hope, remember that we have a God that is far beyond our understanding. What a wonderful and loving God we serve: A Father who hears and answers every prayer. We must continue to be built up in Him, strengthened in the faith that we were taught and overflowing with thankfulness.

May 14-15

WATER FOR THE WEEKEND

LONGING TO BE WITH CHRIST
by William Cowper

To Jesus, the crown of my hope,
My soul is in haste to be gone;
O bear me, ye cherubim, up,
And waft me away to His throne!

My Saviour, whom absent I love,
Whom, not having seen I adore;
Whose name is exalted above
All glory, dominion, and power;

Dissolve thou these bonds that detain
My soul from her portion in thee.
Ah! strike off this adamant chain,
And make me eternally free.

When that happy era begins,
When arrayed in Thy glories I shine,
Nor grieve any more, by my sins,
The bosom on which I recline.

Oh then shall the veil be removed,
And round me Thy brightness be pour'd,
I shall meet Him whom absent I loved,
Shall see Him whom unseen I adored.

And then, never more shall the fears,
The trials, temptation, and woes,
Which darken this valley of tears,
Intrude on my blissful repose.

Or, if yet remember'd above,
Remembrance no sadness shall raise,
They will be but new signs of Thy love,
New themes for my wonder and praise.

Thus the strokes which from sin and from pain
Shall set me eternally free,
Will but strengthen and rivet the chain
Which binds me, my Saviour, to Thee.

May 16

A REASON TO REJOICE

Luke 10:19-20 I have given you authority to trample on snakes and scorpions and to overcome all the power of the enemy, nothing will harm you. However, do not rejoice that the spirits submit to you, but rejoice that your names are written in heaven.

We may not be trampling on snakes and scorpions, but God has given us power to do all kinds of things, even to overcome the power of the enemy. He has given us power to do whatever He asks us to do. He wants us to live a life of service.

God has given each one of us a place to serve Him. We may be walking the path where Jesus is leading us. We may be fulfilling the task that He has set before us. All of these things are admirable and wonderful, but we must remember that God, because we are His children, has given us the power to do all of these things. We should not rejoice in the things that we have done. We should rejoice in the fact that we are a child of God.

Christ died on the cross for our sins. If we believe Him and receive Him as our personal Lord and Savior, we can rejoice in the fact that our names are written in the book of life. Let us rejoice in what God has done for us, not what we have done for Him.

May 17

FINDING GOD'S PURPOSE

Proverbs 19:21 Many are the plans in a man's heart, but it is the Lord's purpose that prevails.

I am convinced that God has a purpose for each of us. The question is, are we seeking His purpose or are we bent on our own? We get so caught up in our lives doing the things that we want to do that we miss God's direction. We stay so busy doing our own thing that we don't hear God. We run to and fro doing even good things, but are they the things that God has called us to do? God has a perfect plan for us, far better than we can dream up for ourselves. *Hebrews 11:40 God had planned something better for us so that only together with us would they be made perfect.*

God has a path He wants us to travel. He will never lead us astray. He can and will do miraculous things in our lives that we can't even imagine. He empowers us to use even those areas in our lives where we feel the most inferior. *Exodus 4:10 Moses said to the Lord, "O Lord I have never been eloquent, neither in the past nor since you have spoken to your servant. I am slow of speech and tongue.* Because of his human frailties, Moses doubted that he could do what God had called him to do but God found a way to use him in spite of it. God had a purpose for his life.

Never underestimate the power of the Lord. He will equip us with everything we need to carry out His plan and purpose for each of us. It is through our weakness that we are made strong in Christ. *2 Corinthians 12:9 But he said to me, "My grace is sufficient for you, for my power is made perfect in weakness."*

Ask Him to show you what He has for you to do. I promise you, if you are seriously looking to Him for guidance, He will show you the way. *Jeremiah 33:3 'Call to me and I will answer you and tell you great and unsearchable things you do not know.'* Are you earnestly seeking His purpose?

May 18

COMPASSIONATE LORD

Isaiah 49:13 Shout for joy, O heavens; rejoice, O earth; burst into song, O mountains! For the Lord comforts his people and will have compassion on his afflicted ones.

I have had several calls this week from Christian sisters asking for prayer for those who are hurting; for God's people who have major health problems, and those who have lost loved ones. In this world we are going to face all kinds of sorrow; that is just a matter of fact. God's word tells us so. But praise God, we will not go through them alone.

We serve a God of all comfort. He sees, feels, and knows exactly what we are going through. There is nothing that we face that He has not faced. There is no pain so great that He has not experienced, and more. He can identify with every heartache. He has compassion for everyone who is going through trials of all kinds.

If you are experiencing heartache, Our Lord wants to comfort you. He alone truly understands your pain. You are not alone in your grief. Turn to Him; He is your source of strength and comfort. He has compassion like no other and His compassion never fails.

May 19

FORGIVENESS

Colossians 3:13 Bearing with one another, and forgiving one another, if anyone has a complaint against another; even as Christ forgave you, so you also must do.

Have you ever been hurt so badly by someone that you thought you just couldn't forgive them? Most of us have at some time or another. Our very human response is to either retaliate or pull away from the one who has caused us pain with an un-forgiving attitude. The problem with that is we end up hurting ourselves much more than the person who caused us pain. Harboring grudges is very destructive because it takes our mind and our hearts away from our relationship with the Lord. We wallow in self-pity instead of letting the Lord heal our pain.

I just read a story about a Christian woman who was paralyzed with an un-forgiving spirit, because of a man who had molested her as a child. For many years she had hated this person and refused to let it go. She became clinically depressed and suffered anxiety attacks. And then one day through the help of a Christian counselor and her husband (a minister); she was able to release her pain and give it to the Lord. It was then and only then that she obtained the peace that only God can provide. Today God is using her in a mighty way because she was able to release her pain and forgive the man who had caused it. She is free to be the woman God intended her to be.

Christ came to this earth for one purpose; to die on the Cross for our sins. Not just for the sin of our enemies and those who have hurt us, but for our own personal sins. He has graciously forgiven us and continues to forgive over and over again every time we sin against Him. He died on the Cross for my sin and your sin. He rose again so that we could have eternal life with Him.

Then Peter came to Him and said, "Lord, how often shall my brother sin against me, and I forgive him? Up to seven times?" Jesus said to him, "I do not say to you, up to seven times, but up to seventy times seven." Matthew 18:21-22. We must learn to forgive.

May 20

LOVE AND PROTECTION

Isaiah 65:24 And it shall come to pass that before they call, I will answer; and while they are yet speaking, I will hear. KJV

Yesterday I put a roast on to cook in preparation for a pot of vegetable soup; then I left the house forgetting to turn the stove off. I was gone about an hour when suddenly, I had a flash (or should I say a lightening bolt) of remembrance. I hurriedly headed for home. As I was coming out of the parking lot where I had been, I heard the fire engines and I instinctively knew that they were on their way to my house. I was so panicked and scared that the only thing I could pray was Jesus, Jesus, Jesus. I repeated His name all the way home. I had visions of my house being in flames.

As I turned on to my street, sure enough I saw two fire trucks in front of my house. I pulled up in the drive, jumped out of the car, opened the door leading in to my kitchen, and the smoke just rolled out. I ran to the stove, shoved the pan with the roast off of the burner, turned it off, and then ran back outside for breath. All the time thanking Jesus that all the damage that was done was a house that disgustingly smelled of smoke.

As I pondered the whole situation this morning and was thanking the Lord for His magnificent mercy and grace, I was lead to this scripture and I knew that I must write a devotional about my embarrassing negligence. How can I explain what happened any better than the above scripture. Even before I knew what was going on, God brought to my mind the memory of the stove being left on. He answered my call even before I asked Him. And all of the way home He heard me speak His Name. How great is our God! He is awesome and worthy to be praised.

May 21-22

WATER FOR THE WEEKEND

LOOKING UPWARDS IN A STORM
by William Cowper

God of my life, to Thee I call,
Afflicted at Thy feet I fall;
When the great water-floods prevail,
Leave not my trembling heart to fail!

Friend of the friendless and the faint,
Where should I lodge my deep complaint,
Where but with Thee, whose open door
Invites the helpless and the poor!

Did ever mourner plead with Thee,
And Thou refuse the mourner's plea?
Does not the word still fix'd remain,
That none shall seek Thy face in vain?

That were a grief I could not bear,
Didst Thou not hear and answer prayer:
But a prayer-hearing, answering God
Supports me under every load.

Fair is the lot that's cast for me;
I have an Advocate with Thee;
They whom the world caresses most
Have no such privilege to boast.

Poor though I am, despised, forgot,
Yet God, my God, forgets me not:
And he is safe, and must succeed,
For whom the Lord vouchsafes to plead.

May 23

HELPING HANDS

Exodus 17:11, 15 As long as Moses held up his hands, the Israelites were winning, but whenever he lowered his hands the Amalekites were winning. When Moses hands grew tired, they took a stone and put it under him and he sat on it. Aaron and Hur held his hands up—one on one side, one on the other—so that his hands remained steady till sunset. Moses built an altar and called it The Lord is my Banner. He said," For hands were lifted up to the throne of the Lord."

Once upon a time in my youth I sang solos, but did not use my voice for many years and I lost it. I have recently acquired a desire to sing again but I am terribly fearful when faced with singing alone. I was asked to sing a solo in the evening service one Sunday. The Lord gave me a song to sing along with a testimony. I prayed for two plus weeks that God would give me courage, clarity, and peace so that I would get through it in a manner so that the words would be heard. I had complete peace until minutes before I was to sing. I was trying to run through the music in my head but I could not grasp the tune, I was in a state of panic. Satan was trying to destroy my peace. As our Pastor was giving the offertory prayer, two of my precious sisters obviously sensed my anguish and they stepped up beside me. One of them took my hand and the other laid her hand on my back. I knew that they were lifting me up in prayer and immediately my peace was restored.

Satan was trying to win the battle, but God sent His enforcements in to lift me up in my weakness. The above scripture came to my mind. Isn't it a wonderful thing to have Christian sisters and brothers who are forever ready to help us fight our battles? I, like Moses can say that The Lord is my Banner—for hands were lifted up to the throne of God for me. God heard and delivered me from my fears.

We all need help at times, we need each other. Let's always lift our brothers and sisters to the Lord in prayer when we see they are in trouble.

May 24

LEARNING LESSONS

Daniel 5:18, 19a, 20, 22, 23, 30, 31 "O king, the Most High God gave your father Nebuchadnezzar sovereignty and greatness and glory and splendor. Because of the high position he gave him, all the peoples and nations and men of every language dreaded and feared him. But his heart became arrogant and hardened with pride; he was deposed from his royal throne and stripped of his glory. But you his son, O Belshazzar, have not humbled yourself, though you knew all this. Instead, you have set yourself up against the Lord of heaven. You had the goblets from his temple brought to you, and you and your nobles, your wives and your concubines drank wine from them. You praised gods of silver and gold, of bronze, iron, wood and stone, which cannot see or hear or understand. But you did not honor the God who holds in his hand your life and all your ways. That very night Belshazzar, king of the Babylonians was slain, and Darius the Mede took over the kingdom, at the age of sixty-two.

Wouldn't you think after Belshazzar had seen what happened to his father, Nebuchadnezzar; he would have learned a lesson? He didn't and it cost him his life. There are many lessons we could learn just by seeing the results of someone else's sins. But Satan will blind us and lead us down paths of destruction. We can choose to go our own way and ignore the things that God has for us. We can worship the things of this earth if we so desire—or we can learn from the mistakes of others, and worship God, and choose to serve Him and Him only.

How many times have we seen the change in those who have turned from their own sinful ways to follow the Lord? What a difference God makes in our lives when we choose to walk with Him and allow Him to lead us in the paths of righteousness. We don't have to walk down that path of destruction, we can look at the lives of others that have turned from their wicked ways; we can see the changes that God has brought; we can learn from them and choose to walk with God.

May 25

LIGHTING THE PATH

Psalms 119:105 Your word is a lamp to my feet and light for my path.

Are you at a crossroad in your life? Are you contemplating which way to go? Perhaps there is a decision in your workplace that needs to be made. Or maybe you are considering a move to another job, or another home. Or perhaps God is calling you to a ministry, but you aren't sure if you want to follow that path. There are so many different roads to take as we travel on this journey of life. And if we aren't careful, we can make the wrong turn, leading us to a disastrous end, and missing the treasure God has for us.

How would you feel if you knew that you could be assured of success in every decision that you make? Did you not know that you have the road map to a hidden treasure right in your grasp? It is in The Bible: God has mapped out everything you and I need to lead us to victory. All we have to do is open it and read it and apply it to our life.

We may not travel the road we want, but when we seek God and His wisdom, He will lead us on the right path. Only He knows what lies ahead.

Why then do we fret about every decision that must be made? Because we are not leaning on the Lord and searching His Word for the path that lights our way. God has given us His Word to help us travel the road to victory. But it is up to us to open it up to find the treasure map therein.

May 26

PARTIAL OBEDIENCE

1 Samuel 15:3a Now go, attack the Amalekites and totally destroy everything that belongs to them. 15:9a But Saul; and the army spared Agag and the best of the sheep and cattle, the fat calves and lambs—everything that was good. 15:11a I am grieved that I have made Saul king, because he has turned away from me and has not carried out my instructions."

When I read this account of Saul, I ask myself how he could have ignored the command that God had given him. God had made him king of Israel, you would think that he would heed every word that came from God. He was successful in defeating the Amalekites as God directed him to do, but he withheld what he wanted for himself. The worst part of it is that he used the excuse of doing it to sacrifice to God.

How many times do we hold things back from God that He has asked us to get rid of? Do we pick and choose what we will get rid of or do we give it all to God? Do we make a commitment to God and then hold on to the things that we desire—and try to disguise our sin by making our offerings to Him?

God grieves when we aren't obedient and then offer our flimsy sacrifices to Him. He desires our obedience above sacrifices. *"Does the Lord delight in burnt offerings and sacrifices as much as in obeying the voice of the Lord? To obey is better than sacrifice, and to heed is better than the fat of rams. 1 Samuel 15:22*

Are you hanging on to something that God has asked you to get rid of? If we are not willing to get rid of everything He asks us to, He is not pleased. God desires our obedience—partial obedience is no obedience at all.

May 27

MATURITY

1 Timothy 4:12 Don't let anyone look down on you because you are young, but set an example for the believers in speech, in life, in love, in faith and in purity.

Our physical age or how long we have been a Christian has nothing to do with our maturity in the Lord. It has everything to do with the relationship we have established with Him. I have seen so many young people serving the Lord as if they are elders of the church. They have gone beyond the baby Christian stage of living on milk, to the meat stage where they are consuming God's word with a hearty appetite. They have gained a wealth of knowledge through their desire to feed on His word. He is using them in a mighty and powerful way, because they are hearing from Him and serving Him in obedience. They are indeed setting an example not only to their contemporary brothers and sisters, but to the older Christians who have not yet reached maturity in the Lord.

On the other hand, I have seen Christian people who are advanced in age both in the physical and spiritual realm but have never gone beyond the baby stage in their walk with the Lord. Why is that? *In fact though by this time you ought to be teachers, you need someone to teach you the elementary truths of God's word all over again. You need milk, not solid food! Anyone who lives on milk, being still an infant, is not acquainted with the teaching about righteousness. Hebrews 6:12-13.* If we aren't searching for knowledge we are not likely to attain the wisdom that God has planned for us.

No matter what our age is, let's move on in the knowledge of the Lord. Let's set an example as children of God — in our speech, in our life, in our love, and in our faith and purity. Let's become mature Christians.

May 28-29

WATER FOR THE WEEKEND

LOVE CONSTRAINED TO OBEDIENCE
by William Cowper

No strength of nature can suffice
To serve the Lord aright:
And what she has she misapplies,
For want of clearer light.

How long beneath the law I lay
In bondage and distress;
I toll'd the precept to obey,
But toil'd without success.

Then, to abstain from outward sin
Was more than I could do;
Now, if I feel its power within,
I feel I hate it too.

Then all my servile works were done
A righteousness to raise;
Now, freely chosen in the Son,
I freely choose His ways.

"What shall I do," was then the word,
"That I may worthier grow?"
"What shall I render to the Lord?"
Is my inquiry now.

To see the law by Christ fulfilled
And hear His pardoning voice,
Changes a slave into a child,
And duty into choice.

May 30

PRAISE GOD IN LOW PLACES

Habakkuk 3:17-19 Though the fig tree does not bud and there are no grapes on the vines, though the olive crop fails and the fields produce no food, though there are no sheep in the pen and no cattle in the stalls, yet I will rejoice in the Lord, I will be joyful in God my Savior The Sovereign Lord is my strength; he makes my feet like the feet of a deer, he enables me to go on the heights.

There are times in our lives that we experience unpleasant things—low places—difficult situations: Perhaps illness, loss of a loved one, loss of a job, broken relationships, and spiritual battles. None of us are immune to times such as these. They are real and they hurt. Sometimes we feel like we are all alone. Sometimes we feel like just giving up.

Life has a way of striking extremely difficult blows. In those times we can either retreat to an empty place of despair—or we can reach for the hand of God to pull us up to higher ground. Perhaps you are going through a low place right now: If you are, reach out and clasp the hand of God. And like Habakkuk, rejoice in the Lord. He is your strength and He will carry you to higher ground where you will find peace and comfort, even in times of distress.

May 31

PRAYER, PEACE & PRAISE

Philippians 4:6-7 Do not be anxious about anything, but in every-thing, by prayer and petition, with thanksgiving, present your requests to God. And the peace of God which transcends all under-standing will guard your hearts and your minds in Christ Jesus.

Why do we spend so much of our time agonizing over what might or might not happen? Does it do any good at all to wring our hands in agonizing fear? The is an absolute NO. Nothing we say or do can change the circumstances around us. It is when we take our cares to the Lord, and leave them with Him, that we receive the peace that passes all understanding.

I once read a statement that said if you pray with doubt, you might as well not pray at all. There is a lot of truth in that. If we pray with that kind of doubt, we are not putting our trust and faith in God. His word says to pray with thanksgiving. I believe that when we pray we should give Him immediate thanks for what He is going to do. He hears our every prayer, and He already has the answer.

We can praise God for all things. When we are trusting in Him, we have the assurance that He will answer in due time and according to His will. When we grasp that with understanding, we will attain the peace that Paul is talking about.

June 1

FAITH AND HOPE

Psalm 25:20-22 Guard my life and rescue me, let me not be put to shame, but I take refuge in you. May integrity and uprightness protect me, because my hope is in you. Redeem Israel, O God, from all their troubles.

It seems to me that most people are living in fear these days. Fear of what is going to happen in the world around us-fear of the economy-fear for our children- fear for our tomorrows. It isn't difficult to understand the fear that prevails. Satan is working in every area of our lives to discourage us and make us think there is no hope. We need to keep our faith and trust in the Lord because He is our hope.

As the song says, 'My hope is built on nothing less than Jesus blood and righteousness.' That tells the entire story of how we can find peace in the midst of the madness of our world today. Nothing will give us hope except for Jesus. We know that no matter what goes on in the world around us, we don't have to worry. We are in God's hands. He is our peace, our strength, our redeemer, our comforter, our friend, our HOPE. Let's keep our faith and trust in Him, because the day is coming when He will take us out of this world of chaos and sin, and we will live eternally with Him. HE IS OUR HOPE!

June 2

CALLED TO THE LIGHT

1 Peter2:9 But you are a chosen people, a royal priesthood, a holy nation, a people belonging to God that you may declare the praise of him who called you out of darkness into his wonderful light.

Isn't it amazing when we think about the fact that we are chosen people, and because of that we are part of a royal family: A family that belongs to God? Why would He choose us? Well the word says it is so we can declare His praises to others. Are we living like His chosen people? Are we praising Him to the world around us?

We have been called out of darkness into light Are we truly living in the light that He has given us? His light shines in our hearts so that we can see clearly and live the life that He called us to. Before we were called by Him, we lived in darkness; not able to see His truth. Now we are children of light. We are children of the King. Let's let His light shine through us and go out and praise His Holy Name to the world around us.

June 3

GO FOR THE GOLD

1 Corinthians 9:24-27 Do you not know that in a race all the runners run, but only one gets the prize? Run in such a way as to get the prize. Everyone who competes in the games goes into strict training. They do it to get a crown that will not last; but we do it to get a crown that will last forever. Therefore I do not run like a man running aimlessly; I do not fight like a man beating the air. No, I beat my body and make it my slave so that after I have preached to others, I myself will not be disqualified for the prize.

I look forward to every four years when the Olympic Games are on. I am always in awe of the fitness and dedication that these athletes display. It is obvious that they put in many hours of training. They are all hopeful that they will get a medal. There are some who do not want to settle for just any medal—they want the gold.

As I was watching the men's figure skating competition during the last winter Olympics, I was very impressed by the performance of the young man that represented America, It was obvious that he had done all that he could possibly do to prepare himself for this very moment. His efforts were rewarded with the coveted gold award. As I was listening to the commentators, they were talking about the fact that he was the most dedicated skater there; they talked about the hours that he put in daily, even to the point that his own coach would have to tell him to stop and take a rest. Wow! It's not often that we see that kind of dedication.

God has given us all a vision for what He has called us to do. Are we training ourselves to win the race we are in? Do we give it our all? Do we train daily so that we might win the prize set before us? We need to be doing all in our power to learn everything we need to know, to strengthen our bodies and our spirits so that we might finish the race and not be disqualified. We are training for a prize that will last forever. Let's not settle for less than 'the gold'.

June 4-5

WATER FOR THE WEEKEND

NOT WORKS
by William Cowper

Grace, triumphant in the throne,
Scorns a rival, reigns alone;
Come and bow beneath her sway;
Cast your idol works away!
Works of man, when made his plea,
Never shall accepted be;
Fruits of pride (vainglorious worm!)
Are the best he can perform.

Self, the god his soul adores,
Influences all his powers;
Jesus is a slighted name,
Self-advancement all his aim:
But when God the Judge shall come,
To pronounce the final doom,
Then for rocks and hills to hide
All his works and all his pride!

Still the boasting heart replies,
What the worthy and the wise,
Friends to temperance and peace,
Have not these a righteousness?
Banish every vain pretence
Built on human excellence;
Perish everything in man,
But the grace that never can

June 6

HIDING SIN

Genesis 3:8-9 Then the man and his wife heard the sound of the Lord God as he was walking in the garden in the cool of the day, and they hid from the Lord God among the trees of the garden. But the Lord God called to the man," Where are you?"

Adam and Eve had sinned against God when they disobeyed the command that He had given them—not to eat from the tree of knowledge of good and evil. So when they heard the Lord walking in the garden they hid themselves. They didn't want God to see them in their sin.

Isn't that the way we do when we sin against our Lord? We want to hide ourselves by not being in the presence of God. We avoid spending time with Him—we avoid church—we avoid Christian people who just might possibly say something that would convict us of our sin. We try to hide ourselves from the very one who could bring us back into fellowship—Our Lord.

We cannot hide our sins from God. He knows and sees all that we do. He will not banish us forever. He wants to restore our salvation. Perhaps you have sinned against God and think that you need to hide from the Lord. Don't try to hide, face Him and ask His forgiveness. He is a loving and forgiving God. He will welcome you back with open arms. He is calling you back. Just like He did with Adam and Eve—He is asking "Where are you." Answer Him and allow Him to restore your fellowship.

June 7

CRY OF THE RIGHTEOUS

Psalms: 34:17-18 The righteous cry out, and the Lord hears them; he delivers them from all their troubles. The Lord is close to the brokenhearted and saves those who are crushed in spirit.

There are just some things in this life that are hard to take. Recently there was an attack made against one of my sisters-in-Christ, which left me brokenhearted and discouraged. To say that I was crushed in spirit is an understatement. Satan at once pounced on the chance to bring me down. But praise God, He delivered me from the defeat that could have ensued. God is greater than he who is in the world trying to rob us of our peace and joy.

Is there something in your life that has left you brokenhearted and discouraged? Don't let another day go by without crying out to God. He knows, He hears, and He understands: And He is the only one who can restore your peace. He will lift your spirit and mend your broken heart if you cry out to Him.

Satan hangs around trying to destroy our peace and joy every time we become discouraged. Don't let that happen, we have the power in Jesus to defeat him at all times. *The God of peace will soon crush Satan under your feet. The grace of our Lord Jesus be with you. Romans 16:20.*

June 8

BE STILL -WAIT-LISTEN

Psalms 27:13 I am still confident of this: I will see the goodness of the Lord in the land of the living. Wait for the Lord; be strong and take heart and wait for the Lord.

It seems as if every Christian I talk to is concerned about a wayward child or grandchild. It is so disheartening to see your children being led astray by the pull of the world. Even some of those who walked with the Lord in a close relationship at one time are now going their own way. They seem to have turned their back on the Lord. It seems as if they want nothing to do with the things that they were taught as children.

The question everyone asks themselves is, "What can I do to point them to Jesus?" We can't forcefully bring them back: But we have a Savior who understands our heartache: He understands our fears: He understands our feeling of helplessness. God has given us a great and powerful tool in prayer. He hears our every plea for our children. He loves them even more than we do and His desire is to bring them back to Himself.

There are times when we even become angry with our children and have thoughts of giving up on them: But that is not the response that God wants us to have. *My dear brothers, take note of this: Everyone should be quick to listen, slow to speak and slow to become angry, for man's anger does not bring about the righteous life that God desires. James 1:20.* We must be patient with them and wait on the Lord to do the work in them that only He can do.

God's Word says to *"Be still and know that I am God." Psalm, 46:10a.* We must be still, we must wait on the Lord, and we must listen to every word that the Lord tells us. And we must pray constantly for our children to be convicted by the Lord through His plan and according to His will. He sees every move they make, He knows everything about them: And only He knows the right way to get their attention. Let's put our complete faith and trust in Him and be confident that we will see the goodness of God in the land of the living.

June 9

CONSEQUENCES OF SIN

Numbers 14:30-34 Not one of you will enter the land I swore with uplifted hand to make your home, except Caleb son of Jephunneh and Joshua son of Nun. As for your children that you said would be taken as plunder, I will bring them in to enjoy the land you have rejected. But you—your bodies will fall in the desert. For forty years —one year for each of the forty days you explored the land—you will suffer for your sins and know what it is like to have me against you.

Sin has far reaching affects on people, even those innocent ones that are caught up in the consequences. God had told Moses that he was going to give the Israelites the land of Canaan, a land flowing with milk and honey. But because of their fear of others, they refused to go. As a result of their disobedience and lack of faith, they and their children wandered in the desert for forty years.

What a different life they would have had if they had believed God and trusted Him. They could have immediately entered the land of Canaan. It was a lush land and would have provided all they needed. God would have protected them against those who would have fought against them.

I wonder how often we miss out on wonderful blessings that God has for us because we fear to go where He leads us. How many of our bad choices affect those around us? When we don't obey the Lord, it not only hurts us, but it may hurt those we love. One thing we can know for sure—there will be consequences. We either trust God or we don't, and our choices should be considered very carefully.

June 10

ANTICIPATE EXCITEMENT

Hebrews 10:24-25 And let us consider how we may spur one another on toward love and good deeds. Let us not give up meeting together as some are in the habit of doing, but let us encourage one another— and all the more as you see the Day approaching.

While on the way to Sunday school one day, my 3 year old granddaughter, Ellison, was very excited about going, and talked about it all the way there. I was wondering how many of us are always excited to enter the house of God. We should be. It is there that we share the love of God so freely. It is there that we develop relationships with our spiritual family, and to encourage one another in our walk with the Lord.

We should always enter God's house with excitement and anticipation to worship and praise God. *Praise God in the great congregation; praise the Lord in the assembly of Israel. Psalm 68: 26.* God desires us to inhabit our place in His house. He wants us to come with joy and an open heart to accept His blessings. The church is a sanctuary in which to come and share in God's Love with our Christian family, and most of all to worship God. Let's get excited about it and thank God for the opportunity and the freedom that we have to praise His name.

June 11-12

WATER FOR THE WEEKEND

O LORD I WILL PRAISE THEE
by William Cowper

I will praise Thee every day
Now Thine anger's turn'd away;
Comfortable thoughts arise
From the bleeding sacrifice.

Here, in the fair gospel-field,
Wells of free salvation yield
Stream of life, a plenteous store,
And my soul shall thirst no more.

Jesus is become at length
My salvation and my strength;
And His praises shall prolong,
While I live, my pleasant song.

Praise ye, then, His glorious name,
Publish His exalted fame!
Still His worth your praise exceeds;
Excellent are all His deeds.

Raise again the joyful sound.
Let the nations roll it round!
Zion, shout! for this is He;
God the Saviour dwells in thee

June 13

CHAINS OF DEPRESSION

God is our refuge and strength, an ever present help in trouble. Therefore we will not fear, though the earth give way, and though the mountains fall into the heart of the sea, Though its waters roar and foam, and the mountains quake with their surging. Psalm 46:1-3

I have a friend who has been struggling with depression because of Satan's attack on her and her family. We all suffer those attacks from time to time. Even the strongest of Christians are not immune to them. But praise God we do not have to linger there. God is our refuge and strength. He will guide us through the darkest times.

On those days that seem so dark, and our hope is dim, and our faith is weak, we can look up and know that God is near. He is ready, willing, and able to renew our strength and to break those chains of depression. What a wonder—to know that our Heavenly Father knows our heartaches and our struggles. He wants to take our hands and lead us out of the depression that Satan wants us to remain in.

When we are feeling like God has forsaken us, let us remember His promise to keep us in perfect peace. Look to the Lord for the support that only He can give us. He wants to restore the joy of our salvation. *When I said, "My foot is slipping," your love, O Lord, supported me. When anxiety was great within me, your consolation brought joy to my soul. Psalm 94:18-19*

June 14

AN ABUNDANCE OF FOOD

2 Kings 4:43-44 "How can I set this before a hundred men?" his servant asked. But Elisha answered, "Give it to the people to eat. For this is what the Lord says: 'They will eat and have some left over.'" Then he set it before them, and they ate and had some left over, according to the word of the Lord.

Have you ever noticed when reading about the miracles that God performed concerning food, that not only was there plenty to fill them up, but there was some left over? God's provisions are never skimpy, they are always abundant. He never gives us just enough to satisfy our hunger temporarily, He always gives us more than we need.

Just imagine going to a banquet where the most delicious food is set before you, and you are invited to partake of it all: I doubt that you would hold back, but rather you would eat your fill. God's banquet table is like that: It is full of the choicest food, and it is ours for the taking. *Jesus answered, "It is written: 'Man does not live on bread alone, but on every word that comes from the mouth of God.'" Matthew 4:4* When we partake of His food on a regular basis, we have more than enough. He will fill us up with much left over. Let's linger at the banquet table that God has set for us: We will never be hungry again.

June 15

CHANGES

Matthew 18:3 *And he said: "I tell you the truth, unless you change and become like little children, you will never enter the kingdom of heaven."*

We hear a lot of rhetoric these days from our politicians about change. They have a lot of ideas about how we need to change our government, our policies, our choices, our strategies, etc. All of them promise that if they are elected, they will change our entire country to the utopia of excellence. Wouldn't that be wonderful? Unfortunately, that is not going to happen, no matter who comes in to power. No man has that ability— only God can bring that about.

I totally agree with them when they say we need change. The change we need however, does not have anything to do with who is in control of our government, but rather who is in control of our hearts. God is the only one who can make the changes that we need to turn our county around. I fear that people are trying to kick God out of this country. It is not politically correct to talk about Jesus because we might offend someone.

We have seen the attacks being made on Christians who stand up and proclaim the Word of God. How can God be pleased with this country when some of our politicians stand up and blatantly say that they think it is ok to kill babies and it's ok to allow same-sex marriage when God's word says it is an abomination?

We, as Christians have the opportunity to change the direction of the way things are going in our country. Will we obey what God tells us in His Word? *If my people, who are called by my name, will humble themselves and pray and seek my face and turn from their wicked way, then will I hear from heaven and will forgive their sin and will heal their land. 2 Chronicles 7:14*

June 16

CRY OUT THE WARNING

Ezekiel 3:17-19 "Son of man, I have made you a watchman for the house of Israel; so hear the word I speak and give them warning from me. When I say to a wicked man, 'You will surely die,' and you do not warn him or speak out to dissuade him from his evil ways in order to save him from his life, that wicked man will die for his sin, and I will hold you accountable for his blood. But if you do warn the wicked man and he does not turn from his wickedness or from his evil ways, he will die for his sin; but you will have saved yourself.

If we saw someone crossing the street in front of an oncoming vehicle, wouldn't we cry out to them so they would save themselves from certain death? If we saw someone drowning, would we not throw out a lifeline to them? Of course we would.

Would we hesitate to cry out a warning to those we see living in sin? Would we throw out a life line to them? When we see another in the throes of sin and don't warn them, they will die in their sin. *John 8:24 I told you that you would die in your sins; if you do not believe that I am the one I claim to be, you will indeed die in your sins."*

They may not listen, but we must warn them anyway. *Ezekiel 2:5 And whether they listen or fail to listen—for they are a rebellious house—they will know that a prophet has been among them.* If they do not listen, at least we know that we have done what Jesus has commanded us to do. We have given them warning.

God says we will be held accountable. That is a pretty serious thing to contemplate. If we see others living in sin, we need to warn them of their fate and try our best to point them to Jesus. It may be the only way they will ever find their way to The Cross. We may be the only one who will plant the seed that could save their life. I don't think any of us want to be accountable for one lost soul.

June 17

DECEIVING SPIRITS

1 Timothy 4:1 The Spirit clearly says that in later times some will abandon the faith and follow deceiving spirits and things taught by demons. Such teachings come through hypocritical liars, whose consciences have been seared as with a hot iron.

My daughter and her family were extremely joyous when they chose to join a church about 6 months ago. They thought they had found the one that they had been looking for: Until Laura (their 13 year old) came home from a youth meeting one night greatly disturbed. The conversation they had in that meeting led to a debate on homosexual issues. When Laura discovered that this particular denomination they were in sanctioned them not only through uniting them in marriage, but allowing them in the pulpit, she spoke up and defended God's Word on the matter and she was called a Gay Basher. The entire family, of course was devastated. They have realized that they can no longer stay in a denomination that approves of something that is directly against the Word of God.

It is very sad that society today has stamped what is an abomination to our Lord with their approval. But it is even sadder that the churches have bought into the lies and also have turned their back on the Word of God. All because they want to be politically correct instead of biblically correct.

We should not align ourselves with any church that sanctions sin in the pulpit. Let us stand firm on the Word of God.

June 18-19

WATER FOR THE WEEKEND

OLD TESTAMENT GOSPEL
by William Cowper

Israel in ancient days
Not only had a view
Of Sinai in a blaze,
But learn'd the Gospel too;
The types and figures were a glass,
In which thy saw a Saviour's face.

The paschal sacrifice
And blood-besprinkled door,
Seen with enlighten'd eyes,
And once applied with power,
Would teach the need of other blood,
To reconcile an angry God.

The Lamb, the Dove, set forth
His perfect innocence,
Whose blood of matchless worth
Would be the soul's defence;
For he who can for sin atone,
Must have no failings of His own.

The scape-goat on his head
The people's trespass bore,
And to the desert led,
Was to be seen no more:
In him our surety seem'd to say,
"Behold, I bear your sins away."

Dipt in his fellow's blood,
The living bird went free;
The type, well understood,
Express'd the sinner's plea;
Described a guilty soul enlarged,
And by a Saviour's death discharged.

Jesus, I love to trace,
Throughout the sacred page,
The footsteps of Thy grace,
The same in every age!
Oh, grant that I may faithful be
To clearer light vouchsafed to me!

June 20

CROSSING THE LINE

The sacrifices of God are a broken spirit; a broken and contrite heart, O God, you will not despise. Psalm 51:17

While doing a bible study written by Ginni Hawley, she told a story that happened to her. I would like to quote her (with her permission)

Quote: 'Many years ago at a weekend conference in a small church in rural Missouri, I was praying with a woman who was responding to the Lord's convicting presence. She wept at the altar as I prayed with her, confessing her desperate need for Jesus. I will never forget the line over which she would not cross when I encouraged her to give the Lord all of her life, good and bad, just as she was. She stiffened and narrowed her eyes as she looked at me and said, "No, I cannot go that far. All of me is too much. Some of us just can't do it, Ginni." And before I could respond, she was gone.' Unquote

Why won't we cross that line and give it all to Jesus? What is in our life or in our minds that makes us think we can't trust Him? There is nothing, absolutely nothing, so big or so small that He cannot and will not forgive. There is nothing that we are going through that He doesn't understand, and that He cannot handle. There is nothing that His grace won't cover. Let us grasp the truth of how deep and wide his love and grace is. *And God raised us with him in the heavenly realms in Christ Jesus, in order that in the coming ages he might show the incomparable riches of his grace, expressed in his kindness to us in Christ Jesus. Ephesians 2:-7*

God wants to give us peace and the only true peace we will find is when we cross that line and give Jesus everything. Let's not hold anything back or we will miss the peace and joy that God has set before us. There's a song I love that says 'give it all to Jesus and He will turn your sorrows in to joy.' Why on earth wouldn't we want that? There is nothing that compares to the joy and peace that we find when we give it all to Jesus. *The Lord is my strength and my shield; my heart trusts in him, and I am helped. My heart leaps for joy and I will give thanks to him in song. Psalms 28:7*

GOD LOVES A CONTRITE HEART.

June 21

DENYING JESUS

Mark 14:27-31 "You will all fall away," Jesus told them. "For it is written: "'I will strike the shepherd, and the sheep will be scattered.' But after I have risen, I will go ahead of you into Galilee." Peter declared, "Even if all fall away, I will not." "I tell you the truth," Jesus answered, "today-yes; tonight-before the rooster crows twice you yourself will disown me three times." But Peter insisted emphatically, "Even if I have to die with you, I will never disown you." And all the others said the same.

As we all know, Peter did in fact, deny knowing Jesus. *Mark 14:71 He began to call down curses on himself, and he swore to them, "I don't know this man you're talking about."* As we read the account of Peter and his denial of Christ, we gasp and we are appalled. How could he have done that to the man that he had declared an undying friendship with?

Let's ask ourselves if we would have the strength and the determination to stand firm in our commitment to Christ if our lives were in question. If someone was standing in front of you with a loaded gun, and they asked you to deny Christ or die, would you have the strength to stand firm for Jesus?

How could we possibly deny Christ after what He has done for us? It is very possible that we might be put to that very test one day. How will you respond? Do you know Jesus as your personal Lord and Savior? Would you be ready to die before you would deny Him?

June 22

ENCOURAGING OTHERS

Luke 22:31-32 "Simon, Simon, Satan has asked to sift you as wheat. But I have prayed for you Simon, that your faith may not fail. And when you have turned back strengthen your brothers."

Has there ever been a time in your life when you have faltered in your faith. I don't know about you, but it sure has happened to me. Satan has a way of discouraging us in our weaknesses. But praise God; he is always there to put us back on our feet. He will strengthen us; He will forgive us and He will give us strength once again.

What an amazing God we serve. Even in our weaknesses He will use even that to encourage others who are going through the same trials. Only He can use our weaknesses to make us strong enough to help others. And that is exactly what He wants us to do. *Praise be to the God and Father of our Lord Jesus Christ, the Father of compassion and the God of all comfort, who comforts us in all our troubles, so that we can comfort those in any trouble with the comfort we ourselves have received from God. 2 Corinthians 1:3-4.* Don't you think that when others see that we have had the same struggles and yet overcome them through Christ, that they will be more likely to believe that there is hope for them also? Let's be willing to confess our weaknesses so that others may be encouraged.

June 23

FAITH AND BELIEF

1 John 1:2 The life appeared; we have seen it and testify to it, and we proclaim to you the eternal life, which was with the Father and has appeared to us.

On July 20, 1969, thirty-five years ago, Neil Armstrong stepped foot on the moon. Everyone who was born at that time remembers the words that he spoke; "That's one small step for a man, one giant leap for mankind."

I don't think anyone doubted the fact that it happened, even though they didn't experience it for themselves. Everyone believed, and still does, that Neil Armstrong did indeed experience this most extraordinary feat. Yet when it comes to our Lord Jesus being who He says He is, and the fact that He came to earth as a man and walked among men, people question the validity of it. How can they believe that a man can walk on the moon, but they can't believe in the existence of the one who created this universe? They put their faith in ordinary men, but refuse to put their faith in God.

But not all the Israelites accepted the good news. For Isaiah says, "Lord, who has believed our message?" Consequently, faith comes from hearing the message, and the message is heard through the word of Christ." Romans 10:16-17 There you have it: If one does not believe in the Word of God, he will never have faith in Him. What a tragedy; to live ones life without faith in our Creator, is the saddest thing in the world. Without faith in our Lord Jesus Christ, what in the world are we here for?

June 24

FROM UGLINESS TO BEAUTY

Ecclesiastes 3:11a He has made everything beautiful in its time.

We have made many trips across the desert area of Arizona. There was a time when I dreaded it because it seemed like what we mostly saw was cactus which I considered ugly. I will never forget the first time I saw cactus in bloom. It was beautiful. It was hard for me to imagine that it was the same plant that I had always viewed as being ugly. I never look at cactus anymore without realizing that in due time those ugly plants will be gorgeous.

It is the same with people. When we come to know Jesus as our personal Savior, He takes the ugliness in our hearts and begins to turn it into something beautiful. If we see someone with an ugly spirit, we need to think about the beauty that is just waiting to be displayed, and pray that those people will allow Jesus to come into their heart. That is the time when their beauty will be revealed. God is able to take the ugliest spirit and turn it into something beautiful.

June 25-26

WATER FOR THE WEEKEND

MOURNING AND LONGING
by William Cowper

The Saviour hides His face;
My spirit thirsts to prove
Renew'd supplies of pardoning grace,
And never-fading love.

The favor'd souls who know
What glories shine in Him,
Pant for His presence as the roe
Pants for the living stream.

What trifles tease me now!
They swarm like summer flies!
They cleave to everything I do,
And swim before my eyes.

How dull the Sabbath day,
Without the Sabbath's Lord!
How toilsome then to sing and pray,
And wait upon the Word!

Of all the truths I hear,
How few delight my taste!
I glean a berry here and there,
But mourn the vintage past.

Yet let me (as I ought)
Still hope to be supplied;
No pleasure else is worth a thought,
Nor shall I be denied.

Though I am but a worm,
Unworthy of His care,
The Lord will my desire perform,
And grant me all my prayer.

June 27

DO YOU HAVE A VISION?

Daniel 10:1, 7a, 8, 9, 10, 12 In the third year of Cyrus king of Persia, a revelation was given to Daniel (who was called Belteshazzar). I, Daniel was the only one who saw the vision; the men with me did not see it. So I was left alone, gazing at this great vision; I had no strength left, my face turned deathly pale and I was helpless. Then I heard him speaking, and as I listened to him, I fell into a deep sleep, my face to the ground. A hand touched me and set me trembling on my hands and knees. "Do not be afraid, Daniel. Since the first day that you set your mind to gain understanding and to humble your-self before your God, your words were heard, and I have come in response to them.

Has God ever given you a vision for service? Have others seen it? I doubt it, it is usually a vision that God has given you only. It is difficult to explain it to others. In fact others may think you are strange and delusional. When God gave Daniel his vision, he was the only one who saw it. The others with him fled and he was left alone. When God calls us, we are never alone. He is always with us, directing our path.

When God has given you a vision have you felt frightened and totally helpless? Daniel did. But then God, through His angel, spoke to him and he listened. When we open our hearts and get in God's word, He will speak to us and direct us in the ways that He wants us to go. Have you been afraid that you couldn't carry out the plan that God has set before you? God told Daniel not to fear because from the first day that he humbled himself and set his mind to under-standing, God heard him and responded.

Whatever our vision is, we have nothing to fear. God would never give us a vision and then desert us to carry it out on our own. He will equip us with all that we need. *2 Timothy 3:16-17 All Scripture is God-breathed and is useful for teaching, rebuking, correcting and training in righteousness, so that the man of God may be thoroughly equipped for every good work.*

We may never have a vision like Daniel, but I believe that God has a vision for each one of us. When we get in His Word and diligently seek Him, He will reveal Himself to us and show us where He wants to use us. What an exciting adventure!

June 28

APPROACHING IN LOVE

John 4:7-10 When a Samaritan woman came to draw water, Jesus said to her, "Will you give me a drink?" (His disciples had gone into the town to buy food.) The Samaritan woman said to him, "You are a Jew and I am a Samaritan woman. How can you ask me for a drink?" (For Jews do not associate with Samaritans.) "Sir," the woman said, "you have nothing to draw with and the well is deep. Where can you get this living water?

The woman at the well experience is one of the most beautiful stories in the bible. What a wonderful example of Christ's love for us. She must have been totally shocked when Jesus spoke to her. She was not accustomed to recognition from a Jew. But Jesus loved her in spite of who she was. He reached out to her, even though He knew she was a sinner, He didn't feel like she was unworthy. He saw her need for a Savior and offered her the living water. She accepted what Jesus offered her. He lovingly pointed out her sin and she was amazed that He knew all about her past. He revealed himself to her. Because of her encounter with this wonderful Jesus, she became a living testimony, being filled with the living water, she was able to spread the good news, and many became believers. *Many of the Samaritans from that town believed in him because of the woman's testimony. John 4:39*

Jesus teaches us a wonderful lesson in this story. Can we look beyond a person's past and present sin, to offer them hope in Jesus. Or do we look down on them and feel like they are not worthy? None of us are worthy, aside from God's grace. Give it some honest thought, do you open up in love to those around you who are living a sinful life, or do you feel you might get dirty if you show them the loving kindness that Jesus showed the woman at the well?

We need to drink daily from the living water to be able to refresh ourselves and be filled with the Holy Spirit, so that we can go out and testify of His forgiveness. We were all sinners and it is only because of the grace of God that we have been saved, and have eternal life. Let's not look down on anyone. Let's approach them in love and point them to the same living water that Jesus did for this Samaritan woman.

June 29

FAITH OF A CHILD

Psalms 62:5-8 Find rest, O my soul, in God alone; my hope comes from him. He alone is my rock and my salvation; he is my fortress, I will not be shaken. My salvation and my honor depend on God; he is my mighty rock, my refuge. Trust in him at all times, O people; pour out your hearts to him, for God is our refuge.

I have been following the progress of a little girl for several months on the Caringbridge.org. website. Her name is Abby. I don't know her personally but I got interested in her story when I was following the progress of another little boy suffering from cancer. She has been fighting this for 2 years with a series of very strong chemo. She has not had very many good days. The following paragraph is written by her.

"I am 11 yrs. old. I have a rare form of pediatric lung cancer. But cancer is not who I am. I am a brave and strong girl. God has given me the BEST family and friends. I love to play with my little brother, Ian. He is 3 years old. He makes me laugh and I forget that I have sick lungs. I get scared sometimes. But I know that I have to trust God no matter what."

Sometimes we think we have problems and then we read stories like Abby's and realize that ours pale in comparison. This little girl realizes that her strength comes from God, and she is putting her faith and trust in Him; a lesson we can all learn. I am blessed every time I read an update about her. She makes me bow my head in shame for not always putting her kind of faith in my Heavenly Father. Abby knows who she can trust, she knows God is her refuge and her salvation, she knows that her hope comes from Him. O what wonderful things we can learn from our children. God often uses them to teach us. We need to have the faith of a child.

June 30

FEEDING THE LOST

Luke 5:30-31 But the Pharisees and the teachers of the law who belonged to their sect complained to his disciples. "Why do you eat and drink with tax collectors and sinners?"
Jesus answered them, "It is not the healthy who need a doctor, but the sick. I have not come to call the righteous, but sinners to repentance."

I remember listening to a man who heads up a shelter for the homeless. He said that they always feed them first, before they speak to them about God's saving grace. It makes it much easier for them to believe that they care about their needs

I commend those who work with the homeless, the drunkards, the drug addicts, the sinners: But what about those in our own midst? Are we so involved in our own Christian fellowship that we ignore the ones who are sick in spirit? Are we so self-absorbed in our position as Christians that we ignore those who need to be fed? Do we consider ourselves to be too 'good' to eat with sinners'?

Jesus said it is not the healthy who needs a doctor, but the sick. How can we possibly share the love of God with others, if we deem ourselves too good to eat with them? It is a wonderful thing to fellowship with our brothers and sisters in Christ. I love to share with those people who understand who God is and praise our Lord together: But there are many around us who don't know Christ as their personal Savior. They need to hear the Word. Will you be willing to share your time and your food with them? I think they would be far more willing to listen to what we have to say about the grace of our Lord.

DO YOU NEED HELP?

John 5: 7-9 "Sir," the invalid replied, "I have no one to help me into the pool when the water is stirred. While I am trying to get in, someone else goes down ahead of me. "Then Jesus said to him, "Get up! Pick up your mat and walk. At once the man was cured; he picked up his mat and walked.

This man had been an invalid for 38 years. Surely in all that time, there were many people that saw his plight. They must have seen that he needed help but chose not to help him. There was one however, that saw his need and gave him the help he needed. Just by His very words, the man was healed.

Aren't we glad that Jesus sees all of our needs? We need no other. Do you need help today? Are you thinking that their just isn't anyone to help you? Well, there is one who sees your need and wants to help. Call on the name of Jesus—-He is the only help you need. If it is a physical need, he will heal you according to His will.

Others may not even be aware of the fact that you need help, most especially if it is a spiritual need. But Jesus knows and He is waiting for you to come to Him. Humble yourself and go to the one who knows, who understands and who will help you. You can be assured that you will receive the help and the healing that you need according to His will. If you are honestly seeking Him. He will never let you down. *Psalm 34:17-18 The righteous cry out, and the Lord hears them; he delivers them from all their troubles. The Lord is close to the brokenhearted and saves those who are crushed in spirit.* I encourage you today, if you are broken in spirit. Run to the one you need and receive the healing that He has for you.

July 2-3

WATER FOR THE WEEKEND

PEACH AFTER A STORM
by William Cowper

When darkness long has veil'd my mind,
And smiling day once more appears,
Then, my Redeemer, then I find
The folly of my doubts and fears.

Straight I upbraid my wandering heart,
And blush that I should ever be
Thus prone to act so base a part,
Or harbour one hard thought of Thee!

Oh! let me then at length be taught
What I am still so slow to learn,
That God is love, and changes not,
Nor knows the shadow of a turn.

Sweet truth, and easy to repeat!
But when my faith is sharply tried,
I find myself a learner yet,
Unskilful, weak, and apt to slide.

But, O my Lord, one look from Thee
Subdues the disobedient will,
Drives doubt and discontent away,
And Thy rebellious worm is still.

Thou art as ready to forgive
As I am ready to repine;
Thou, therefore, all the praise receive;
Be shame and self-abhorrence mine.

July 4

FREEDOM'S COST

John 3:16 For God so loved the world, that he gave his only begotten Son, that whosoever believeth in Him should not perish, but have everlasting life.

There have been many wars fought throughout the History of the world for the purpose of gaining freedom for the oppressed. Freedom has never been free. Freedom comes at the cost of much blood shed and many lives. Sadly many of those who have obtained that freedom often become enslaved once again, through their own weakness and lack of determination to live as free men and women.

We were born into a world of sin. We were powerless to fight for our freedom, but God loved us so much that He gave His only Son to die on a cross for our sins. Jesus shed His own blood so that we (you and I) might be set free from the sin that enslaved us. All we have to do is believe in Him and receive Him as our personal Savior.

As we remember those who have fought and are still fighting for the freedom of others, let's remember Jesus sacrifice on the Cross and what it cost Him. Will we live our lives as free men and women? Or will we once again become slaves to sin? *It is for freedom that Christ has set us free. Stand firm, then, and do not let yourselves be burdened again by a yoke of slavery. Galatians 5:1*

July 5

DARKNESS TO LIGHT

Acts 26:17-18 I will rescue you from your own people and from the Gentiles. I am sending you to them to open their eyes and turn them from darkness to light and from the power of Satan to God, so that they may receive forgiveness of sins and a place among those who are sanctified by faith in me.

On the fourth of July, after it was dark, our son was at our house shooting off fireworks, while the rest of us looked on with anticipation of what each one would look like. It was all very innocent and enjoyable. But the next morning when we went outside, we saw what a mess it had made. Apparently every time one of the fireworks exploded it scattered red paper everywhere. It even scarred the blacktop in the street. My husband was out there cleaning up the mess that the morning light revealed to us.

Spiritual darkness is just like that—sometimes sin is enjoyable in fact it is just plain fun. I was thinking about how we live in the darkness of sin until God's light reveals to us the mess that we are making of our lives. And once we see the light, we are appalled at what our lives have become. But then we ask Jesus for His forgiveness and he cleans up the mess we have made. What a wonderful Savior.

Let's not be blinded by the darkness of sin in our lives, but allow God's light to shine so that our sin will be revealed to us. God wants to clean up our messes so that His light can shine through us in this world of darkness. *You are the light of the world. A city on a hill cannot be hidden. Neither do people light a lamp and put it under a bowl. Instead they put it on its stand, and it gives light to everyone in the house. In the same way, let your light shine before men that they may see your good deeds and praise your Father in heaven. Matthew 5:14-16*

July 6

FALSE TEACHERS

1 John 4:1 Dear friends, do not believe every spirit, but test the spirits to see whether they are from God, because many false prophets have gone out into the world.

I am concerned about the fact that there are so many preachers teaching prosperity over television these days. I can't understand how they get such a different message than I do out of God's Word. I must tell you that I believe they are severely misguided and why I believe it. If we fall for the teaching that we can have whatever we want if we just have faith; then what happens to those who don't acquire earthly wealth? Their faith is built on false teaching and of course they are going to lose it.

1. Why would we think that God has ordained us all to be rich? If that were a fact, how do we explain the men of God like Paul and other Godly men throughout the bible, who had no earthly wealth except only what they needed? They certainly were not rich according to the world's standard. If we are chasing after worldly wealth instead of the wealth of knowledge of our Lord, we are doomed. God's word says: *A man who has riches without understanding is like the beasts that perish. Psalm 49:20*

2. When we put faith in false teachers, as so many do, we are taking ourselves out of God's control and His will for us. God's word says; *See to it that no one takes you captive through hollow and deceptive philosophy, which depends on human tradition and the basic principles of this world rather than on Christ. Colossians 2:8.* I believe that we cheapen the faith that our Lord speaks of in His Word when we hang on the words of man instead of God.

3. It is true that we can do all things through Christ. *Philippians 4:13 I can do everything through Christ who gives me strength.* But don't we misuse this scripture to satisfy and justify our

own selfish desires. We put the emphasis too much on the 'I' in this verse than we do on <u>Christ</u>. I believe that Paul was talking about strength to do the things that glorifies the Lord. We need to first look to God's will for our lives.

4. We should not use God's Word to try and acquire everything that we want, but rather what He wants for us. What if it isn't in His will for you to have great wealth? Would you still trust Him? *Matthew 19:23 Then Jesus said to his disciples, "I tell you the truth, it is hard for a rich man to enter the kingdom of heaven.*

So many times we are so consumed with the pursuit of making money that we have no time for God. We are either spending our time trying to acquire it, or we are spending time trying to hang on to it. The faith that our Lord speaks of, is an all consuming trust in God for the spiritual wealth that He has for us. Read *Luke 12:16-21* to see what Jesus had to say about one who is consumed by the desire for worldly wealth.

We need to put our faith and trust in the only one who can give us the things that we need. When we pray, we should pray according to God's will. I don't think we want anything that isn't in His will. Only God knows what's best for us. We can trust Him.

July 7

GLOBAL WARMING — OR GLOBAL WARNING

Isaiah 40:26 Lift your eyes and look to the heavens: Who created all these? He who brings out the starry host one by one, and calls them each by name. Because of his great power and mighty strength, not one of them is missing.

Now I want you all to know right up front, that I know very little about the subject of global warming, and I care very little about educating myself on it. In other words I am not very 'politically correct'. I do know that if our God could create the heavens and the earth and everything in it; the One that has made the stars and even calls them by name certainly has the power to take care of it.

Our real problem is that men have not put their faith and trust in the Lord. Man has a way of imagining that they can do the work of the only one who is able to maintain this universe. God's word says, *Trust in the Lord and do good; dwell in the land and enjoy safe pasture. Psalm 37:3* I find it sad that we worship the creation and not the creator. We are more concerned about the land we live in here on earth, than in the home that Jesus has made ready for His people.

We live in an evil world where people are more concerned about being politically correct than they are of being biblically correct. It's sad to say that even Christian people buy in to the lies of Satan by listening to those who have no knowledge of God. *They exchanged the truth of God for a lie, and worshiped and served created things rather than the Creator-who is forever praised. Roman 1:25* God did not make us robots. He gave us a mind to think with, and the freedom to choose whom and what we will worship. Are we going to put our trust in men or in Our Supreme Maker?

As we continue to kick God out of our hearts, homes and country, He will finally say enough is enough. He will take His Spirit away from those who do not hear and fear Him. He will let those who choose to go their own way, have their own way. He will numb their conscience and turn them over to their own desires, and allow them to accept the lies of Satan. *Romans 1:28 Furthermore, since they did not think it worthwhile to retain the knowledge of God, he gave them over to a depraved mind, to do what ought not to be done.*

His word has warned us about all the things that we see happening in our world today. Let's pray that people will see and heed the Word so that they would be concerned about the <u>warning</u> rather than the <u>warming</u>.

July 8

FIGHTING EVIL

Ephesians 6:12 For our struggle is not against flesh and blood, but against the rulers, against the authorities, against the powers of this dark world and against the spiritual force of evil in the heavenly realms.

There have been so many who have not only served but have given their lives while fighting for the good of the country, and for the rights of the people. They have recognized their enemies and fought against them.

We as Christians fight against our enemy every day. Have you ever noticed when you mention anything about 'spiritual warfare', many people become uncomfortable with the subject? Even many Christian people, who should not be intimidated by it, seem often to try to avoid the subject.

Yet we are told emphatically that we war against the forces of evil rather that that of flesh and blood. Why is that so difficult for some people? We must understand the seriousness of it if we are going to be ready to fight those evil forces. We must face the fact that we do have an enemy that is trying to destroy us, and use every weapon God has given us to fight for our freedom.

Dr. Adrian Rogers once said, "Whether you realize it or not, you are a part of a deadly war between light and darkness. You cannot afford to be ignorant and you cannot be neutral. If you try to be neutral you're going to find yourself in the most dangerous place of all.'

We must understand that it is truth. We must be ready to fight against it; and that means that we must put on our full armor of God so that we will be able to stand against it, just as God's word instructs us to do. *You dear children are from God and have overcome them, because the one who is in you is greater than the one who is in the world. 1 John 4:4.* Let's not bury our heads in the sand and pretend that evil doesn't exist: It does, but we serve a Savior that is bigger than any evil force. Let's recognize our enemy, put on our full armor and fight against those evil forces.

July 9-10

WATER FOR THE WEEKEND

PLEADING FOR AND WITH YOUTH
by William Cowper

Sin has undone our wretched race;
But Jesus has restored,
And brought the sinner face to face
With his forgiving Lord.

This we repeat from year to year
And press upon our youth;
Lord, give them an attentive ear,
Lord, save them by Thy truth!

Blessings upon the rising race!
Make this a happy hour,
According to Thy richest grace,
And thine Almighty power.

We feel for your unhappy state
(May you regard it too),
And would a while ourselves forget
To pour our prayer for you.

We see, though you perceive it not,
The approaching awful doom;
Oh tremble at the solemn thought,
And flee the wrath to come!

Dear Saviour, let this new-born year
Spread an alarm abroad;
And cry in every careless ear,
"Prepare to meet thy God!"

July 11

GIVE UP AND PRAY

Philippians 4:6 Do not be anxious about anything, but in everything, by prayer and petition with thanksgiving, present your requests to God.

I have talked to so many people lately who seem to be in a battle of some kind. Some are struggling with health problems; some are dealing with relationship issues, some with marital problems, and some with spiritual battles. Many times we try to carry the weight on our own shoulders. We do everything in the world to try and fix the problems—to no avail. We forget our source of help

The following is a stanza from a poem written by M. S. Lowndes.

> I get so sick of constantly repeating
> The same failures day after day
> I feel so worn down by the constant battle
> Maybe I should give up and 'Pray'

Why do we constantly try to handle situations on our own? Won't we ever learn to go to the Lord in prayer with our concerns and our battles first? Perhaps there have been times when you just didn't know how to pray for a certain situation. I have felt that way many times. But we have an advocate in Jesus. *In the same way, the Spirit helps us in our weakness. We do not know what we ought to pray for, but the Spirit himself intercedes for us with groans that words cannot express. Romans 8:26*

Let's remember where our source of help comes from. Jesus wants us to put our cares on Him. He is the one who will give us peace in the midst of every storm. And He is the only one who has the power to change anything. So let's quit trying to fix things ourselves—let's give up and pray.

July 12

GOD'S ANGER

The Lord's anger was aroused that day and he swore this oath: 'Because they have not followed me wholeheartedly, not one of the men twenty years old or more who came up out of Egypt will see the land I promised on oath to Abraham, Isaac and Jacob—not one except Caleb son of Jephunneh the Kenizzite and Joshua son of Nun, for they followed the Lord wholeheartedly.'

For some reason or another, we don't like to talk about God's anger. But it is a fact, and we might as well face it. The same God that was angry with the disobedient Israelites is the same God we serve today. If He was angry with them, why wouldn't He be angry with us when we disobey Him? *Jesus Christ is the same yesterday and today and forever. Hebrews 13:8* God is angry when we don't obey Him.

Sometimes I think when we disobey God, we think He pats us on the head and says "I understand and it's ok; just try not to do it again." Well I don't believe that is true, He does forgive us, but there is a penalty to pay for sin. The Israelites were denied the blessing of entering the Promised Land because they disobeyed God and broke the covenant that Moses made with God. *"Now if you obey me fully and keep my covenant, then out of all nations you will be my treasured possession. Although the whole earth is mine, you will be for me a kingdom of priests and a holy nation. These are the words you are to speak to the Israelites." Exodus 19:5* Notice he says "if you keep my covenant".

On the other hand God rewards those who follow Him and obey Him wholeheartedly, just as He did with Joshua and Nun. They were led into the Promised Land. Are we keeping the covenant that we made with the Lord? Will we be led into the land that God has promised us? God desires our obedience more than anything else. Our obedience to Him shows our love for Him. *And this is love: that we walk in obedience to his commands. As you have heard from the beginning, his command is that you walk in love.*

July 13

FIGHTING TOGETHER

Nehemiah 4:16 From that day on, half of my men did the work, while the other half were equipped with spears, shields, bows and armor. The officers posted themselves behind all the people of Judah who were building the wall. Those who carried materials did their work with one hand and held a weapon in the other, and each of the builders wore his sword at this side as he worked. But the man who sounded the trumpet stayed with me.

Nehemiah reported that when their enemies heard that God had frustrated their plot, the people went back to their work on building the wall. They were not afraid. They each had their own job to do, and each one of them did it. Notice that some of them worked with one hand and carried a weapon in the other hand. They were working together, each one doing his own job, and they were prepared to fight to the finish.

As they worked, they were widely spread out and separated from each other and Nehemiah said to them, *"Wherever you hear the sound of the trumpet, join us there. Our God will fight for us!"* *Nehemiah 4:20.* They were listening for the sound of the trumpet, telling them that they were in danger. When they heard the sound they gathered together to fight, knowing that God would fight for them.

These men all worked together to rebuild the wall. They were not working alone. God was in the middle of it all. Can we take a lesson from this wonderful example? There is nothing we can't accomplish by working together to fulfill the things God is calling us to do as a family of God. He will provide us with all we need. When we hear the sound of the Trumpet of God in our hearts, let's respond by pulling together and helping each other to finish our mission, no matter what it is. God will be in the midst of it all, if we call on His Name.

July 14

GOD'S COMFORT

2 Corinthians 1:3-4 Praise be to the God and Father of our Lord Jesus Christ, the Father of compassion and the God of all comfort who comforts us in all our troubles, so that we can comfort those in any trouble with the comfort we ourselves have received from God.

I got an email from my great-niece who had just lost her 18 year old son in a tragic and unexpected time and manner. Here is a statement she made to me in that email: Quote- "Losing Derek has crushed my heart. But, because of God's love and what he is using this situation for, it comforts me. God is good."- Unquote. There were many young people touched by Derek's death. Some of them have chosen to give their heart to Jesus as a result of this horrific tragedy.

As I sat watching Sandra and James on the evening of Derek's visitation, I witnessed a most amazing thing. They had great peace and composure, and as a result of that, they were able to console those young people who were in distress. *And the peace of God, which transcends all understanding, will guard your hearts and your minds in Christ Jesus Philippians 4:7* The strength that they demonstrated could only have come from their faith and love for God.

One could not witness this great mystery of peace without real-izing that it was not a natural reaction to such a tragic circumstance. There strength was coming directly from the Heavenly Father. They have the knowledge that they will one day be reunited with their son again, they have hope for the future. Without hope, it is impossible to bear this kind of heartache with such grace. How amazing, that even after what Sandra has just been through; she can still say "God is good."

Some allow God to comfort them and others turn their backs on Him. Some face the reality that bad choices may end in heartache, while others blame God for every circumstance. Sandra and James have put their trust and faith in the only one who can comfort them: The Comforter himself. *Blessed are those who mourn, for they shall be comforted. Matthew 5:4*

God's promises are true: I have been a witness to this very scripture through Sandra and James.

July 15

FILLING THE EMPTINESS

Matthew 5:6 "Blessed are those who hunger and thirst for righteousness, for they will be filled."

Have you ever been so hungry that you thought you were going to die if you didn't get something to eat soon? I would bet that as soon as the opportunity arose to feed that gnawing in your stomach, you quickly satisfied it. Fortunately most of us are able to eat anytime we want and however much we want. But there are those who starve to death for lack of food.

How is it we are so quick to satisfy our physical hunger while we are starving to death spiritually? Is it because we don't take the time to feed on The Word? Is it because we don't take the time to communicate with our Lord? Is it because we are consumed with other interests that take our thoughts away from the only things that can nurture us spiritually? What would happen if we ignored our hunger for physical food? If we let it continue for long, we would starve to death. The same thing will happen if we ignore our spiritual hunger. We must feast on God's Word and seek His presence and allow Him to fill us up. I believe there is a craving in our spirits that will not be satisfied until we feast at His table.

July 16-17

WATER FOR THE WEEKEND

PRAISE FOR FAITH
by William Cowper

Of all the gifts Thine hand bestows,
Thou Giver of all good!
Not heaven itself a richer knows
Than my Redeemer's blood.

Faith too, the blood-receiving grace,
From the same hand we gain;
Else, sweetly as it suits our case,
That gift had been in vain.

Till Thou Thy teaching power apply,
Our hearts refuse to see,
And weak, as a distemper'd eye,
Shut out the view of Thee.

Blind to the merits of Thy Son,
What misery we endure!
Yet fly that Hand from which alone
We could expect a cure.

We praise Thee, and would praise Thee more,
To Thee our all we owe:
The precious Saviour, and the power
That makes Him precious too.

July 18

FLEEING FROM SIN

Psalms 149:7 Where can I go from your Spirit? Where can I flee from your presence?

One night as I was driving home from church with Tahlia, my eight year old granddaughter, I was headed east and had just started through a busy intersection as the light turned green, trusting that the southern bound drivers were observing their red light. Then out of the corner of my eye I saw a car barreling through the red light and I knew that he was going too fast to avoid colliding with me. I stomped on the break in time for him to plow into the front drivers side of my car instead of (Thank the Lord) the side of my door which would have been a much worse accident. The driver then proceeded to take off and run away from the scene of the accident. I later found out that the police were looking for this very driver that had hit another car and ran away. He was later caught and will now have to pay the consequences.

I was thinking about how we try to run away from our sins. We may be able to avoid others knowing of our sin but we can never flee from God. He sees and knows everything we do. We couldn't run hard enough nor could we hide anywhere to escape from God. If we don't obey God's commands, there will surely be consequences. *But if you fail to do this, you will be sinning against the Lord, and you may be sure that your sin will find you out. Numbers 32 23*

One of the worse things about sin is that it usually involves hurting others in one way or another. Tahlia and I could have suffered great injury, had it not been for God's protection over us. As it was, the only thing we suffered was shock and trauma.

The young man that hit me broke the law for running a red light; but if he would have confessed what he had done instead of running away and trying to hide, he would not have had to face the consequences of running. Let's not try to run away from our sins, let's confess them and avoid the penalty we will have to pay if we run away.

July 19

FORGET THE PAST—LOOK TO THE FUTURE

Isaiah 43:18:21 Forget the former things; do not dwell on the past. See, I am doing a new thing! Now it springs up; do you not perceive it? I am making a way in the desert and streams in the wasteland. The wild animals honor me, the jackals and the owls, because I provide water in the desert and streams in the wasteland, to give drink to my people, my chosen, the people I formed for myself that they may proclaim my praise.

How do you feel about past sins; yours or anyone else's? Are you judging yourself or others on the past? Do you feel like you are not worthy to proclaim yourself or others to do the work of the Lord? If you are, you are buying into the lies of Satan.

For all have all sinned and fallen short of the glory of God Romans 3:23. But because of God's great love for us we have been saved. No sin is greater than another. All we need do is look to see what God has done for others to see how He can use us to further His plan for our lives.

Moses was a murderer—Exodus 2:12, but God used him to lead the Israelites out of bondage in Egypt.

Rahab was a prostitute—Joshua 2:1, but she became the great, great grandmother to David.

David was a premeditated murderer—2 Samuel 11:14-17—but he spent the rest of his life serving the Lord. Christ was of his lineage.

Paul was a persecutor of Christians—Acts 9:1 but led many people to the Lord.

Peter denied Christ—but was used enormously to lead others to Christ.

These are just a few people who, probably at one time, thought that God could never use them because of their past. We are wrong when we think that because of our past, God could never use us. When God forgives us, we need to forgive ourselves and instead of looking back, we need to look ahead because God is doing a new thing in us.

God forgives everyone every sin. When we finally realize the graciousness of God, and when we let our past go, He will use us also in a powerful way. And then we can proclaim his praise to the whole world.

July 20

GOD'S FAITHFULNESS

Matthew 6:33 But seek first his kingdom and his righteousness, and all these things will be given to you as well.

How many ways have we searched for things in our lives that will make us happy? I don't know about you, but in the past I have pursued many things. Things that maybe made me happy for a short time, but the happiness soon faded, and then I was pursuing other things in other directions.

We try to put our hopes and faith in things. We have a tendency to live in an 'if only' attitude. If only I had this, then I would be happy. We spend our time and money in the pursuit of happiness that only lasts for a little while. The truth is the only one who can fulfill all of our needs, the only one who is faithful, the only one who will make us happy in all things, is Jesus.

The above scripture tells us to seek first His kingdom and His righteousness and all these things will be given to you as well. That doesn't mean everything we want will be given to us, but everything we need. And who we need is Jesus. He is the one who supplies what we need to make us happy. God's promises are true. *The Lord is faithful to all his promises and loving toward all he has made. Psalms 145:13b.* Our happiness lays in our trust and faith in Christ.

July 21

FORGIVING HURTFUL PEOPLE

Genesis 50:18:21 His brothers then came and threw themselves down before him. "We are your slaves," they said. But Joseph said to them, "Don't be afraid. Am I in the place of God? You intended to harm me, but God intended it for good to accomplish what is now being done, the saving of many lives. So then, don't be afraid I will provide for you and your children." And he reassured them and spoke kindly to them.

Here is a picture of God's mercy and His kindness working through others. Joseph had been sold in to slavery by his own brothers, and had suffered many things as a result of their sin against him. If anyone ever had the right to say that they wouldn't forgive, it would have been Joseph. But Joseph knew that God's plan had been worked out. He also recognized that God is the one who could forgive them of their sins: He couldn't do it, but he could forgive the hurt that he had suffered as a result of their sin.

Have you ever been hurt by those close to you? We might suffer sometimes as a result of others sins, but God will see us through. God is in control of all things. God will use every circumstance in our lives for our good, even a hurtful person. He would not allow his children to be lead down a path that He was not walking with them. We may not be able to see the end of our journey, but we can trust God for our future.

Others may intend us harm but God intends it good to accomplish what he wants done. God can use these hurtful things to grow us into the person that He wants us to be. Just like Jesus forgives all of those who ask for forgiveness, Joseph forgave his brothers. And we dear friends must forgive ours also

July 22

FROM START TO FINISH

Exodus 40:33 Then Moses set up the courtyard around the taber-
nacle and altar and put the curtain at the entrance to the courtyard.
And so Moses finished the work.

Exodus chapter 40 is focused on the instructions to Moses as
he was building the Tent of Meeting. After each instruction it is
recorded that Moses did just as the Lord commanded him. He followed everything he was asked to do until the job was finished.

Paul talks about finishing the race we have begun in *2 Timothy*
4:7. I have fought the good fight, I have finished the race. I have kept
the faith. And again in *2 Corinthians 8:11 Now finish the work, so*
that your eager willingness to do it may be matched by your com-
pletion of it, according to your means. James talks about finishing
your work in perseverance as we put our faith in God. *James 1:4*
Perseverance must finish its work so that you may be mature and
complete, not lacking anything.

Do you suppose there were times in these men's lives that they
became discouraged to the point of giving up? Don't you think they
thought that their work would never be accomplished? I don't doubt
that they had their times of doubt and frustration. But they never
gave up, they never quit. I believe that as they went through the
times of discouragement, God was right by their side encouraging
them to keep on keeping on. I also believe that through it all God
was teaching them and building their faith and trust in Him as they
determinedly finished the job that God called them to do.

In your pursuit of fulfilling the job God has called you to do, are
you tempted to quit because things aren't going the way you think
they should? I would venture to say that every one of us has gone
through all of these doubts and fears. But God tells us not to give
up. He uses those times to build up our faith and trust in Him. It is in

those times of doubt and fear that we see our weaknesses and learn to lean on Him. Like the little children's song says, "We are weak but He is strong." Don't give up until God tells you that you have completed the work.

July 23-24

WATER FOR THE WEEKEND

PRAISE FOR THE FOUNTAIN OPENED
by William Cowper

There is a fountain fill'd with blood,
Drawn from Emmanuel's veins;
And sinners, plunged beneath that flood,
Lose all their guilty stains.

The dying thief rejoiced to see
That fountain in his day;
And there have I, as vile as he,
Wash'd all my sins away.

Dear dying Lamb, Thy precious blood
Shall never lose its power,
Till all the ransom'd church of God
Be saved, to sin no more.

E'er since, by faith, I saw the stream
Thy flowing wounds supply,
Redeeming love has been my theme,
And shall be till I die.

Then in a nobler, sweeter song,
I'll sing Thy power to save;
When this poor lisping stammering tongue
Lies silent in the grave.

Lord, I believe Thou hast prepared
(Unworthy though I be)
For me a blood-bought free reward,
A golden harp for me!

'Tis strung and tuned for endless years,
And form'd by power divine,
To sound in God the Father's ears
No other name but Thine.

July 25

GO AND TELL

Mark 5:18-20 As Jesus was getting into the boat, the man who had been demon-possessed begged to go with him. Jesus did not let him but said, "Go home to your family and tell them how much the Lord has done for you, and how he has had mercy on you. So the man went away and began to tell in the Decapolis how much Jesus had done for him. And all the people were amazed.

No wonder this man wanted to go with Jesus. He had been demon possessed his entire life and separated from others. He had led a life of misery until he met Jesus. He recognized Jesus the moment he saw him. And he ran to him and fell on his knees. Because of Jesus he was set free from his torture.

Jesus told him to go to his family and tell them what He had done for him. He not only told his family, he told the entire Decapolis (10 cities) around the region, all that Jesus had done for him and they were amazed.

Of course they were amazed. What a miracle Jesus had performed in his life. Others couldn't help but see the change in him. Don't you know that because of his testimony, others were inspired to meet this blessed Savior?

I wonder what an inspiration our testimonies would be to the people around us. When we are washed in His blood, others can definitely see the difference in our lives. But we must be willing to share our stories about what Jesus has done for us. If just one person would come to The Cross as a result of our testimony, just think how many we would see in Heaven if we were all willing to share the good news. Wow, what a sight to see.

July 26

GOD'S GRACE

Ephesians 2:8 For it is by grace you have been saved, through faith and this not from yourselves, it is the gift of God-not by works, so that no one can boast.

I was raised in a very strict legalistic denomination and for many years I thought I had to be perfect to be a Christian. Because the church I was brought up in taught certain things I couldn't understand, I ran from the Lord. I knew I couldn't measure up to their standards. I portrayed God as one who would punish me for doing anything that the church said was a sin. Don't get me wrong, there were many precious Christian people in that church and I know I will see them in heaven one day. However I was totally confused by the legalistic views that clouded my perception of God. AND THEN I MET THE LORD!

I started reading my bible and was amazed when God opened my eyes and I seemed to see everything so clearly. Until that time, when I tried to read His word, it seemed so confusing that I would become discouraged and just give up. I read *Philippians 2:12b-13 Work out your own salvation with fear and trembling, for it is God who works in you to will and to act according to His good purpose.* I realized that God's Word is truth and it is God who would tell me through the scriptures what He desired of me. I realized that being a true Christian was not a religion but a personal relationship with the Lord. I started to see the God that loved me so much that He sent His son to die on the cross for my salvation, instead of an angry God who was ready to condemn me at every turn. I praise God for His Word that teaches us all we need to know. Our salvation is not dependent on what we do, but what Jesus did for us. I truly began to understand Ephesians 2:8

It is a dangerous thing to rely on men instead of God for our knowledge and understanding. I'm not saying that there aren't

225

Godly men who can give Godly counsel, but we must know God's word and be able to test what is being told us. God's word is perfect and when we bathe ourselves in it, God will lead us to knowledge and understanding.

If you are confused about what others tell you, go to God's Word and seek His counsel. He will never fail you. *John 17:17 Sanctify them by the truth; your word is truth.*

July 27

HATRED AND LOVE

Isaiah 53:6 We all, like sheep, have gone astray, each of us has turned to his own way; and the Lord has laid on him the iniquity of us all.

Along with several others from our church, I attended a Women of Faith conference. I was appalled, as we waited at the door, by the protestors across the street from the arena. There were people standing there holding up the most hateful signs against our Lord and His people. I was angry and disgusted when I noticed that they had children among them, holding up their signs. As I stood there, with my own judgmental attitude, God reminded me that He loved them and died for their transgressions as much as He did for mine. I was impressed to pray for their blinded eyes. I would guess that I wasn't the only one who was impressed to pray for them. I feel sure that God reminded the others of the same thing.

Just imagine the kind of love that sent our Savior to the cross for those who absolutely hated Him. Why would people hate someone that they don't even know? Why would they go out of their way to condemn those who have faith in the God of the universe? There is only one reason—they have been blinded by Satan's lies. They have no knowledge of the kind of love that Christ has for <u>everyone</u>. They wouldn't understand why Christians would pray for them as they stand there with their signs of hate.

For God so loved the world that he gave his one and only Son, that whoever believes in him shall not perish but have eternal life. John 3:16. It is truly amazing to think about a love so great that He would die on a cross for the sins of those who hated Him. What an awesome God.

July 28

GOD'S PERFECT TIMING

Psalm 121:7-8 The Lord will keep you from all harm-he will watch over your life; the Lord will watch over your coming and going both now and forevermore.

A few years ago Bill and I pulled off of I-25 going toward Denver to get something to eat. The restaurant was full, and they said it would be a 45 minute wait. We were grumbling to ourselves after we got back in the car because the only thing we got out of the stop was a 5 minute delay in our trip. We hadn't gone far until we came upon a 15 car pile-up that resulted in several deaths and injuries. It had just happened and it occurred to both of us that if it had not been for the timely stop we had made, we more than likely would have been involved in the accident.

I wonder how many times God has spared us from tragedy by circumstances that we deemed as hindrances to our plans. I would venture to say more times than we could count. *1 Thessalonians 5:18 Give thanks in all circumstances for this is God's will for you in Christ Jesus.* I have learned to give thanks in the times that we have been detained: And for those times that we had to change our plans because something prevented us from fulfilling them. Only God sees what lies ahead. He goes before us and behind us to protect us

Instead of groaning and complaining about plans that must be changed, let's give thanks to God for looking out for us. There is a reason why some plans should not be carried out. God knows why and that's good enough for me.

Take the time to read all of Psalm 121.

July 29

HAVING FAITH

2 Chronicles 20 Early in the morning they left for the Desert of Tekoa. As they set out Jehoshaphat stood and said, "Listen to me, Judah and people of Jerusalem! Have faith in the Lord your God and you will be upheld; have faith in his prophets and you will be successful.

In a study of Mark that I am participating in, written by Ginni Hawley, she tells a story about George Mueller, a wonderful man of God; a man who put his complete faith and trust in the Lord. This is the story I would like to share with you also.

"I went to America some years ago with the captain of a steamer, who was a very devoted Christian. When off the coast of Newfoundland he said to me, 'The last time I crossed here, five weeks ago, something happened which revolutionized the whole of my Christian life. We had George Mueller of Bristol on board. I had been on the bridge twenty-four hours and never left it. George Mueller came to me, and said, "Captain, I have come to tell you that I must be in Quebec Saturday afternoon." "It is impossible," I said. "Very well, if your ship cannot take me, God will find some other way. I have never broken an engagement for fifty-seven years. Let us go down into the chart-room and pray." I looked at that man of God, and thought to myself, what lunatic asylum can that man have come from? I never heard of such a thing as this, "Mr. Mueller," I said, "do you know how dense this fog is?" "No," he replied "my eye is not on the density of the fog, but on the living God, who controls every circumstance of my life." He knelt down and prayed one of the simplest prayers, and when he had finished I was going to pray; but he put his hand on my shoulder, and told me not to pray. "First, you do not believe He will answer; and second I BELIEVE HE HAS, and there is no need whatever for you to pray about it." I looked at him, and he said. "Captain, I have known my Lord for fifty-seven years, and there has never been a single day that I have failed to get audience with the King. Get up, Captain and open the door, and you will find the fog gone." I got up and the fog was indeed gone. On Saturday afternoon, George Mueller was in Quebec for his engagement.' (From <u>Streams In The Desert</u> by Mrs. Charles E. Cowman.)"

I was truly blessed by this story and at the same time I was challenged on my faith in prayer. How many times do we pray with total confidence that God is going to answer that prayer? I fear that many times we pray without truly believing that God will answer. God is a God of His Word and He will answer every prayer, if we are praying in faith and according to His will. Nothing is too difficult for Him. We can trust that the answer we receive when we pray trusting in God will be forthcoming and will be the perfect answer. *He answered their prayers because they trusted in him 1 Chronicles 5:20b*

July 30-31

WATER FOR THE WEEKEND

PRAYER FOR PATIENCE
by William Cowper

Lord, who hast suffer'd all for me,
My peace and pardon to procure,
The lighter cross I bear for Thee,
Help me with patience to endure.

The storm of loud repining hush;
I would in humble silence mourn;
Why should the unburnt, though burning bush,
Be angry as the crackling thorn?

Man should not faint at Thy rebuke,
Like Joshua falling on his face,
When the cursed thing that Achan took
Brought Israel into just disgrace.

Perhaps some golden wedge suppress'd,
Some secret sin offends my God;
Perhaps that Babylonish vest,
Self-righteousness, provokes the rod.

Ah! were I buffeted all day,
Mock'd, crown'd with thorns and spit upon,
I yet should have no right to say,
My great distress is mine alone.

Let me not angrily declare
No pain was ever sharp like mine,
Nor murmur at the cross I bear,
But rather weep, remembering Thine.

August 1

GODLY CHARACTER

Esther2:20 But Esther had kept secret her family background and nationality just as Mordecai had told her to do, for she continued to follow Mordecai's instructions as she had done when he was bringing her up.

As I was preparing for a bible study this morning, something was brought out about the character of Esther. If you are familiar with the book of Esther; you know that Mordecai was her cousin who raised her from a child because she was left orphaned.

In the above scripture, this orphan girl has become a queen: Yet she was still obeying Mordecai. If she hadn't been the respectful, obedient woman that she was, she could have had the attitude that she was a powerful woman and no longer had to observe the lessons that she had learned from her adopted father. But Mordecai had taught her well.

God had put her in her position, and I believe that she was aware of it, even though scripture doesn't record that. I believe that she knew that her uncle had given her Godly wisdom as she was growing up under his roof, and she knew that she could trust him.

Do we show respect for those who have taught us Godly wisdom? Are we obedient to follow that wisdom? We are children of a king: A good reason to remember what we have been taught and respect the ones who have helped us along our spiritual walk. For everything we have learned from God and His people will reveal God's character in us, if we listened and took it to heart.

August 2

HEARING FROM GOD

Isaiah 59:1-2 Surely the arm of the Lord is not too short to save, nor his ear too dull to hear. But your iniquities have separated you from your God; your sins have hidden his face from you, so that he will not hear.

Do you feel like your prayers are not heard? God always hears our prayers if we are praying with the right motives and with the right heart. Are we walking in the ways of the Lord? Or are we so deep in sin that He has hidden His face from us. It is a sad thing when God hides His face. He doesn't do it because He is tired of hearing our prayers. He wants to hear from us when we are seeking His wisdom in the fullness of our repentant heart.

Have you been to the cross? Have you surrendered your heart to the Lord? If not, I want to encourage you to do so. God is waiting with open arms to bring you in to His family. He will immediately forgive you of yours sins. His word says that he even forgets our sins. He will hear from you and answer you when you call on His Name.

For those of us who are Christians and feel like God is not hearing our prayers, let's ask ourselves if we are praying in the will of God, and are we living the life that glorifies Him? God wants to hear from us and is interested in everything we say and do, but we have a responsibility to live the way Christ has instructed us to live. God hears and answers every Christian's prayers according to His will. He doesn't always answer the way we want Him to, but He will answer—either with a yes, no, or wait.

August 3

HELP

Psalm 34:17 The righteous cry out, and the Lord hears them; he delivers them from all their troubles.

Have you ever noticed how many self-help books are being written? There are books on how to solve your financial problems, marital problems, how to overcome low self-esteem, there's one on how to quit worrying, and there is even one on how to love yourself. The list goes on and on. It is enough to boggle the mind for sure. One could spend dollar after dollar on books that supposedly has all the help we need to overcome every obstacle in life. I have a secret to tell you——none of them work. There is only one book that we need and it has the answer to every problem in our lives. It is the Bible, the inerrant word of God.

It doesn't matter what we are going through in this life; God has the answer. We don't have to search through books in the book stores or in the libraries for our help. All we have to do is open God's word and search for His wisdom and knowledge. *As for God, his way is perfect; the word of the Lord is flawless. He is a shield for all who take refuge in him. 2 Samuel 22:31.* There is absolutely no way that we can solve our problems on our own; and there is no book written by man that will be able to help us. Only our heavenly Father has the help we need for every circumstance in life. Not only does He have an answer, He has the perfect answer. Look to God and get in His word to find the solution to your problems. I guarantee you, He is all you need.

August 4

GOD IS ON HIS THRONE

Psalm 46:4-11 There is a river whose streams make glad the city of God, the holy place where the Most High dwells. God is within her, she will not fall; God will help her at break of day. Nations are in uproar, kingdoms fall, he lifts his voice, the earth melts. The Lord Almighty is with us, the God of Jacob is our fortress. Come and see the works of the Lord, the desolations he has brought to the earth. He makes wars cease to the ends of the earth; he breaks the bow and shatters the spear, he burns the shields with fire. "Be still, and know that I am God, I will be exalted among the nations, I will be exalted in the earth." The Almighty is with us; the God of Jacob is our fortress.

As we awake this morning, we may have a feeling of discouragement because of the turn of events in our country. But how can we remain discouraged when we realize that our God was, is, and always will be in control. He is still on His Throne. When we serve a God who loves us and will walk with us every day of our lives, we have nothing to fear. *He is our refuge and strength, a very present help in trouble. Psalm 46:1*

He changes times and seasons; he sets up kings and deposes them. Daniel 2:21a. We don't know why God allows certain ones to be put in the positions that they are in, but we do know that we can trust Him and that He does absolutely have a purpose. We must keep on keeping on with faith, hope and trust in the one who is above all others—Our wonderful Father, Counselor and Almighty God—Our everlasting Prince of Peace, King of Kings and Lord of Lords.

August 5

HIDING FROM SIN

Numbers 32:23 But if you fail to do this, you will be sinning against the Lord; and you may be sure that your sin will find you out.

While watching my 3 year old granddaughter one day, I suddenly realized that she was no where to be seen. When I looked for her she was hiding because she was doing something that she knew she wasn't supposed to be doing. She was hoping that she wouldn't be caught.

Aren't we like that. We try to hide our sins hoping that God will not notice. There is nothing we do that God does not see. There is nothing we say that God does not hear. There is nothing we think that God does not know. It is utterly ridiculous to think that we can hide from the Lord.

Against you, you only, have I sinned and done what is evil in your sight, so that you are proved right when you speak and justified when you judge. Psalms 51:4 God's word tells us how to live our lives in such a way that His name will be glorified. When we sin we sin against God, not against man, therefore He has every right to judge us. Don't try to hide from your sin, because you can't. Confess it and let God's forgiveness fill your heart with joy and a determination not to hide in sin anymore.

August 6-7

WATER FOR THE WEEKEND

PRAYER FOR CHILDREN
by William Cowper

Gracious Lord, our children see,
By Thy mercy we are free;
But shall these, alas! remain
Subjects still of Satan's reign?
Israel's young ones, when of old
Pharaoh threaten'd to withhold,
Then Thy messenger said, "No;
Let the children also go!"

When the angel of the Lord,
Drawing forth his dreadful sword,
Slew with an avenging hand,
All the first-born of the land;
Then Thy people's door he pass'd,
Where the bloody sign was placed:
Hear us, now, upon our knees,
Plead the blood of Christ for these!

Lord, we tremble, for we know
How the fierce malicious foe,
Wheeling round his watchful flight,
Keeps them ever in his sight:
Spread Thy pinions, King of kings!
Hide them safe beneath Thy wings;
Lest the ravenous bird of prey
Stoop and bear the brood away.

August 8

GOD IS THE GREATEST

1 John 4:4 You, dear children, are from God and have overcome them, because the one who is in you is greater than the one who is in the world.

One day I wrote a devotional with an acronym that was misspelled. It left me with a red face, and a feeling of discouragement. First of all I knew how to spell commission, but had spelled it wrong. Now why did that happen? I did not realize it until I sent it out over the internet. The minute I sent it, I was compelled to go back to my document and review it. I was appalled by what I had done. Immediately I started thinking that I was just fooling myself about the devotionals that I had been writing. Satan was telling me that they weren't really coming from the Lord, or the mistake I made wouldn't have happened. I immediately thought about abandoning the whole thing.

There are only two things that I fear: Doing anything for the Lord that He hasn't commissioned me to do, and not giving Him the glory when I do what He has asked me to do. As I was whipping myself mentally for my mistake, God spoke to my heart. I realized that Satan had tried to use my mistake to take my eyes off of what God has asked me to do. I also was reminded that I could not do anything without the Lord, proving that it is only because of His grace and guidance that I could ever write the devotionals in the first place.

All at once I was reminded of the above scripture. I don't have to give in to my fears. God is greater than Satan, and He is the one who will give me strength in my weakness. *That is why, for Christ's sake, I delight to weaknesses, in insults, in hardships, in persecutions, in difficulties. For when I am weak, then I am strong. 2 Corinthians 12:10.* I will not be discouraged because of something Satan has tried to use against me.

Let's recognize that Satan is trying to destroy us. We need to put on our armor and fight against the evil thoughts that he brings against us. Most of all, remember that God is greater than Satan, and He will fight our battles for us. He will restore us and revive us, and enable us to carry out the tasks that He has asked us to do.

August 9

LET US REJOICE!

Psalm 118:24 This is the day the Lord has made; let us rejoice and be glad in it.

This is one of my favorite verses from Psalms. I use it on my personal cards, I sing the song with exuberance, but sadly, I do not always live my days with the truth of the scripture reigning in my heart. Every day is a gift from God. When we awaken each morning we ought to rejoice and determine to meet the day with gladness instead of dwelling on the things that have a tendency to drag us down.

No matter what comes our way each day, if we have been saved by God's grace by the shed blood of Jesus, and if we rely on Him, we can in all things, truly rejoice. God will give us peace and grace to face what lies ahead. Whatever comes our way; God has allowed it and will see us through. We can rejoice in every circumstance, knowing that God walks with us every minute of every day.

If you are down today over something that Satan is trying to defeat you with—read the whole chapter of Psalms 118. Let it soak through your mind and soul. What a wonderful God we serve, He is there for us everyday, we can rely on Him for all things. Let's truly rejoice in this day.

August 10

HOPE OF GLORY

Romans 15:13 May the God of hope fill you with all joy and peace as you trust in him, so that you may overflow with hope by the power of the Holy Spirit.

Have you ever watched a movie or read a book only to find out that the ending was sad? I have, and it always leaves me with a depressed feeling. I always wonder why the author couldn't have given it a happy ending. Unfortunately there are many real life stories that have sad endings.

The author of the book of our life has written a happy ending for each of us, if we choose to believe. We can actually be assured of it: And that assurance comes through Jesus death on the cross and through His resurrection. What a Savior. No matter what we go through in the life, our hope is in the Lord. Because of His great love for us, we can know that the end result will be happy when we put our complete trust in Him. We don't have to be mystified about the end of our story. *To them God has chosen to make known among the Gentiles the glorious riches of this mystery, which is Christ in you, the hope of glory. Colossians 1:27*

Do you have that hope and assurance? Do you know Jesus as your personal Savior? If not choose this day to have everlasting life through the blood of Christ.

August 11

INSTITUTION OF MARRIAGE

Genesis 2:10, 21, 22 The Lord God said, "It is not good for the man to be alone. I will make a helper suitable for him. So the Lord God caused the man to fall into a deep sleep; and while he was sleeping, he took one of the man's ribs and closed up the place with flesh. Then the Lord God made a woman from the rib he had taken out of the man, and he brought her to the man.

When God made Eve from Adam's rib, He did it so that Adam would have a helpmate. It was at that time that God instituted marriage. He created Eve to be Adam's wife. He said that the two should be as one flesh. How then have we fallen so far down, that there are those who are trying to say that it is ok for people to marry those of the same sex?

If God had approved marriage between the same sexes, He wouldn't have been so precise in why and how He created the woman for the man. It is most disturbing to hear people say that there is nothing wrong with same sex marriage. It is even more disturbing to witness so many 'Christian people' being so apathetic toward it.

Why are we accepting things that are so blatantly against God's word? Only a few years back, we would have stood up for the word of God, and vehemently denied these kinds of abominations. Are we so concerned about being 'politically correct' that we have hardened our hearts to the sins that are destroying our world? So many Christians have bought into the lies, that we are guilty of being prejudiced and close-minded about such things.

I don't know about you, but I am more concerned with what my Father says about such things, than I am with what the world thinks. Let's get back to the basics of His Holy Word, and let others opinions go. Let's be brave enough to say that marriage between same sexes is a sin—God did not intend it so.

August 12

HEALTHCARE ASSURANCE

Proverbs 4:20-22 My son, pay attention to what I say; listen closely to my words. Do not let them out of your sight, keep them within your heart; for they are life to those who find them and health to a man's whole body.

You can't go anywhere these days without the subject of health-care coming up. It seems as though the leaders of our country want to control every aspect of our lives, including our choices of health-care provision. It is rather disconcerting to think that our choices of insurance, Doctors, medication and healthcare concerns in general, may soon be taken away. In fact it is downright frightening to think that it has come to this in our beloved country, a country that has been free from government control, but is now on the brink of socialism.

The choice of healthcare may be taken out of our hands and we may not be able to make the choices that we want. But one thing is a certainty; and that is that we alone can control our spiritual health. Nobody or nothing in this world has control of that choice except us. When we make the choice to become a child of God, when we make the choice to follow Jesus, our future is secure. No matter what happens in the world around us, those who have made the right choice will listen to the word and gain health to the entire body. We can rest in the promise of God's Word. We are in good hands with God. We may not have good insurance, but we have the guaranteed assurance that we will have eternal life. How much better can it be than that?

August 13-14

WATER FOR THE WEEKEND

SEEKING THE BELOVED
by William Cowper

To those who love the Lord I speak;
Is my Beloved near?
The Bridegroom of my soul I seek,
Oh! when will He appear?

Though once a man of grief and shame,
Yet now He fills a throne,
And bears the greatest, sweetest name,
That earth or heaven have known.

Grace flies before, and love attends
His steps where're he goes;
Though none can see Him but His friends,
And they were once his foes.

He speaks; — obedient to His call
Our warm affections move:
Did He but shine alike on all,
Then all alike would love.

Then love in every heart would reign,
And war would cease to roar;
And cruel and bloodthirsty men
Would thirst for blood no more.

Such Jesus is, and such His grace;
Oh, may He shine on you!
And tell him, when you see His face,
I long to see Him, too.

August 15

JEALOUSY

Proverbs 27:4 Anger is cruel and fury overwhelming, but who can stand before jealousy?

While visiting with a friend one day, she was telling me about a traumatic event in the life of one in her family. This wonderful man is going through extremely hurtful trials as a result of lies and defamation of character. As she was relating the story to me, it became very clear in my mind that the core reason for the earthly hell that is taking place in this man's life is a result of the jealousy that another has for him. I listened with extreme sympathy, as she revealed the hurt that was being placed on him and his family. I felt a great need to pray that God would give them peace and that the truth would be revealed.

Jealousy can be one of the most poisonous sins in life. It can lead to the destruction of marriage, families, friendships, reputations and much, much more. Let's be on the alert for any kind of jealousy that enters our mind and ask God to rid us of it. Through God's grace we can overcome it. We should never be jealous of another. God created each of us in His image, and that image should never reflect a jealous nature. Jealousy comes from a lack of security, and why should we be insecure when we are in Christ?

If you have been the recipient of another's jealousy, take comfort in the fact that God is on your side and that He will use it for good. Joseph is one of my favorite stories in the bible. It was jealousy that his brothers had for him that led to his being sold into slavery. His brothers meant it for harm, but God allowed it for ultimate good. *Genesis 50:20 You intended to harm me, but God intended it for good to accomplish what is now being done, the saving of many lives.*

August 16

HOPE IN HELPLESSNESS

Psalms 33:18-22 But the eyes of the Lord are on those who fear him, on those whose hope is in his unfailing love, to deliver them from death and keep them alive in famine. We wait in hope for the Lord; he is our help and our shield. In him our hearts rejoice, for we trust in his holy name. May your unfailing love rest upon us, O Lord, even as we put our hope in you.

I read an email this morning about two families who have children with cancer. My heart goes out to them. Cancer is a terrible enemy, and it is difficult to see our loved ones go through the pain and anguish that it brings. It must be an incredibly helpless feeling watching a child go through such suffering, knowing that you can do nothing for them.

The only way that one could have peace in these kinds of circumstances is when we put our faith, hope and trust in our Lord. He is the only one who can fill our hearts with unfailing hope. He is the only one who truly understands the pain. He watched His only Son die on a cross so that we might gain eternal life. And because of that we can have hope. When we know Christ as our personal Savior we know that our spirits will never die. Our body will die, but we will be raised with a new perfect one as we enter the presence of Jesus Our Lord and Savior. Our hope is that we will see our loved ones once again. PRAISE HIS HOLY NAME.

August 17

LOOKING FOR WISDOM

Proverbs 2:1-5 My son, if you accept my words and store up my commands within you, turning your ear to wisdom and applying your heart to understanding, and if you call out for insight and cry aloud for understanding and if you look for it as for silver and search for it as for hidden treasure, then you will understand the fear of the Lord and find knowledge of God.

It has been said that 'if' is the biggest word in the dictionary. As you read this passage in scripture, you will see that it is indeed a very big word. In fact, it is impossible for us to attain knowledge and understanding without that 'if'. God's word says if we accept His words, if we store up His commands. if we open our ears, if we apply our hearts, and if we call out for insight and understanding; then we will understand the fear of the Lord and find the knowledge of God.

We will never find the knowledge and understanding that God has for us, unless we get in His word and search earnestly for it. I have heard so many say that they just don't understand God's word. I myself have said it (before I met my Savior). They don't understand it because they are not truly searching for it. Are you one of those who can't seem to grasp what God has for you? Look to Him for the wisdom that eludes you. Earnestly seek Him through His Word and through talking with Him. I can guarantee you, that if you do, He will enlighten you and lead you to knowledge and understanding.

August 18

FORGIVE AND FORGET

2Timothy 4:16-18 At my first defense, no one came to my support, but everyone deserted me. May it not be held against them. But the Lord stood at my side and gave me strength, so that through me the message might be fully proclaimed and all the Gentiles might hear it. And I was delivered from the lion's mouth. The Lord will rescue me from every evil attack and will bring me safely to his heavenly kingdom. To him be glory for ever and ever. Amen

Does this remind you of another man at another time? It does me. As I was reading this I thought about Jesus and how everyone had deserted Him and yet He asked His Father not to hold it against them. That is a picture of how we should be when someone hurts us. It would probably never happen if left up to us: But through the grace that God gives us we can not only forgive but we can forget. Even if everyone forsakes us God will stand beside us.

Have you ever been slandered by another? Has your name ever been unjustly defamed? Do you feel as if God has deserted you? Jesus had suffered all of these things and yet He said, "Father, forgive them for they do not know what they are doing." God not only forgives those who have sinned against Him, He doesn't even remember their sins. That's how I want to be, I want to forgive and forget. If we don't, we are the only ones who are hurt. If you are hurt by others, remember that God protects those who love Him and serve Him. He will bring you safely to His heavenly kingdom.

August 19

LOOK UP TO THE FUTURE

Psalm 121:1-2 I will lift up mine eyes unto the hills, from whence cometh my help. My help cometh from the Lord, which made heaven and earth.

It seems as though everyone I talk to is facing heartache of one kind or another right now. Some are hurting desperately as a result of a death in their family, some are facing severe health problems, some are having financial problems, others are having marital problems, and some are having problems with a wayward child. The list just goes on and on.

We can get so caught up with our struggles that we start to lose hope that life will ever be the same again. But don't despair; we have a helper with us at all times. The very one who made the heavens and the earth is the same one who will help us through every struggle in our life.

When we lift our eyes to the one who is our help, we can overcome every struggle, every worry and all heartache. He is able to give us the strength to carry on. When we are God's children we know that our sufferings here are temporary and they don't compare to the glory set before us. *"For I reckon that the sufferings of this present time are not worthy to be compared with the glory which shall be revealed in us" Romans 8:18*

Isn't it wonderful to know that we have help to see us through the heartaches and troubles in this world? One day we will never have troubles, worries, heartaches or tears again. We will reign with our Heavenly Father in a place so wonderful that even in our wildest imagination; we cannot comprehend or understand it. But God has given us that promise and His promises are true.

August 20-21

WATER FOR THE WEEKEND

SELF-ACQUAINTANCE
by William Cowper

Dear Lord! Accept a sinful heart,
Which of itself complains,
And mourns, with much and frequent smart,
The evil it contains.

There fiery seeds of anger lurk,
Which often hurt my frame;
And wait but for the tempter's work,
To fan them to a flame.

Legality holds out a bribe
To purchase life from Thee;
And Discontent would fain prescribe
How Thou shalt deal with me.

While Unbelief withstands Thy grace,
And puts the mercy by,
Presumption, with a brow of brass,
Says, "Give me, or I die!"

How eager are my thoughts to roam,
In quest of what they love!
But ah! when duty calls them home,
How heavily they move!

Oh, cleanse me in a Saviour's blood,
Transform me by Thy power,
And make me Thy beloved abode,
And let me roam no more.

August 22

HOPE FOR THE LIVING

His servants asked him, "Why are you acting this way? While the child was alive, you fasted and wept, but now that the child is dead, you get up and eat!" He answered, "While the child was still alive, I fasted and wept. I thought, 'Who knows? The Lord may be gracious to me and let the child live.' But now that he is dead, why should I fast? Can I bring him back again? I will go to him, but he will not return to me."

We had a tragic thing happen in our area this past week. A mother accidentally ran over her child and killed him. How sad it is for a parent when a child is taken away. I can't imagine anything worse, especially under the circumstances that this family is experiencing.

As I was praying for them this morning, it occurred to me that there is nobody who could understand the pain that this mother is feeling except God. He actually sent His Son to die on the cross for our sins. But His death was not the end of the story; He rose again to eternal life. That's what His death on the cross means for us when we have chosen to accept Jesus. We shall rise again and we will live eternally with those who have gone before us. Those children who have been taken are with the Savior, awaiting the arrival of their Christian parents.

Nobody knows the reason God allows little children to be taken from this life at such an early age. But we can have the assurance that we will see them again. David understood this and chose to rejoice in the future reunion in Heaven, instead of mourning the physical death.

August 23

TO FEAR OR NOT TO FEAR

Psalms 111:10 The fear of the Lord is the beginning of wisdom; all who follow his precepts have good understanding. To him belongs eternal praise.

There are 2 types of fear mentioned in the bible. One is beneficial, and the other is detrimental. Let's look at the difference in God's word. The scripture above is not talking about being frightened of God; rather it is saying that we will gain wisdom and understanding of God. There are many scriptures in the bible that talks about the fear of the Lord. They are all encouraging us to see the awesomeness of God and to recognize His power and strength and His holiness.

I wonder if you, like me have a tendency to give way to fear: fear of failure, fear of the future, fear for your family, etc. We must recognize the fact that this kind of fear does not come from the Lord. *2 Timothy 1:7 For God did not give us a spirit of timidity, but a spirit of power, of love and of self discipline.*

God's word tells us not to fear. *So do not fear, for I am with you; do not be dismayed for I am your God. I will strengthen you and help you. I will uphold you with my righteous right hand. Isaiah 41:10*

Wow! When we really look into the difference, how we can miss the point that the fear of the Lord gives us wisdom and provides the power that we need to combat all of the detrimental fears that paralyze us. Let's quit agonizing in fear. We have absolutely nothing to fear. *In God I trust; I will not be afraid. What can man do to me? Psalms 56:11*

August 24

UN-CONFESSED SIN

Psalms 32:5 Then I acknowledged my sin to you and did not cover up my iniquity. I said, "I will confess my transgressions to the Lord"—and you forgave the guilt of my sin.

As I was sitting in church one Sunday morning listening to the truth of God's Word, I was convicted on a particular point in my life and I knew I had to address it as quickly as possible. I could not wait to make amends for my sin—yes sin. Just because we are Christians doesn't mean that we are immune to sin in our life. We need to be on guard, because the evil one will use our words and thoughts to harm our relationship with Him and with others. If we let that happen, we certainly will sin. I am so thankful that I serve a God who loves me unconditionally, and His love reveals the truth to me and shows me where I am wrong and tells me to make it right.

None of us are immune to the lies Satan tries to put in our heads, but praise God, he is bigger than the evil one. God alone is omnipotent, omnipresent, and omniscient. Nothing and no one can compare to Him. We must not let sin prevail in our hearts; but rather confess it to our Lord and ask Him to lead us in the paths of righteousness.

August 25

LIGHTEN THE BURDEN

*Matthew 11:28-30 "Come to me all you who are weary and bur-
dened and I will give you rest. Take my yoke upon you and learn
from me, for I am gentle and humble in heart, and you will find rest
for your souls. For my yoke is easy and my burden is light.*

For the past several weeks I have been carrying a very heavy
burden. I hasten to add the fact that it was unnecessary. I have ago-
nized over a job that God has asked me to do; a job that I feel most
unqualified for. This morning as I was praying about my situation,
the above scripture came across my mind in several different ways.
It is a most familiar scripture to most of us, but it turned on a bright
light in my spirit this morning.

Many times while studying the word of God, I will go to the
dictionary to see what its meaning says, hoping that I might get a
better picture of what God is saying to me. Sometimes it helps me
to understand a little better and sometimes it doesn't. This morning
I was blown away as I read what it said about a yoke. And I realized
that it was exactly for me at this time. Isn't it wonderful how God
has different ways to lead us to clarity and understanding of His
word?

This is what Webster had to say about a yoke.

1 a: a wooden bar or frame by which two draft animals (as oxen)
are joined at the heads or necks for working together b: an arched
device formerly laid on the neck of a defeated person c: a frame
fitted to a person's shoulders to carry a load in two equal portions

Immediately I realized that when I take His yoke upon me, I
am no longer carrying my burden alone. He is walking beside me
sharing my burden and making it light and easy. What a beautiful
picture I have in my mind as I write this devotional: A picture of
Jesus walking right beside me. And what a load has been lifted from

my shoulders. And what rest for my soul—what peace I have. For the first time I understand what Jesus has been telling me all along.

God never intends for us to carry our heavy burdens by ourselves. He invites us to put on His yoke so that He can give us the help we need. Are you carrying a heavy load today? You don't have to carry it alone. Take His yoke upon you and learn from Him; you will find rest for your soul.

August 26

LISTENING EARS—RECEIVING HEARTS

Nehemiah 8:2-3 So on the first day of the seventh month Ezra the priest brought the Law before the assembly, which was made up of men and women and all who were able to understand. He read it aloud from daybreak till noon as he faced the square before the Water Gate, in the presence of the men, women and others who could understand. And all the people listened attentively to the Book of the Law.

What a group of people. Can you imagine how exciting that revival must have been? Just imagine an entire group of people so eager to hear from God that they endured a sermon that lasted from daybreak until noon. That tells me that each one of them knew their God intimately; so much so that they were willing to listen to His word no matter what the clock said.

Further on in this wonderful book, verse 6 says—*Ezra praised the Lord, the great God; and all the people lifted their hands and responded, "Amen! Amen!" Then they bowed down and worshiped the Lord with their faces to the ground.* These people of God were not only listening, they were receiving. They were bowing down in worship with their faces to the ground.

Wouldn't it be wonderful to set in on a church service where the entire congregation was there to receive everything God had for them? Wouldn't it be great to be so enthralled with the word of God that we wouldn't be watching the clock to see when we could leave? Wouldn't it be wonderful to be fed by God's word and filled with His Spirit to the point of bowing face down to worship him in total abandonment?

Maybe the reason we do not experience that kind of revival is because there are too many who just don't understand. Let's think about it. Do we go to the house of our Lord with the understanding of who God is and that He wants to fill us up to the point that we will fall on our knees to worship Him? Let's ask God to give us the kind of understanding that would cause us not only to listen but to receive and respond with total adoration to our Lord.

August 27-28

WATER FOR THE WEEKEND

SUBMISSION
by William Cowper

O Lord, my best desire fulfil,
And help me to resign
Life, health, and comfort to Thy will,
And make Thy pleasure mine.

Why would I shrink at Thy command,
Whose love forbids my fears?
Or tremble at the gracious hand
That wipes away my tears?

No, rather let me freely yield
What most I prize to Thee;
Who never hast a good withheld,
Or wilt withhold, from me.

Thy favor, all my journey through,
Thou art engaged to grant;
What else I want, or think I do,
'Tis better still to want.

Wisdom and mercy guide my way,
Shall I resist them both?
A poor blind creature of day,
And crush'd before the moth!

But ah! my inward spirit cries,
Still binds me to Thy sway;
Else the next cloud that veils the skies
Drives all these thoughts away.

August 29

MORE THAN ENOUGH

Mark 8:6-8 He told the crowd to sit down on the ground. When he had taken the seven loaves and given thanks, he broke them and gave them to his disciples to set before the people, and they did so. They had a few small fish as well; he gave thanks for them also and told the disciples to distribute them. The people ate and were satisfied. Afterward the disciples picked up seven basketfuls of broken pieces that were left over.

There were four thousand men in attendance that day, not to mention how many women and children there might have been. That must have been an awesome time. These people had spent three days with the Lord. He not only fed them food for their bodies, think about the food that He gave them for their spirits.

There is a song entitled 'Your Enough for Me.' God isn't only enough He is more than enough. Just as there was more than enough food for the body on that particular day Jesus fed the 4,000, I am convinced that for those who were feeding on His word, they were more than filled up. I find it amazing that His Word says that there was food left over. I have to ponder whether or not there were those in attendance that didn't eat their fill. There was plenty left for them and for many more that could have been there. When we enter into the presence of God, are we allowing Him to fill us up?

August 30

FIGHTING THE GIANT

1 Samuel 17:45-47 David said to the Philistine, "You come against me with sword and spear and javelin, but I come against you in the name of the Lord Almighty, the God of the armies of Israel, whom you have defiled. This day the Lord will hand you over to me and I'll strike you down and cut off your head. Today I will give the carcasses of the Philistine army to the birds of the air and the beasts of the earth, and the whole world will know that there is a God in Israel. All those gathered here will know that it is not by sword or spear that the Lord saves; for the battle is the Lord's and he will give all of you into our hands."

Every time I read the story of David, I am blessed anew: The man after God's own heart. David was ridiculed not only by his opponent 'Goliath' but by his own brother. I suppose it was understandable — looking at David's stature and comparing it to a giant of nine feet tall. I imagine most of us would have had our doubts that he would be successful in a battle against all of the odds of a giant equipped with every weapon and armor available, and David equipped only with a sling shot and five stones. Looking at the whole scenario, it would look like an impossible situation. But God knew David and He knew his heart. *The Lord does not look at the things man looks at. Man looks at the outward appearance, but the Lord looks at the heart. 1 Samuel 16:7b*

David knew that God was on his side and it would be Him who would fight the battle. He wasn't daunted by the fact that he was small and unequipped with armor. He knew that God would not only fight the battle but that He would win it. He needed nothing else. Not one time did the scripture even hint that David was fearful: To the contrary; he was confident that he was going to win the battle because God was with him.

Is there a 'Goliath' in your life? Are you facing a battle that looks like it will be impossible to win? Do you feel like you are not equipped to fight against the odds that are facing you? Well take heart; Put your faith and trust in The One who wants to fight the battle for you. Keep your eyes on the Lord and His mighty power. He will fight every battle in your life and He will win it, if like David you go into the battle with full assurance that you have put it in God's hands. What a wonderful encouragement David is for us today. We are no different than David was if we are confident in our position with the Lord. He is the Rock of our Salvation, He is our Strength. He is our Deliverer. He is our Hope. We can put our faith in Him, knowing that He cares for us.

August 31

MAKING MEMORIES

Deuteronomy 4:9 Only be careful, and watch yourselves closely so that you do not forget the things your eyes have seen or let them slip from your heart as long as you live. Teach them to your children and to their children after them.

I think one of the biggest joys in my life is my grandchildren. They just seem to be interested in everything I say and do. I love to talk to them, especially about God. They are all ears and I have their undivided attention. I was talking to my 8 year old granddaughter the other day and she said she just loved to come over and spend the day with me: And I told her that is the way you make memories.

My 13 year old granddaughter spent several days with us this summer and I had the opportunity to talk to her about some spiritual things that she had on her mind and it blessed my heart because I don't have the opportunity to spend much time with her since she doesn't live in close proximity to do so. It is not the quantity of time that we have together but rather it is the quality of time.

Of all the things I could give to my children and grandchildren, I would hope and pray that the things they remember when I am gone is what I might have taught them about my Lord. Unfortunately I didn't know the Lord as my personal Savior when my own children were growing up and I missed that opportunity to do so. But hopefully I will inspire them from this time on, to walk with the Lord all of the remaining days of their lives

If you are parents of small children and you know the Lord, you and your children are blessed beyond measure. Don't miss the opportunity to teach them the things of God. It is the most important mission in your life.

September 1

NEEDS MET

Philippians 4:19 And my God will meet all your needs according to his glorious riches in Christ Jesus.

Our business involves loading and unloading heavy merchandise. My husband has a bad back and it sometimes presents a problem if there is not a parking place in close proximity to the area where we need to load and unload.

We recently worked a show in Las Vegas. I had gone to retrieve the car from the hotel parking area to move it to the convention center where we had worked the show. When I entered the underground parking area next to the exit doors, there were no available parking places anywhere, which would mean that Bill would have to push a heavy cart for quite a distance. I began to pray that God would provide a space for us. As I drove around trying to find a space, I noticed a man getting into his car. I stopped and asked him if he was getting ready to leave and he said yes, and if I would just wait on him to load his car, he would gladly make sure that I would get the spot. Not only did God provide a parking place, but guess what? He provided one directly in front of the exit door.

Now I know that some may think that it might be stretching the above scripture a bit; but I'll tell you my thoughts on the matter. I don't think so. God cares about all of our needs—even down to a parking place. He also hears and answers our prayers. *If you believe, you will receive "whatever you ask for in prayer." Matthew 21:22.* We serve an awesome God. He loves His children and He sees our needs. I immediately realized that God understood that Bill needed help that day and He provided and met our need. Sometimes we just don't see the small miracles that He works in our lives on a daily basis.

September 2

LIVING VESSELS

2 Corinthians 4:7 But we have this treasure in jars of clay to show that this all-surpassing power is from God and not from us.

Isn't it odd how we can read a scripture over and over again, and then all of a sudden God opens our eyes to see what He is really saying. I was overwhelmed with awe as I read 2 Corinthians 4. Verse 7 just jumped out to me. I suddenly realized that we are all empty vessels, susceptible to brokenness, but usable in so many different ways. We are worthless in serving the Lord unless He fills us up. No wonder Paul used this as an example of what God can do through us. Without God the Father, sending Jesus as the propitiation for our sins, and without the Holy Spirit filling us up, we would remain just an empty vessel.

Only through Christ and His Holy Spirit can we be filled with the knowledge, wisdom, and desire to shed the light of His love. Only through Him are we able to show and tell the world of His magnificent grace. How humbling it is to know that God is willing to take a plain, ordinary clay vessel and fill it with treasure to use it for His purpose. We would never be able to do all that He wants us to do without His grace. Are we willing to allow Him to fill us up and use us as vessels to be poured out for Him?

September 3-4

WATER FOR THE WEEKEND

TEMPTATION
by William Cowper

The billows swell, the winds are high,
Clouds overcast my wintry sky;
Out of the depths to Thee I call, —
My fears are great, my strength is small.

O Lord, the pilot's part perform,
And guard and guide me through the storm;
Defend me from each threatening ill,
Control the waves, — say, "Peace! be still."

Amidst the roaring of the sea
My soul still hangs her hope on Thee;
Thy constant love, thy faithful care,
Is all that saves me from despair.

Dangers of every shape and name
Attend the followers of the Lamb,
Who leave the world's deceitful shore,
And leave it to return no more.

Though tempest-toss'd and half a wreck,
My Saviour through the floods I seek;
Let neither winds nor stormy main
Force back my shatter'd bark again.

September 5

LOOK STRAIGHT AHEAD

Hebrews 12:2 Let us fix our eyes on Jesus, the author and perfector of our faith, who for the joy set before him endured the cross, scorning its shame and sat down at the right hand of the throne of God.

I once wondered why they put blinders on horses; it seemed to me that it limited their vision. Well guess what, it does. Blinders are used to keep the horse focused on what is in front of it. Without the blinders, they might become distracted by things around them. Horses are easily frightened, and when that happens, they sometimes bolt and run.

As Christians, sometimes we look at the circumstances around us and become frightened and discouraged, and just like horses; we might be tempted to bolt and run. Or we might just look at the things around us and simply take our eyes off of Jesus and wander down the wrong path. Satan would love nothing more than for us to do that. We must keep our eyes focused on Jesus; the author and perfector of our faith. Don't let the circumstances around you distract you or discourage you. Look straight ahead to the Cross of Jesus.

September 6

WALKING ON WATER

Matthew 14:28-31 "Lord, if it's you," Peter replied, "tell me to come to you on the water." "Come," he said. Then Peter got down out of the boat, walked on the water and came toward Jesus. But when he saw the wind, he was afraid and, beginning to sink, cried out, "Lord, save me!" Immediately Jesus reached out his hand and caught him. "You of little faith," he said, "why did you doubt?"

Have you ever been in the middle of a seemingly impossible task and prayed that the Lord would take control and help you do the impossible: You think that you have put your complete faith and trust in Him; then all of a sudden you become scared and your faith starts to waver until you feel as though you are sinking. I have done that very thing just recently, so it is no surprise that God has been talking to me about a faith that does not waver. I had complete trust and faith in God to see me through the task ahead of me until I let doubt come in and threaten to destroy it. But praise God, He has delivered me out of the fear that was about to take control.

Fear the Lord, you his saints, for those who fear him lack nothing. Psalm 34:9

There are two different types of fear. Webster's dictionary says that there is a fear in oneself, and there is a reverential fear (awe) of God. When we take our eyes off of the Lord and we see the dangers around us, we become fearful and our faith starts to waver. But when we look to God with an awesome fear, we realize that His power will sustain us. I believe that all of us at sometime have had the 'walking on water' experience that Peter had. We can put our complete faith and trust in God. He won't leave us out there to drown in our fears, if we look to Him for our help.

September 7

THE GOD OF MIRACLES

Psalms 77:13-15 Your ways, O God are holy. What god is so great as our God? You are the God who performs miracles; you display your power among the peoples. With your mighty arm you redeemed your people, the descendants of Jacob and Joseph.

We live in troubling times. We see our nation going down the tubes as those who seemingly don't walk with the Lord, make the decisions for our country. We sit and wring our hands and talk about our dubious future and discuss what we can do about it all. Those of us who are Christians can take heart in the fact that our God is the God of miracles. He is able to do all things. Remember all of the times that He has redeemed you and me from despair. He hears our cry for help. The question is: Are we crying out to God with a sincere heart to bring this country back to our Christian values? Sitting around wringing our hands and talking about our situation will do no good at all. But God has told us to humble ourselves and pray. *2 Chronicles 7:14 If my people who are called by my name, will humble themselves and pray and seek my face and turn from their wicked ways, then will I hear from heaven and will forgive their sin and will heal their land.* How about you? Are you seeking God with all your heart and crying out to Him with sincere humility to save our country?

Perhaps you have need of a miracle in your own life. God is able to bring about that miracle. There is hope in every circumstance when we serve our Lord and Savior. Cry out to Him and ask him to give you what you need according to His will. He will hear your voice and deliver you out of your troubles. He will give you exactly what you need, not necessarily what you want, but certainly what you need. Trust in Him for all things.

September 8

LOOK UP AND LIVE

Romans 7:21-25 So I find this law at work: When I want to do good, evil is right there with me. For in my inner being I delight in God's law, but I see another law at work in the members of my body waging war against the law of my mind and making me a prisoner of the law of sin at work within my members. What a wretched man I am. Who will rescue me from this body of death? Thanks be to God-through Jesus Christ our Lord! So then, I myself in my mind am a slave to God's law, but in the sinful nature a slave to the law of sin.

Did you know that if you put a bumble bee in a container, it will never get out? It looks for ways all around the container to escape but never looks up. It becomes a prisoner there until it dies, unless someone sets it free.

What a picture that is of us when we find ourselves deep in sin. We can't pull ourselves out; we become slaves to that sin until it destroys us. The only way we can get out is to look up to the one that will rescue us, and lift us out of the pit of slavery; slavery to the sins we are in.

Just like the bumble bee, all we have to do is look up to find our way to life everlasting. Look to the one that made a way for our escape from certain death; the Lord Jesus Christ. If you feel like you are trapped in a life of sin, look up to the one who will break those chains and set you free.

September 9

NO LOOKING BACK

Genesis 19:26 But Lot's wife looked back and she became a pillar of salt.

Everybody has memories from the past; some good and some bad. Satan has a way of bringing up the bad things from our past to discourage us. When we allow that to happen, we are not fit to do the things that God calls us to do.

Sometimes it is fun to relive the wonderful things of the past, but even then it can be a tool of Satan's to take our eyes off of what God is calling us to do.

God may call us to a place where we must give up some things that we enjoy. Do we argue with Him, or are we obedient to follow Him? *Luke 9:61-62 Still another said "I will follow you Lord; but first let me go back and say good-by to my family." Jesus replied, "No one who puts his hand to the plow and looks back is fit for service in the kingdom of God."*

Jesus himself said we must not look back but move on with Him. If we are serious about serving our Lord, we must determine in our hearts to give up the past things and look ahead to what God has for us. We should be so excited about what God is calling us to do, that our past pales in comparison. If we don't, we might become like Lot's wife, and become an inanimate object, useless in our future work for the Lord.

September 10-11

WATER FOR THE WEEKEND

THE CONTRITE HEART
by William Cowper

The Lord will happiness divine
On contrite hearts bestow;
Then tell me, gracious God, is mine
A contrite heart or no?

I hear, but seem to hear in vain,
Insensible as steel;
If aught is felt, 'tis only pain,
To find I cannot feel.

I sometimes think myself inclined
To love Thee if I could;
But often feel another mind,
Averse to all that's good.

My best desires are faint and few,
I fain would strive for more;
But when I cry, "My strength renew!"
Seem weaker than before.

Thy saints are comforted, I know,
And love Thy house of prayer;
I therefore go where others go,
But find no comfort there.

Oh make this heart rejoice or ache;
Decide this doubt for me;
And if it be not broken, break —
And heal it, if it be.

September 12

THE GREEN EYED MONSTER

1 Samuel 18:6-9 When the men were returning home after David had killed the Philistine, the women came out from all the towns of Israel to meet King Saul with singing and dancing, with joyful songs and with tambourines and lutes. As they danced, they sang: "Saul has slain his thousands, and David his tens of thousands." Saul was very angry; this refrain galled him. "They have credited David with tens of thousands," he thought, "but me with only thousands. What more can he get but the Kingdom?" And from that time on Saul kept a jealous eye on David.

Look at this! Saul, the king who had said to David just before he went to fight the Philistines, "Go, and the Lord be with you" is now jealous of the very one who had just defeated the Philistines. David had never taken glory for himself but made it known to all that it was God who would fight the battle and win. Yet Saul was furious because the people were praising David more than himself. He was so angry that from that day on he wanted to kill David. It is difficult to understand how someone who had been successful in a pursuit that won such a huge victory over the enemy could now be the target of the one who sent him to do the job. Saul's jealousy destroyed the relationship that he had with David.

No wonder they call jealousy 'the green eyed monster'. I'm sure that most of us at some time in our life have been envious of others. But to be so jealous of someone to the point of wanting to kill them is unthinkable. And to be jealous of one of God's people who have surrendered their life to His call is beyond the wildest imagination. How could anyone want to harm a man or woman of God? I doubt that anyone reading this would ever be that hateful and jealous, but have you ever been mean spirited enough to slander one of God's people just because of what they are doing for the Lord? I have heard people say unkind, hurtful and unmerited things about those who are serving God. Why would anyone be jealous of those who are obeying the Lord, especially one of their own brothers or sisters in Christ? God has a purpose for everyone's life. All we have to do is ask Him to show us what He wants us to do. No purpose is greater than another. It is our obedience to follow the Lord that He desires. God must be very sad to see His children bad-mouth another because of a jealous spirit.

Have you ever been hurt by someone that you thought was a friend, I have and I would guess that you have also. It hurts tremendously, doesn't it? The only explanation that I can think of is that they are consumed with jealousy and feel threatened in one way or another. Jealousy is very destructive to relationships. Families have been split apart because of jealousy. And churches have been divided because of it. Let's be very careful not to allow a jealous nature to destroy a relationship with others.

September 13

LOVING CORRECTION

2 Timothy 4:2 Preach the Word; be prepared in season and out of season; correct, rebuke and encourage with great patience and careful instruction.

Because of my husband's back surgery, we carry a handicap sign in our car. There was a time, and occasionally still is when we have had a legitimate excuse to use it. But there have been many times when I have used it for convenience sake. One day while shopping with a wonderful Christian sister, I pulled into a handicap parking space, and she said, "You aren't going to park here are you". I looked at her and said, "Yes, I have a permit". I immediately saw the look of disappointment in her face, and she lovingly chastised me for taking a space that someone else might truly need. I felt so ashamed, most of all because I had not considered other's needs first. Needless to say I moved the car and parked in a legitimate parking place.

I am so grateful for my sister who does not compromise her Christian values, and is not afraid to tell a friend, in a loving manner, that she is doing wrong. She truly has encouraged me to be more considerate and thoughtful of others. She made me see what a poor witness it would be, for others to see me getting out of a car parked in a handicap space, with no apparent handicap of my own. No matter how you try to put a tag on it—it is being dishonest.

I had certainly compromised my Christian witness. But because of a sister who loved me enough to point out my fault, God has used it to teach me. Believe me; I will never again park in a handicap space without cause. It also taught me to think about the things I do that are seemingly harmless, that could cause others to stumble, or doubt my faith. I realized also just how deep her love was for me, as a sister-in-Christ, and it humbled me to think that she would risk my anger by rebuking me. Now that is a true friend.

September 14

PROTECT THE CHILDREN

Deuteronomy 31:11-13 When all Israel comes to appear before the Lord your God at the place that he will choose, you shall read this law before them in their hearing. Assemble the people, men, women, and children, and the aliens living in your towns, they can listen and learn to fear the Lord your God, and follow carefully all the words of this law. Their children, who do not know this law, must hear it and learn to fear the Lord your God, as long as you live in the land that you are going over the Jordan to possess."

When I witness little children who have such a tender heart for the Lord, it truly blesses my heart. It is hard to believe that one day they might not have that kind of open excitement and enthusiasm for God. It is hard to imagine that these sweet, innocent little ones might be caught up in the world and into peer pressure that would lead them astray. Unfortunately this scenario happens many, many times. What can we possibly do to protect them from this happening?

We can't control the lives of another person when they reach the age of making their own choices. But we can and should follow God's word in the way we can lead them. The scripture above tells us to assemble together, with our children in tow, to hear the Word of the Lord. We have an obligation to take them to church regularly. We are instructed to teach them the ways of God. How do we teach them?—by reading the Word to them and by telling them all of the wonderful things of God and His word on a daily basis. *Teach them to your children, talking about them when you sit at home and when you walk along the road, when you lie down, and when you get up. Deuteronomy 11:19* We need to cover them with prayer from the time they are born. Pray that God would protect them from the arrows that Satan throws at them. Teach them to put on the armor of God so that they will be able to stand against the evil powers of this world.

275

Sometimes we can do all that is in our power to show them the way, and still when they are older they might go astray. But we won't have to look back and say that we didn't teach them God's ways. Our hope is in the Lord and so is our children's. Let's do what God instructs us to do. *Train a child in the way he should go, and when he is old he will not turn from it. Proverbs 22:6*

September 15

MARRIAGE RELATIONSHIP

Matthew 19:4-6 "Haven't you read," he replied, "that at the beginning the Creator made them 'male and female,' and said, 'For this reason a man will leave his father and mother and be united to his wife and the two will become one flesh'? So they are no longer two, but one. Therefore what God has joined together, let man not separate.

As I was thumbing through a magazine one day, I was taken aback when my eye caught a Lawyers advertisement with the headline—'Divorce with Dignity.' How in the world can a divorce with dignity be possible? The answer to that question is—never. God's Word emphatically states, what He has joined together, no man should separate. Our society today actually promoting divorce should offend everyone, especially Christians. It has become so easy to demolish marriages, separating husbands and wives, and in most cases, leaving children in a broken home, which generally causes everlasting problems.

The problem in marriage today is that self is put before anyone else. Our happiness becomes the central theme. The big question is "How will you meet my need." It is so unfair to expect our happiness to be the responsibility of another person. The truth is—the only real happiness comes from our relationship with the Lord. If we are looking for someone else to provide that, it will not happen. When we are seeking a right relationship with our Lord, we won't have time or the desire to wreck our relationship with our mate. When we find peace with our Lord, we will find peace in our homes.

There is absolutely nothing in our marriage that God cannot heal. If you are having a problem in your marriage, go to the Lord for the help you need, don't let Satan destroy what God has joined together. Let's realize that our happiness comes from our relationship with the Lord—then and only then will the relationship with our spouse be strengthened.

September 16

SAVED BY GRACE

Romans 3:22-24 This righteousness from God comes through faith in Jesus Christ to all who believe. There is no difference, for all have sinned and fall short of the glory of God, and are justified freely by his grace through the redemption that came by Christ Jesus.

I love to hear people give their testimonies, don't you? We each have our own story to tell about the grace of God; every one of them different. Some may be more dramatic than others, but they all tell about God's grace. By telling our stories, others are touched by them. I truly believe that when people can identify with the sinful life of another, and can hear them tell about the grace that has saved them, they will understand that they can receive the same grace. It gives them hope for a future of being freed from the sin that entangles them.

There is not a grading curve on our sins. Sin is sin, no matter what it is. We are all sinners saved by the grace of God. There is nothing that we can do ourselves to earn the gift of life. It is only through God's grace: The grace that sent His Son to die for our sins.

O what hope, O what peace, O what grace.

Easter should be the most important Holiday in our lives: The one that we should celebrate with joy. God's Grace sent His Son to die for us. He rose again three days later. Because of His death and resurrection, we can have eternal life. Hallelujah to The King!

September 17-18

WATER FOR THE WEEKEND

THE COVENANT
by William Cowper

The Lord proclaims His grace abroad!
"Behold, I change your hearts of stone;
Each shall renounce his idol-god,
And serve, henceforth, the Lord alone.

"My grace, a flowing stream, proceeds
To wash your filthiness away;
Ye shall abhor your former deeds,
And learn my statutes to obey.

"My truth the great design ensures,
I give myself away to you;
You shall be mine, I will be yours,
Your God unalterably true.

"Yet not unsought or unimplored,
The plenteous grace I shall confer;
No — your whole hearts shall seek the Lord,
I'll put a praying spirit there.

"From the first breath of life divine
Down to the last expiring hour,
The gracious work shall all be mine,
Begun and ended in my power."

September 19

MAY GOD BE EXALTED

Luke 18:11-14 The Pharisee stood up and prayed about himself: 'God, I thank you that I am not like other men—robbers, evildoers, adulterers—or even like this tax collector. I fast twice a week and give a tenth of all I get.' But the tax collector stood at a distance. He would not even look up to heaven, but beat his breast and said, 'God, have mercy on me a sinner.' I tell you that this man rather than the other, went home justified before God. For everyone who exalts himself will be humbled, and he who humbles himself will be exalted.

One day I was listening to a young minister on television. He was a 'rising star' in the world of ministers. I had heard many things about his success in building a huge church, but I had never heard him preach a sermon until that particular day. As I sat there listening to him, I noticed how many times he said 'I'. It seemed to me that he was praising himself for the things that he had done rather than the things that God had done. I was not impressed with him and could never allow myself to listen to another of his messages again.

A short time later, I read where he was in all kinds of trouble. He was now in the headlines of the newspaper, not because of the greatness of his ministry, but because of the misuse of it. It is a dangerous thing to exalt ones self instead of exalting God. God uses us as instruments to spread His word. He and only He has the power to save. To think otherwise is a sin. Even to suggest that it is because of something we have said or done is to exalt ourselves instead of God.

I sometimes think we have a tendency to exalt those who preach the word of God, not understanding that it is the Holy Spirit inspiring them who should be exalted. To speak the word as He gives it to us, is wonderful, as long as we realize that it comes from God. God's name should be exalted and glorified above all others. *My soul will boast in the Lord; let the afflicted hear and rejoice. Glorify the Lord with me; let us exalt his name together. Psalm 34:2-3*

September 20

MOLDING THE MAN

Jeremiah 18:3-6 So I went down to the potter's house, and I saw him working at the wheel. But the pot he was shaping from the clay was marred in his hands; so the potter formed it into another pot, shaping it as seemed best to him. Then the word of the Lord came to me: "O house of Israel, can I not do with you as this potter does:" declares the Lord. "Like clay in the hand of the potter, so are you in my hand, O house of Israel.

I have watched pottery being made and it is a most amazing process. If the potter isn't satisfied with his piece of work, he just re-forms it to his satisfaction. As I was reading the above passage of scripture in Jeremiah, I started thinking about some of the pottery that I have seen and a most interesting thought came to my mind. Most pottery, on close examination is not perfect; but apparently it was made to the satisfaction of the potter. The thought came to me that when God molds us, he does so to His satisfaction, and as the above scripture says, as seems best to Him. It doesn't say we are perfect, only Jesus was perfect.

God wants to mold us to His ways. He molds each of us individually, and to His satisfaction if we are willing to let Him. Not any of us are designed and molded exactly alike. But God in His infinite wisdom knows just how to mold each one of us according to His desire. Are we pliable in the hands of God, allowing Him to mold us and make us in to exactly what He wants us to be. *Does not the potter have the right to make out of the same lump of clay some pottery for noble purposes and some for common use? Romans 9:21.*

The potter doesn't throw away the clay; he just keeps molding and re-shaping until he is satisfied with His piece of work. That's the way God does with us, he just keeps molding us and shaping us as we need it. Let's allow Him to mold us to His satisfaction whether it is for a noble purpose or a common purpose.

September 21

VENGEANCE

Matthew 5:38-39 You have heard that it was said, 'Eye for eye, and tooth for tooth.' But I tell you, do not resist an evil person. If someone strikes you on the right cheek turn to him the other also.

What is your first inclination when someone has hurt you? I think if we are honest, most of us would say vengeance and retaliation. It is a natural human reaction, to want to strike back at those who have harmed us. But God says to turn the other cheek. Many times those same people will continue to hurt us over and over again. Are we supposed to keep turning the other cheek? Yes, we are. My mother used to say, "Two wrongs don't make a right." Usually when vengeance and retaliation is put into place, it causes conflict in the heart. I don't think we ever feel good about ourselves when we retaliate.

It is very difficult to turn the other cheek when someone just keeps on slapping us. But that's what God tells us to do. God's word says to pray for our enemies. He wants us to allow Him to take care of those things. *Romans 12:19 Do not take revenge my friends, but leave room for God's wrath, for it is written: "It is mine to avenge; I will repay, says the Lord.*

September 22

NEVER FEAR—THE LORD IS NEAR

Isaiah 51:7-8 "Hear me, you who know what is right, you people who have my law in your hearts: Do not fear the reproach of men or be terrified by their insults. For the moth will eat them up like a garment, the worm will devour them like wool. But my righteousness will last forever, my salvation through all generations."

I was listening to the news when they were discussing the resignation of Sarah Palin, Governor of Alaska. They were talking about what affect it would have on her political future and how people would react to her decision. I was taken aback when I heard one of them say that their fear is that it would be her downfall, and cited one of the reasons being that there are so many liberals who don't like her, simply because she is an 'evangelical'. And they will use their hatred against her to attack her in every way possible. After giving it some thought, I think he is absolutely right.

We live in a sinful world, and never before have I seen such disdain and even hatred for Christian people as I do today. This world has come to the place where sinful people are placated to everyday, and the rights of the Christians are continually being trampled underfoot. Many Christians live in fear of what is going on in the world. But we should never fear, it is the ones who don't fear the Lord that have something to worry about. They are the ones who have no hope for a future. God's word says that they will be eaten up like a moth eats a garment and that the worm will devour them.

Praise the Lord for His protection and His defense on our behalf; for His righteousness will last forever and His salvation through all generations. Because of Him we can have perfect peace. *You will keep in perfect peace, him whose mind is steadfast, because he trusts in you. Isaiah 26:3*

September 23

RELEASING ANGER

1 Corinthians 13:5 It is not rude, it is not self-seeking, it is not easily angered, it keeps no records of wrongs.

There are many times in our life that we experience anger over something someone has said or something they have done to us. It is a fact that we will all face those kinds of things fairly regularly. The question is how we will handle the anger. So many times I have heard people say, "I don't get angry, I get even." Now that is an oxymoron if I ever heard one. If they weren't angry, they wouldn't be contemplating hurtful retaliation.

1 Corinthians 13 is known as the 'Love Chapter'. It tells us how to show our love to others. The above verse says that it keeps no record of wrongs. If our love for others was based on never being hurt, we would be in deep trouble. Even the loveliest of people say and do hurtful things at times. Have you ever hurt someone by your actions or your words? I certainly have, and I would hope that they would forgive me and move on. If we live with the attitude of getting even, we need to look into our hearts and ask ourselves where that comes from. It certainly doesn't come from God. God is a forgiving God, He keeps no record of wrongs and we should do the same.

September 24-25

WATER FOR THE WEEKEND

THE FUTURE PEACE AND GLORY OF THE CHURCH
by William Cowper

Hear what God the Lord hath spoken,
"O my people, faint and few,
Comfortless, afflicted, broken,
Fair abodes I build for you.
Thorns of heartfelt tribulation
Shall no more perplex your ways;
You shall name your walls, Salvation,
And your gates shall all be Praise.

"There, like streams that feed the garden,
Pleasures without end shall flow,
For the Lord, your faith rewarding,
All His bounty shall bestow;
Still in undisturb'd possession
Peace and righteousness shall reign;
Never shall you feel oppression,
Hear the voice of war again.

"Ye no more your suns descending,
Waning moons no more shall see;
But your griefs forever ending,
Find eternal noon in me:
God shall rise, and shining o'er ye,
Change to day the gloom of night;
He, the Lord, shall be your glory,
God your everlasting light."

September 26

NOTHING CAN BE EVERYTHING

2 Kings 4:2 Elisha replied to her, "How can I help you? Tell me, what do you have in your house?" "Your servant has nothing there at all," she said, "except a little oil."

Are you familiar with the story of the widow who was about to lose her sons to slavery because she couldn't pay her bills? When Elisha asked her what she had in her house, her answer was that she had nothing except a little oil. Elisha told her to collect all of the empty jars that she could and start filling them with what little oil she had. As she began to pour, the oil just kept coming until every jar was full. *She went and told the man of God, and he said, "Go, sell the oil and pay your debts. You and your sons can live on what is left." 2 Kings 4:7*

I love this account of the widow and her need. I wonder if any of us can identify with her story. Have there been times in your life when you felt you were down to nothing and didn't know where to turn? The widow didn't doubt at all when Elisha told her what to do. She didn't argue or waste time asking questions; she just obeyed him and started collecting and filling the empty jars until she had all that she needed.

Do you feel like you are empty? When we are down to empty God will fill us up with everything we need; all we have to do is ask and believe. We might think we have nothing, but God multiplies what we have to supply every need for our entire lifetime.

September 27

TRUE LOVE

John 15:13 Greater love has no one than this, that he lay down his life for his friends.

I remember as a little girl, every time we had fried chicken, my mother would pass the platter around to everyone else before she took a piece for herself. Of course, being the selfish children that we were, the best pieces would be gone by the time it got back to mother. She would always take the back part of the chicken and proclaim that it was one of her favorite pieces. As I got older, I realized that it wasn't because the back was my mother's favorite piece of chicken; it was because she loved us so much that she wanted us to have the best.

That is a picture of The Father's love for us. God wants the best for His children. I'm not talking about the best as the world sees it. In the world, we think the best things in life are found in our own selfish desires for food, clothes, friends, houses, positions, etc. Mothers and fathers think they are doing there children a favor by giving them all of the best earthly things, rather than the things of God. I am sorry to say that I was guilty of this before I surrendered my life to Jesus. Now I can truly say that I am no longer concerned about their earthly wealth. I want the best that my Father has for them—-and the best is JESUS. How much better can it get than to trust in our Lord and Savior to care for our children? It can't, there is no greater love.

Are we teaching our children to find their contentment in the empty things of life that we term as the best, or are we showing them the very best that God has for them. God sent His best to us in Jesus. *For God so loved the world that he gave his one and only Son, that whoever believes in him shall not perish but have eternal life. John*

3:16. I want to see my children and my grandchildren in heaven. I want to spend eternity with them, don't you? Let's point them to the very best thing; the only lasting thing that will full-fill their every need, the only one who will give them peace and contentment and eternal life: JESUS†

September 28

OBEYING GOD

Acts 8:26-27a. Now an angel of the Lord said to Philip, "Go south to the road—the desert road—that goes down from Jerusalem to Gaza." So he started out.

God told Philip to go out into the desert. He didn't know why God called him to go, and he didn't ask questions. But because of his faith and trust in the Lord, he immediately responded. He met a eunuch sitting in a chariot reading from the book of Isaiah. After conversing with the eunuch, Philip led him to the Lord.

I wonder how many of us would immediately respond to the Lord if He was calling us to a remote land without the knowledge of why we were going. That particular situation is probably not going to happen to us. But God does call each of us to share His word with others. It might be a friend, a neighbor, a colleague, or someone in our own family. Will we immediately respond without question?

If God calls us to go and share the gospel with another, we should immediately respond. It might be the last opportunity for that person to hear the word. How would we feel if God had asked us to share the good news with someone and we failed to do so, then later hear that they had died? I know from first hand experience, it is not a good feeling. I once missed an opportunity to share the gospel with another and when they died, I was devastated that I had not done so. I learned later that this man had found the Lord, because someone else had listened to God's call and responded. Let's not miss the opportunity to share the Good News.

September 29

THE SHEPHERD AND THE SHEEP

Psalm 23:1 The Lord is my shepherd; I shall not be in want.

This is such a familiar verse that we rarely stop to think how much it really means to us as Christians. We all know what a shepherd is—-Webster's dictionary describes it as one who leads sheep, a pastor. We Christians are His sheep. We hear His voice and we follow Him. At least we should.

When we are following our Shepherd he leads us in the right paths, He leads us to green pastures and quiet waters, He restores our soul, and He guides us in the paths of righteousness. We can walk in the shadow of death without fear, we are comforted by Him. He prepares a table for us in the presence of our enemies, He anoints our head with oil and our cup overflows. Goodness and mercy will follow us all of our days. We will live with the Lord forever.

Why on earth would we not want to be one of His sheep? Why don't we recognize the comfort that would be ours if we followed where He leads? I wonder how victorious we would be in our daily walk, if we would let God lead us each and every day. I don't believe we would suffer the anxiety that we do if we were following Him instead of trying to take the lead.

So many times we take our own path. We get lost and sometimes it is difficult to find our way back to the path of Jesus. Satan is always ready to devour the sheep that go astray. He tries to get us to follow in his ways, which leads to sin and heartache.

What about you? Are you following the path of Jesus? Or have you gotten off the path where Jesus was leading you. Do you hear His voice calling you back? If you are, don't turn your back and walk the other way; turn around and follow Him. He is waiting for you. *I have strayed like a lost sheep. Seek your servant, for I have not forgotten your commands. Psalm 119:176*

September 30

BLOOD ATONEMENT

Leviticus 17:11 For the life of the flesh is in the blood and I have given it to you upon the altar to make atonement for your souls; for it is the blood that makes atonement for the soul.

Leviticus has always been a difficult book for me to read: Simply because it is mind boggling to think of all the laws, regulations and sacrifices that had to be made. But the one thing that is very, very clear is the fact that it was necessary that blood sacrifice was to be made as atonement for sin. It is recorded in Hebrews 9:21-22: *Then likewise he sprinkles with blood both the tabernacle and all the vessels of the ministry. And according to the law almost all things are purified with blood, and without shedding of blood there is no remission.*

How can we not understand the need for a scapegoat, one who would pay the price for our sins once and for all? Jesus was that ONE. He took our sins to the cross. He shed His precious blood as atonement for us. What kind of love is it that someone would lay down their life for our sins? Not just laying down and dying without pain; but being tortured and nailed to a cross suffering agony for all sinners. It is a kind of love that I can't even comprehend. Probably most of us would lay down our lives for our children, but not for the whole world. What a Savior!

Read the book of Leviticus to appreciate what JESUS did for us on that cross. HE was the living sacrifice; HE was our scapegoat; HE is the Savior. Let's just stop and think about the reality of the eternal sacrifice Jesus made for us. His blood was shed as the atonement for my sins and yours. Have you accepted Him? Or have you rejected the ONE who poured out His blood on the cross as atonement for your sins?

WATER FOR THE WEEKEND

THE HAPPY CHANGE
by William Cowper

How bless'd Thy creature is, O God,
When with a single eye,
He views the lustre of Thy Word,
The dayspring from on high!

Through all the storms that veil the skies
And frown on earthly things,
The Sun of Righteousness he eyes,
With healing on His wings.

Struck by that light, the human heart,
A barren soil no more,
Sends the sweet smell of grace abroad,
Where serpents lurk'd before.

The soul, a dreary province once
Of Satan's dark domain,
Feels a new empire form'd within,
And owns a heavenly reign.

The glorious orb whose golden beams
The fruitful year control,
Since first obedient to Thy Word,
He started from the goal,

Has cheer'd the nations with the joys
His orient rays impart;
But, Jesus, 'tis Thy light alone
Can shine upon the heart.

October 3

ONE SAVIOR

Isaiah 43:11 I, even I, am the Lord, and apart from me there is no savior.

Who in all this earth can save you from eternal destruction? There may be times when others can protect you from immediate dangers, but even then, it is only by God's grace. Why then do we look to others for help before we go to our heavenly Father? Do we not know that He is the only one who can save us from disaster?

In the midst of everything that is going on in our country, people are terribly frightened and are looking for a savior. Unfortunately many of them do not give our Father a thought. Without knowing Him as their personal Savior they are to be pitied like no other. I can't imagine what hope people have in a world that has gone wild in every area, without our Lord and Savior. There is no other who can protect us and deliver us from the evils of this world. I am not saying that God's people won't go through some of the same trials that the non-believers do, but we have hope for the future with our Lord, as He walks with us through the trials.

People are more concerned about their finances and riches today than ever before. They are looking for someone, anyone who will save them from the financial disaster that is certain to come. They are not looking for the only one who can save their souls. Those of us who know Christ will not be moved by the fact that the days of impending crisis are coming. We will put our faith and trust in the Lord because we know that He is our Redeemer and our Savior. *Why should I fear when evil days come, when wicked deceivers surround me-those who trust in their wealth and boast of their great riches? Psalms 49:5*

Isn't it wonderful that we can praise our Father in uncertain days, knowing that no matter what comes; we will be safe from harm? God will deliver us and like Paul, we can say—*I consider that our present sufferings are not worth comparing with the glory that will be revealed in us. Romans 8:18*

October 4

RECOGNIZING TRUE FRIENDS

Proverbs 27:6 Wounds from a friend can be trusted, but an enemy multiplies kisses.

Who are your friends? How do you rate them? Are you offended when a friend tells you the truth or do you recognize and accept the truth of what they say? Or do you prefer those who flatter you and say only things that are pleasing to your ears?

A true friend will always tell you the truth. God's word says that your enemy multiplies kisses. In other words they aren't concerned with your soul; they say things to build your own personal ego up. Those who truly love you are more interested in the fellowship you share with them and the Lord. Sometimes we are carried away by those so called friends who flatter our egos. Perhaps we could measure in our heart a true friend by asking ourselves this hypothetical question—If we were facing a major crisis in our life, if we or one of our loved ones were dying, who would we go to for comfort and prayer?

You adulteress people, don't you know that friendship with the world is hatred toward God? Anyone who chooses to be a friend of the world becomes an enemy of God. James 4:4 A true friend is always there to help you in the direst of circumstances; others are there for the good times. Our brothers and sisters in Christ will lift us up in times of crisis, whether physical or spiritual, if we don't shut them out. I was reading this morning about a woman who suffered from clinical depression. She told about how her Christian family had surrounded her with love and compassion and how they had helped her and her family out in concrete ways at a time when she really needed help—some of them took care of her children, some of them came to clean her house, others brought food in. They were true friends and they showed their love for her by being there when she needed them. Let's learn to recognize who our true friends are.

October 5

ORDAINED TIMING

Esther 4:14 For if you remain silent at this time, relief and deliverance for the Jews will arise from another place, but you and your father's family will perish. And who knows but that you have come to royal position for such a time as this?

The story of Esther is so encouraging to anyone who doubts that God could or would use them for any reason or purpose. Esther was a Jewish orphan, raised and adopted by her cousin, Mordecai. There had been a plot to kill all of the Jews in the Kingdom by Haman. Because of Esther being made Queen, and the favor she had found with the King, and because of her obedience to Mordecai and to God, she was able to avert the plot, saving the entire Jewish community. God had a purpose for her, and because of her willingness to serve, she fulfilled that purpose.

It is very obvious as you read the story of Esther, that God put her in the right place, at the right time to carry out His plan. Why do you think that God would choose one like her to save her people from annihilation? She wasn't one that you would imagine that God would use in a situation like hers. I am convinced that God can and will use anyone to carry out His plan, if we are obedient to His calling.

Do you wonder why you are here at this time? It is because God ordained it to be. He has put you here for a reason and He has something special for each one of us. Ask Him what He has for you to do, and then be obedient to what He tells you. Who knows what changes might be brought in another's life because of your obedience.

October 6

SUFFERING AND STRIFE

1Peter 4:16 However, if you suffer as a Christian, do not be ashamed, but praise God that you bear that name.

Have you ever suffered insults because you are a Christian? Has anyone ever misunderstood the work that you do for the Lord? Have you ever been ridiculed because of it, sometimes even from other Christians. I would venture to say that most of us can answer yes to that question.

It is disturbing when the world attacks us for serving our Savior, but when those from our own family (blood or Christian) ridicule us, it is hurtful beyond measure. The question is how will we handle the situation? Will we become angry and allow Satan to get a hold of our minds and entangle us in the chains of un-forgiveness: Or will we allow God to speak to our hearts with a sweet spirit of forgiveness? *"Therefore, if you are offering your gift at the altar and there remember that your brother has something against you, leave your gift there in front of the altar. First go and be reconciled to your brother, then come and offer your gift.*

God's Word tells us to praise Him that we bear His name. When we bear His name we also carry with us the weapons He gives us to fight the battles that Satan brings in to our lives. We have every weapon to become victors. We must put on our armor and fight not only for us but for our families. *Put on the full armor of God so that you can take your stand against the devil's schemes. Ephesians 6:11*

Don't give in to the attacks of Satan and allow him to control our minds; rather put on the armor of Christ. We may have suffering and strife in this world but we will overcome. *Do not be overcome by evil, but overcome evil with good. Romans 12:21*

October 7

OUR PROTECTION

"Because he loves me," says the Lord, "I will rescue him; I will protect him, for he acknowledges my name. He will call upon me, and I will answer him, I will be with him in trouble, I will deliver him and honor him. With long life will I satisfy him and show him my salvation." Psalm 91:14-16

What a wonderful promise. When we are being attacked, God will protect us. Satan may fling his arrows at us but they will never penetrate those who love the Lord. He has provided the protection we need. We must remember his promise to us and call on Him in our days of trouble. He will honor our prayers for deliverance. He alone can protect us from the enemy. Satan's plan is to try to defeat us by any evil scheme, but praise God— He will never leave us nor forsake us. *Be strong and courageous. Do not be afraid or terrified because of them, for the Lord your God goes with you; he will never leave you nor forsake you. Deuteronomy 31:6* Jesus is the rock of our salvation and in Him we have no fear.

There is a song that says "Praise the Lord, He never changes, we call to Him, and He's always there." If you are being attacked right now by the evil one, as we all are from time to time, remember to call on the Lord and he will deliver you and protect you.

October 8-9

WATER FOR THE WEEKEND

THE HEART HEALED AND CHANGED BY MERCY
by William Cowper

Sin enslaved me many years,
And led me bound and blind;
Till at length a thousand fears
Came swarming o'er my mind.
"Where," said I, in deep distress,
"Will these sinful pleasures end?
How shall I secure my peace
And make the Lord my friend?"

Friends and ministers said much
The gospel to enforce;
But my blindness still was such,
I chose a legal course:
Much I fasted, watch'd, and strove,
Scarce would shew my face abroad,
Fear'd almost to speak or move,
A stranger still to God.

Thus afraid to trust His grace,
Long time did I rebel;
Till despairing of my case,
Down at His feet I fell:
Then my stubborn heart He broke,
And subdued me to His sway;
By a simple word He spoke,
"Thy sins are done away."

October 10

SPIRIT AND TRUTH

1 Corinthians 2:13 This is what we speak, not in words taught us by human wisdom but in words taught by the Spirit, expressing spiritual truths in spiritual words.

Our minister is always praying that God will speak to us in Spirit and in Truth.

Since the first of the year, he has been preaching a series of sermons on Holiness. Ouch, boy has he stepped on my toes more than once. In preparation for this particular series, he warned us that he would preach sermons that might make us angry. I suppose if one wasn't wanting to hear the truth, that might be the case: But if we are wanting to be Holy people, we must be willing to hear God's truth even if it convicts us, so that we may live a life that is pleasing to Him—a life that glorifies the name that we carry as Christians.

Let's be thankful for those ministers who are willing to endure the ridicule and suffering that may be theirs for preaching The Truth. Check out what our ministers are teaching us; look in God's Word to see if they are preaching the truth, then you will know whether or not it came from the Spirit. *Then the woman said to Elijah, "Now I know that you are a man of God and that the word of the Lord from your mouth is the truth. 1 Kings 17:24* When a man preaches the truth it will do one of two things, it will either make someone mad, because they don't want to hear the truth—or it will speak words of wisdom to those who are seeking the truth and desire a deeper walk with the Lord; a walk of holiness.

It is not that these men of God want to remind us of our past sins, it is because they are led by the Spirit to preach His Truth: The truth that will set us free from bondage. They must teach the truth of God that enables us to lead a victorious life—a life of holiness. Let's be thankful for those who are willing to listen to the Holy Spirit and preach The Truth. If they are not preaching what the Holy Spirit puts on their hearts, then we might as well not be in church. *God is spirit and his worshipers must worship in spirit and in truth. John 4:24*

October 11

PATIENCE

Galatians 5:22 But the fruit of the Spirit is love, joy, peace, patience, kindness, goodness, faithfulness, gentleness and self-control.

We become so familiar with certain scriptures of the bible, that we sometimes miss what they are saying to us. If we ponder on the fruits of the Spirit, we can see that it is impossible to have them all if we are lacking in one. Do you think that you show all of the fruits of the Spirit on a daily basis? I know I don't. I think each one of us probably fall short of obtaining them all every day. No matter how hard I try, I seem to never attain them all.

Patience seems to be one that I have a difficult time grasping. I lose patience with people I see walking in their own way instead of God's way. But then I think to myself; that very way of thinking is going against God's word. God has patience with me, because He loves me, and he sees my human frailty. As long as I have impatience in my life, I am not experiencing all of the peace and joy that God provides.

What about you? Is there a particular fruit that you are struggling with? We need to confess our weakness and let God do a complete work in our hearts and spirits, so that we can display every one of the fruits of His Spirit every day.

October 12

REWARD FOR SERVICE

2 Kings 4:14-17 "What can be done for her." Elisha asked. Gehazi said, "Well she has no son and her husband is old." Then Elisha said, "Call her," So he called her and she stood in the doorway. "About this time next year," Elisha said, "you will hold a son in your arms." "No, my lord," she objected. "Don't mislead your servant, O man of God!" But the woman became pregnant, and the next year about that same time she gave birth to a son, just as Elisha had told her.

This well-to-do shunammite woman had recognized Elisha as a man of God and she and her husband had provided a place for him to stay when he came to their area. She had seen to it that he was provided everything that he might possibly need. Elisha wanted to reward her in some way and had inquired of her needs. When he found out that they had no children, this man of God told her that she would have a son in her ripe old age. And indeed she did have. In the time that this took place; it was almost an embarrassment for a woman to be barren. But God knew it was the desire of her heart to have one, and He gave it to her as a blessing and a reward for her service to Elisha.

This is not the first time that we have seen God do the impossible for those who have been obedient. I believe that every person who is willing to serve others will be blessed in some way or another. Not that we deserve it or expect it: In fact if we do it to gain rewards for ourselves, then we labor in vain. But God wants to show His appreciation for our faithfulness and obedience.

October 13

PERFECT PEACE

Isaiah 26:3 You will keep in perfect peace him whose mind is steadfast, because he trusts in you.

I listened to a woman's testimony this week. She had been sexually molested by her father from the time she was 6 years old. As a result she had many problems in her life which led her to drugs, alcohol, and prostitution. She told how she had planned to commit suicide by saving up pills. The day she planned to take her life, God got through to her spirit and stopped her. She soon met a young Christian woman who led her to the Lord. But she just couldn't get over the sin that her father had done to her, so she wasn't at peace. She had not seen her father for 19 years, but the Lord told her that she needed to look him up and forgive him. By God's strength, she was able to do that. When she rang the doorbell of her father's home, he answered, and she told him that she had come to forgive him. He fell to his knees and cried and said, "How could you ever forgive me?" She answered him that it was because Jesus had forgiven her. She said the minute that she forgave him, she found sweet peace.

There are some horrific things that mar our lives through things that have been done to us in the past. But we have a choice to make. We can forgive the person who has abused us in any way, or we can carry it with us, allowing it to destroy our peace and possibly our health. God is the only one who can restore the peace that our spirit longs for. If you are still carrying hatred toward someone who has hurt you in the past in anyway, let go and let God give you the peace that passes all understanding. He is able to do that, and He is the only one who can.

October 14

OUR COMMISSION

Acts 1:8-9 "But you will receive power when the Holy Spirit comes on you; and you will be my witnesses in Jerusalem and to all Judea and Samaria, and to the ends of the earth.

Many Christians that I talk to believe that the bible is quickly being fulfilled and that we are nearing the end. Of course no man knows the very time our Lord will return. The signs however, seem to say that it won't be long. Should we sit around and discuss the possibility of His coming soon with the satisfaction that we are ready to go, and therefore we have nothing more to do? Or should we embrace what Jesus taught us, and go out into the world to proclaim the Salvation that Jesus has to offer while there is still time

There are many people hurting in this world today. They need hope for the future. They need a Savior. It is a prime time to point them to the Cross of Jesus. That is our commission. He wasn't just speaking to His disciples; He was speaking to us. As children of God, we are His ambassadors.

The dictionary describes an ambassador in this way: 1: an official envoy; especially: a diplomatic agent of the highest rank accredited to a foreign government or sovereign as the resident representative of his or her own government or sovereign or appointed for a special diplomatic assignment 2 a: an authorized representative or messenger b: an unofficial representative traveling abroad as ambassadors of goodwill

It seems to me that as ambassadors of Christ, we have every authority to proclaim The Word. We are children of the King. Let's go out and do the job that Jesus has commissioned us to do.

October 15-16

WATER FOR THE WEEKEND

THE HIDDEN LIFE
by William Cowper

To tell the Saviour all my wants,
How pleasing is the task!
Nor less to praise Him when He grants
Beyond what I can ask.

My laboring spirit vainly seeks
To tell but half the joy,
With how much tenderness He speaks,
And helps me to reply.

Nor were it wise, nor should I choose,
Such secrets to declare;
Like precious wines their taste they lose,
Exposed to open air.

But this with boldness I proclaim,
Nor care if thousands hear,
Sweet is the ointment of His name,
Not life is half so dear.

And can you frown, my former friends,
Who knew what once I was,
And blame the song that thus commends
The Man who bore the cross?

Trust me, I draw the likeness true,
And not as fancy paints;
Such honor may He give to you,
For such have all His saints.

October 17

THE SPIRITS REVELATION

1 Corinthians 2:9 However, as it is written: "No eye has seen, no ear has heard, no mind has conceived what God has prepared for those who love him" — but God has revealed it to us by his Spirit. The Spirit searches all things, even the deep things of God.

Isn't it the most exciting thing when we are reading God's word and He reveals Himself in a very clear way? I can recall a time when I could not understand anything I read in the bible, therefore I would just give up. That was before I met my Jesus. Wow what a difference it makes when we have the Holy Spirit to enlighten us.

I don't know about you, but I look forward each time I read God's word, to learning something that I have never known before. I thank God that He didn't give up on me. I am so thankful for the Holy Spirit who enlightens me and teaches me, and shows me new and exiting things. The only way we can hear His voice is when we know Him as our personal Lord and Savior. Then He will reveal and enlighten us with His word so that it will penetrate our hearts. Nobody can teach us like our Lord.

October 18

GROWING UP

Colossians 1:10 And we pray this in order that you may live a life worthy of the Lord and may please him in every way; bearing fruit in every good work, growing in the knowledge of God

It can be a pretty traumatic time in a parent's life when their children grow up and leave the nest. I can remember when our daughter left for college, I cried off and on for a week. She also had a difficult time that first week. She called several times crying and it was so tempting to tell her just to pack up and come home. I knew however that it was not the right thing to do. She and I both would be sorry in the long run that we had given in to the loneliness that we both felt. Then again when our son left home; I did the same thing and this time my husband (Bill) and I faced an empty nest. After having children in your home for 20 plus years, the house seems awfully empty and you wonder if you will ever adjust; and you worry about what choices your children will make. We wanted them to stay in our home forever. We knew however, that it was time to let them go to find their own way in the world. As much as parents love their children, we do not know what is best for them. Only God knows. Just like parents realize that their children have to grow up and move on, so does our Heavenly Father. The difference is our heavenly Father knows exactly what we need and where we need to be.

There comes a time in all of our lives when we must grow up in the Lord. *Therefore let us leave the elementary teachings about Christ and go on to maturity. Hebrews 6:1a.* We need to leave our comfort zones and go out and do what God has for us to do. He will not keep us in the same place forever. He wants us to move on in our spiritual walk. He wants to educate us in His ways and to use us where He leads us. He is our heavenly Father and He has a plan for us. Don't be afraid to follow where God leads you. He will go

307

with you wherever He leads. We will never be homeless. Just like our children will always have a home to come to—We also have a dwelling place with our heavenly Father. Wherever we are He is there also. *Blessed are those who dwell in your house; they are ever praising you. Psalm 84:4*

October 19

REST ASSURED

Isaiah 33:5-6 The Lord is exalted, for he dwells on high; he will fill Zion with justice and righteousness. He will be the sure foundation for your times, a rich store of salvation and wisdom and knowledge; the fear of the Lord is the key to this treasure.

We are living in very uncertain times. We could become very distressed as we see all that is going on in our world today. Every newspaper, every television news program, and almost every conversation leads to the perils that we face. If we aren't grounded in God's Word, we would be most miserable people. There is not much hope if we don't have the knowledge of the Lord.

But we have a treasure not known to the sinful world. And that treasure lies in the fear of the Lord. He is the sure foundation for the time we are living in today, just as He was in Isaiah's time. Our Lord dwells on high and we can be assured that He is in control of all things. We know that He will take care of His people. No matter what goes on around us, we know that we will be victors in the end. What a wonderful assurance of the hope for God's children.

October 20

SEEKING WISDOM

James 1:5-6 If any of you lacks wisdom, he should ask God, who gives generously to all without finding fault, and it will be given to him. But when he asks, he must believe and not doubt, because he who doubts is like a wave of the sea, blown and tossed by the wind.

When we are seeking answers for the things of God, we should not be timid about asking for His guidance and help. He is not going to chastise us for our lack of knowledge. He is not going to say, "You should know this by now, don't bother me about it again". No, never will He turn us away from the truth. His word is truth and He will gladly open our eyes and our hearts to reveal it to us, if we are earnestly seeking it. But we must have faith and trust in Him, and believe what He tells us.

Perhaps you are looking for an answer to a particular problem in your life, Are you seeking wisdom from God? The wisdom comes through reading His Word and seeking His face. If you are truly seeking His wisdom, you will obtain it. He will not turn away from your earnest heart.

October 21

SHARING A BLESSING

Genesis 33:10-11 "No, please!" said Jacob. "If I have found favor in your eyes, accept this gift from me. For to see your face is like seeing the face of God, now that you have received me favorably. Please accept the present that was brought to you, for God has been gracious to me and I have all I need." And because Jacob insisted, Esau accepted it.

Talk about a dysfunctional family! I doubt that there will ever be one as dysfunctional as that of Isaac and Rebekah's. You may recall that Esau, their eldest son, sold his birthright to his brother, Jacob. Then with the help of his mother, tricked Isaac into thinking that he was Jacob, and stole the blessing meant for his brother. Jacob had to flee from his home because of Esau's death threat against him. No wonder Jacob was so thankful that Esau had welcomed him with open arms when he retuned home after many years.

There are so many things to ponder in the above scripture. The blessings God had given them both in spite of their sinful ways and thoughts—the forgiveness they offered to one another—God's forgiveness to them both, etc. I am however focusing on the love and relationship that had been restored to them both. A love like that can only come from the Lord. If God could restore the relationship between Esau and Jacob to the point of them wanting to share everything God had blessed them with; surely He can restore any relationship.

Do you feel like you live in a dysfunctional home? I hear stories all of the time from many people talking about the problems they have in their own family. Don't despair; God can restore peace in every home. We must learn to forgive one another to the point of sharing our blessings that God has given us.

October 22-23

WATER FOR THE WEEKEND

THE LIGHT AND GLORY OF THE WORD
by William Cowper

The Spirit breathes upon the word,
And brings the truth to sight;
Precepts and promises afford
A sanctifying light.

A glory gilds the sacred page,
Majestic like the sun;
It gives a light to every age,
It gives, but borrows none.

The hand that gave it still supplies
The gracious light and heat;
His truths upon the nations rise,
They rise, but never set.

Let everlasting thanks be thine,
For such a bright display,
As makes a world of darkness shine
With beams of heavenly day.

My soul rejoices to pursue
The steps of Him I love,
Till glory break upon my view
In brighter worlds above.

October 24

SIN IS A CHOICE

James 1:12-14 (King James Version) Blessed is the man that endureth temptation: for when he is tried, he shall receive the crown of life, which the Lord hath promised to them that love him. Let no man say when he is tempted, I am tempted of God: for God cannot be tempted with evil, neither tempteth he any man: But every man is tempted, when he is drawn away of his own lust, and enticed. Then when lust hath conceived, it bringeth forth sin; and sin, when it is finished, bringeth forth death.

Have you ever been enticed to do something that you know in your heart is not right? Make no mistake; it definitely does not come from God. God does not tempt us to sin. That comes straight from Satan himself. Satan loves nothing more than to tempt us in our weakness. He will not leave us alone until we either give into the temptation or tell him to get behind us because we have decided to follow Jesus.

We are all tempted at some time or another. Are you tempted by someone or something that you know is from Satan? What are you doing about it? You have a choice to make: You can choose to give in to the sin or you can choose to walk away from it. You may think you can't do it; and you can't by yourself, but God's Word says: *No temptation has seized you except what is common to man. And God is faithful; he will not let you be tempted beyond what you can bear. But when you are tempted, he will also provide a way out so that you can stand up under it. 1 Corinthians 10:13*

October 25

THE REFINER

Malachi 3:3-4 He will sit as a refiner and purifier of silver; he will purify the Levites and refine them like gold and silver. Then the Lord will have men who will bring offerings in righteousness and the offerings of Judah and Jerusalem will be acceptable to the Lord, as in days gone by, as in former years.

At one time, I had a poster that said 'Have patience with me, God isn't finished with me yet.' I pondered on the truth of it. Recently, I have been reminded of that very poster. There are times when I become very upset with myself because I haven't reacted to circumstances the way I should have, times when I went ahead of God before consulting Him on an issue—times when I have done or said something that was beneath my Christian standards. Have you had times like that?

Isn't it comforting to know that God has not given up on us? As a matter of fact, He is refining us and molding us into the person that He wants us to be. There are times when we stumble and Satan tells us that we aren't worthy of calling ourselves children of God. Satan is a liar, God still loves us. Even when we feel like a broken vessel, He picks us up and like clay in His hands, He remolds us and renews us. He will continue to refine us until we look just like the vessel He wants us to be.

If you have been thinking that you have blown it and God can't use you anymore; think again. God is there to refine you, and mold you, and make you beautiful, and useable, if you are willing to allow Him to. It is our choice to make. We can go on our own way as a broken vessel or we can be malleable in God's hand and allow Him to reshape us and refine us. You are His and He is never finished with you. He will continue to refine you until you see Him face to face.

October 26

SIN UPON SIN

Numbers 14:41-45 But Moses said, "Why are you disobeying the Lord's command? This will not succeed! Do not go up, because the Lord is not with you. You will be defeated by your enemies, for the Amalekites and Canaanites will face you there. Because you have turned away from the Lord, he will not be with you and you will fall by the sword. Nevertheless, in their presumption they went up toward the high hill country, though neither Moses nor the ark of the Lord's covenant moved from the camp. Then the Amalekites and Canaanites who lived in that hill country came down and attacked them and beat them down all the way to Hormah.

My mother was wise in a lot of things. She said to me many times, "Two wrongs don't make a right." As I was reading the above scripture, I was reminded of mother's great wisdom. This is what the Israelites were doing when they decided to go up to the land that God had promised them. But it was too late; they had rejected God's offer to go up and take the land earlier; they did not believe Him. Moses warned them not to go because the Lord had turned away from them. They were trying to cover up one sin by committing another. They had missed their blessing.

How many times have we disobeyed the Lord in what He has asked us to do? And after realizing that God is displeased with us, we try to do something on our own to regain His favor. Once we have rejected the blessing God had for us, we can never do anything on our own to get it back, and if we try we will surely fail. God does not bless those things that we try to do on our own steam. We need to seek the Lord's counsel. *Plans fail for lack of counsel, but with many advisers they succeed. Proverbs 15:22.*

Let's take a lesson from these scriptures—let's believe God the first time and obey Him when He promises to be with us and give us success. Let's not try to regain His favor by turning around and sinning again by not seeking His council.

October 27

HE HEARS

1 John 5:14 This is the confidence we have in approaching God: that if we ask anything according to his will, he hear us.

I am always an early riser, but for the past 2 weeks I have been waking up extremely early in the morning, even for me. I had become so tired that I didn't think I could go much longer without sleep. I fell into bed last night about 10:00 thinking that surely I would sleep well. I suddenly awakened and looked at the clock and it said 1:30 and I thought 'oh no not again' as I laid there trying to go back to sleep, the thought came to me to pray about it. I asked God to help me go back to sleep for just a little longer. I must have gone back to sleep almost immediately because those were the only words out of my mouth. I don't even remember a thing about even getting sleepy. All I know is when I opened my eyes again it was 5:15. Now to most of you that is probably early, but for me it means I have had a full nights rest.

While I was praising God for a good night's rest, He reminded me that because I asked Him, he honored my request. God heard my plea and He met my need. I wonder why we don't commit every little detail of our life to the Lord. Do we think that God is not concerned about everything in our life? He cares about all things no matter how small. He knows what we need even before we ask Him. Our God provides all that we need; all we have to do is ask for it according to His will.

October 28

SNOW WHITE

Psalms 51:7 Cleanse me with hyssop, and I will be clean; wash me, and I will be whiter than snow.

After the fall season is over and the beautiful colors of the leaves have fallen, it seems as though everything becomes bleak and ugly. And then there is that first beautiful snow. Everything just seems to turn into a winter wonderland. Have you ever noticed just how white snow is? When the ground is covered with new fallen snow, your eyes can hardly look at it without the aid of sunglasses. I think this is truly a beautiful picture of what Jesus did for us on the cross.

In fact it is a picture that we could color in as we ponder the steps God provided for our salvation. Let's pretend that we have a coloring book in our possession with pictures of Jesus life. Open it to the page where Jesus gave His life on the Cross for you. Take a black crayon and color in the picture of your heart before His crucifixion. Then choose a red crayon to color in the red for His blood that was shed for your sins where the picture shows Him hanging on the cross. Now take a white crayon and color your heart after you have chosen to be crucified with Christ and resurrected to eternal life in Him.

Isn't that an amazing picture that God has provided for us? Once your heart was black with sin, but because you have chosen to believe and receive God's gift of salvation, your heart is washed by His red blood until you are whiter than snow. White represents purity: There is only one way we can be pure; and that is through the blood of Christ.

Have you been washed in His blood? If not, don't let another day go by until you make that choice.

October 29-30

WATER FOR THE WEEKEND

THE NARROW WAY
by William Cowper

What thousands never knew the road!
What thousands hate it when 'tis known!
None but the chosen tribes of God
Will seek or choose it for their own.

A thousand ways in ruin end,
One only leads to joys on high;
By that my willing steps ascend,
Pleased with a journey to the sky.

No more I ask or hope to find
Delight or happiness below;
Sorrow may well possess the mind
That feeds where thorns and thistles grow.

The joy that fades is not for me,
I seek immortal joys above;
There glory without end shall be
The bright reward of faith and love.

Cleave to the world, ye sordid worms,
Contented lick your native dust!
But God shall fight with all his storms,
Against the idol of your trust.

October 31

IN THE VALLEY OF BACCA

Psalm 84:5-7 Blessed are those whose strength is in you, who have set their hearts on pilgrimage. As they pass through the Valley of Baca, they make it a place of springs; the autumn rains also cover it with pools. They go from strength to strength, till each appears before God in Zion.

I was visiting with a Christian sister this past week that is going through some trying times. She said even though she and her husband were facing some difficult obstacles, they had along with them, been receiving the biggest blessings from God that they had ever known. The more she said the more she revealed their hearts for God. They were putting all of their trust and faith in Him, even though they were passing through Baca (a trail of tears). They have determined to be strong, no matter what they face in this life, until they meet God face to face. They were putting their faith in God to bring about the things that He wanted for them.

We all have our times in the 'Valley of Baca', but God meets us there to refresh us with springs of water: The living water that gives us strength to go on from day to day. God knows everything that His people are going through. He is walking with us every step of the way and He will give us strength to meet every obstacle. He will meet our needs and we will be blessed. *The Lord gives strength to his people; the Lord blesses his people with peace. Psalms 29:11*

November 1

SPIRITUAL EYES

Ephesians 1:18 I pray also that the eyes of your heart may be enlightened in order that you may know the hope to which he has called you, the riches of his glorious inheritance in the saints, and his incomparably great power for us who believe.

At our Sunday night service at church, I had the privilege of hearing my 8 year old granddaughter sing 'My Father's Eyes' In case you haven't heard it, the following is part of the lyrics:

'When people look inside my life, I want to hear them say' she's got her Father's eyes, eyes that find the good in things, when good is not around, eyes that find the source of help, when help just can't be found. Eyes full of compassion, seeing every pain, knowing what you're going through, and feeling it the same. Just like my Father's eyes.'

Paul talks about this very thing in the first chapter of Ephesians. The eyes of our heart can only be opened by the Holy Spirit living in us. He is the only one who can give us the power to see with the eyes of the Father. It is part of the glorious inheritance in the saints. People's needs are met when they have the 'hope of glory', which is Christ Jesus. The most important thing we can do for others is to point them to the cross. I believe that if we are willing to help them in physical needs, they will be more inclined to respond to their spiritual need as we point them to the cross. Without compassion for others souls, that will not happen.

This has always been one of my favorite songs. And it is truly what I want people to say about me when I have departed this world, don't you? What a legacy! Nothing could be more notable than this. I don't care if I leave this world with anything other than the fact that it knew that I belonged to the Father. What more of a compliment to a life than for people to say, "She had her Father's eyes."

November 2

TEMPTATION

James 1:13-15 When tempted, no one should say, "God is tempting me." For God cannot be tempted by evil, nor does he tempt anyone; but each one is tempted when, by his own evil desire, he is dragged away and enticed. Then, after desire has conceived, it gives birth to sin; and sin, when it is full-grown, gives birth to death.

All of us at some time or another have been tempted to sin. It is not the temptation that is the sin; it is giving in to it. When we are tempted, we make a choice to turn our backs and walk away from it, or give in to it.

Are you being tempted to do that thing which you know in your heart is sin? If you are, turn and run away from it as quickly as you can. If you make the wrong choice, you can never undo it. If you give into that temptation, it will be too late to turn away from the sin. When we are tempted, we must turn our hearts toward Jesus and allow Him to turn us away from the temptation. *So, if you think you are standing firm, be careful that you don't fall! No temptation has seized you except what is common to man. And God is faithful; he will not let you be tempted beyond what you can bear. But when you are tempted, he will also provide a way out so that you can stand up under it. 1 Corinthians 10:12-13*

November 3

STRENGTH FOR THE DAY

Psalms 28:7 The Lord is my strength and my shield; my heart trusts in him, and I am helped. My heart leaps for joy and I will give thanks to him in song.

Do you ever have days when you feel weak and helpless? I think we all go through those periods in our life when troubles seem to get us down: Trials seem so big and answers so illusive. We are weak if we depend on our own strength. There are just some things that are out of our control.

We may not be able to control every situation. But there is one that we can turn to for help. There is one that we can trust emphatically. There is one that will help us through every struggle when we rely on Him. His name is Jesus. We can be joyful in Him even in times of weakness. We can give thanks in every circumstance when we are allowing Him to be our strength and our shield.

November 4

TAMING THE TONGUE

James 3:7 All kinds of animals, birds, reptiles and creatures of the sea are being tamed and have been tamed by man, but no man can tame the tongue. It is a restless evil, full of deadly poison.

I believe there is one thing that we all have in common: And that is not always recognizing when we should speak and what we should speak. How many times have you said something that you wished you hadn't? There are numerous times that I have spoken when I should have kept my mouth shut, and I immediately regretted it.

A word spoken can never be taken back. That is something to ponder, isn't it? We should use our words wisely. Do we speak words to elevate others, or tear them down? Do we speak words that glorify God? If we would just take the time to say a prayer before we speak, we might just save ourselves from a lot of trouble and regret. *A gentle answer turns away wrath, but a harsh word stirs up anger. Proverbs 15:1*

We should never speak words out of anger, for that does not glorify God. *My dear brothers take note of this: Everyone should be quick to listen, slow to speak and slow to become angry, for man's anger does not bring about the righteous life that God desires. James 1:19* Let's pray that God will help us tame our tongue.

November 5-6

WATER FOR THE WEEKEND

THE NEW CONVERT
by William Cowper

The new-born child of gospel grace,
Like some fair tree when summer's nigh,
Beneath Emmanuel's shining face
Lifts up his blooming branch on high.

No fears he feels, he sees no foes,
No conflict yet his faith employs,
Nor has he learnt to whom he owes
The strength and peace his soul enjoys.

But sin soon darts its cruel sting,
And comforts sinking day by day,
What seem'd his own, a self-fed spring,
Proves but a brook that glides away.

When Gideon arm'd his numerous host,
The Lord soon made his numbers less;
And said, "Lest Israel vainly boast,
My arm procured me this success!"

Thus will He bring our spirits down,
And draw our ebbing comforts low,
That saved by grace, but not our own,
We may not claim the praise we owe.

November 7

SURRENDERING

Romans 6:13 Neither yield ye your members as instruments of unrighteousness unto sin: but yield yourselves unto God, as those that are alive from the dead, and your members as instruments of righteousness unto God. (King James Version)

The word surrender is not one that most of us want to think about. We have a misconception of what it implies. We have the idea that it means a form of weakness. In my questioning why we feel that way, I believe it is because we don't like to think about giving up control in our lives.

Webster's dictionary defines surrender as—

1 a: to yield to the power, control, or possession of another upon compulsion or demand <surrendered the fort> **b:** to give up completely or agree to forgo especially in favor of another
2 a: to give (oneself) up into the power of another especially as a prisoner **b:** to give (oneself) over to something (as an influence) *intransitive verb*

We must give up the idea that surrendering to Christ means defeat. In actuality it means freedom. Once we allow Christ to rule in our hearts and minds, we are free to be used by Him. As long as we keep the reigns of control, we will be ineffective in His service.

We do not know the future, only God knows that. How then can we make correct choices if we remain in control? Let's ask ourselves if we want to be in control when it would lead to a disastrous ending; or do we want to let God take the control in our lives, knowing that His will is perfect. Will we surrender to The One who holds our future in His hands? It is the only way that we will ever have complete freedom

November 8

WINNING THE GAME

Psalms 145:14 The Lord upholds all those who fall and lifts up all who are bowed down.

There is a true story about a talented football player, who at the last play of the first half of a game, suddenly became confused and started running the wrong way until one of his own team mates tackled him. He was absolutely mortified. He entered the locker room with a dejected spirit and was at his low point as his confidence drained away. His coach said that he wanted the same players to start the 2nd half of the game, and this guy just sat there. His coach told him that he needed to get up and go back out on the field. The player reluctantly went back out, and played the best game that he had ever played in his life.

Isn't that a perfect picture of our Lord? Even when we turn and run the wrong way, He tells us to turn around and finish what He has for us to do. He gives us the encouragement to carry on. He gives us the confidence to do the things that we feel like we cannot do. He never throws us out because of mistakes that we make. He wants us to get back up and run with courage. There are many times that we learn from the mistakes we have made along the way. God uses them to teach us, He puts His arms of love around us, and tells us not to be discouraged. *The Lord is close to the brokenhearted and saves those who are crushed in spirit. Psalms 34:18*

If you are discouraged because of mistakes that you have made, don't let Satan tell you that you cannot overcome them. Listen to the Lord and turn to Him. He wants you to learn from your past mistakes and become stronger because you have put your faith and trust in Him. Our Lord is a God of second chances and even more. He never gives up on us. He is there to pick us up and lead us on to victory.

November 9

HELPING A FRIEND

Ecclesiastes 4:10 If one falls down, his friend can help him up. But pity the man who falls and has no one to help him up!

Yesterday I told the story about the football player that ran in the opposite direction from the way that he was suppose to go, until one of his team mates tackled him. Today I would like to discuss the one that was brave enough to stop the friend before he got to the end of the field.

My feeling is that the friend had mercy and compassion on him and wanted to help him. Would we be the kind of friend who would step in and stop a brother or sister when we see them going the wrong way? If we aren't, we need to be. God wants us to help restore another gently. *Brothers, if someone is caught in a sin, you who are spiritual should restore him gently. Galatians 6:1a.* There are times when we all get off the path that God wants us to travel. If we have a friend who is willing to help us find our way back, we are blessed beyond measure. We should rejoice in the fact that there is someone who loves us enough to say, "Turn around, and continue on toward the goal that Jesus has for you."

If we are in the family of God, we have a responsibility to help each other. If that means reminding your sister or brother that they have gotten off on the wrong track and going the wrong way, don't hesitate, help them to find their way back. Or if we have been on the wrong track and we have a friend who is willing to help lead us back to the right one, let's thank them and thank God that we have such a friend.

November 10

THE EYES OF FAITH

Numbers 14:36-38 So the men Moses had sent to explore the land, who returned and made the whole community grumble against him by spreading a bad report about it—these men responsible for spreading the bad report about the land were struck down and died of a plague before the Lord. Of the men who went to explore the land, only Joshua son of Nun and Caleb son of Jephunneh survived.

Through God's direction, Moses sent 12 men (one from each tribe) to the land of Canaan to check it out and to report back what they saw. When they returned, 10 of them reported that it was flowing with milk and honey and showed them the fruit of the land. But they said that the people who lived there were powerful and the cities were fortified and very large, and they named all of the people who intimidated them, and they said they shouldn't go there. But Caleb and Joshua said that they should take possession of the land because the Lord would give it to them.

What a difference in the reports that they gave. This was truly in the eye of the beholder. The men who were fearful were not seeing it through the eyes of God. They were seeing it through their own eyes. They didn't believe and trust that God would deliver them from their enemies. They could not see what Caleb and Joshua saw—victory. Caleb and Joshua was not one bit fearful to pursue the land God had promised them.....because they believed God. They knew that God would do what He said He would do. Because of their faith, out of the twelve, they were the only two spared.

What about us? Are we fearful when God calls us to go into unknown territory? Are we afraid to pursue those things that God has called us to do? We shouldn't be. When God calls us to an unfamiliar place, He will go with us. We must believe God; we must trust Him for success in all that he calls us to do.

November 11

THE HEARTBREAK OF REJECTION

Matthew 20:18-19 "We are going up to Jerusalem, and the Son of Man will be betrayed to the chief priests and the teachers of the law. They will condemn him to death and will turn him over to the Gentiles to be mocked and flogged and crucified. On the third day he will be raised to life!"

Have you ever felt rejection? It's a terrible feeling isn't it? Doesn't it sadden your heart when you think about the heartache that Jesus must have felt knowing that He was going to be mocked and betrayed?: God, who came to earth as a man and gave his life on a cross so that you and I could gain eternal life. We who are alive in Him have seen the light, yet there are so many around us who still live in darkness who mock and reject Jesus.

As I read this scripture this morning, I am reminded of 2 men that I am acquainted with who are professing atheists. They know that I am a Christian and every time they see me they tease me about my belief. I have felt lead to engage in conversation with one of them on several occasions because I feel like he is searching for the truth. The other however, is so offensive that I have never felt the call to discuss it with him. It hurts me so much that they mock my Lord, and I think about how Jesus' heart breaks. And I grieve for them and pray that God will reveal Himself to them in such a way that they will see the light and come to the cross.

I wonder if we think Jesus was crucified and mocked only on the day that he was nailed to the cross; as a matter of fact, He is crucified daily every time someone mocks and rejects Him. Jesus still asks the Father to forgive them for they know not what they do. We must continue to spread the good news to those around us.

November 12-13

WATER FOR THE WEEKEND

THE SHINING LIGHT
by William Cowper

My former hopes are fled,
My terror now begins;
I feel, alas! That I am dead
In trespasses and sins.

Ah, whither shall I fly?
I hear the thunder roar;
The Law proclaims Destruction nigh,
And Vengeance at the door.

When I review my ways,
I dread impending doom:
But sure a friendly whisper says,
"Flee from the wrath to come."

I see, or think I see,
A glimmering from afar;
A beam of day, that shines for me,
To save me from despair.

Forerunner of the sun,
It marks the pilgrim's way;
I'll gaze upon it while I run,
And watch the rising day.

November 14

THE IMAGE OF GOD

Genesis 1: 27 So God created man in his own image. In the image of God he created him, male and female he created them.

What is your perception of what God looks like? I'm not talking about His physical appearance. There are those who have painted pictures of Jesus, but since nobody has actually seen him we can't possibly know what he looks like physically.

Although we don't have that knowledge, we do have the knowledge of what His character looks like. He gives us pictures of Himself and His nature all through His Word. I don't believe that it is the physical appearance, but the appearance of our souls that He made in His image. Unfortunately, because of Adam's sin, many no longer look like Him.

While I was talking to my daughter this week she quoted someone she had heard; He said, "God created man in His own image, and man keeps trying to return the favor." I think the man who said that was right on target. I believe that there are many who don't really want to look like their Father, so they try to change His image to look the way that they want Him to look.

If we are His children we most certainly should look like Him. Maybe we should ask ourselves if we are the image of our Father. If we look in our hearts for the answer and the answer is no, we should have a spiritual make-over. I want to look just like my Father, don't you?

November 15

THE MEASURE OF SUCCESS

Ecclesiastes 2:10-11 I denied myself nothing my eyes desired; I refused my heart no pleasure, My heart took delight in all my work, and this was the reward for all my labor. Yet when I surveyed all that my hands had done and what I had toiled to achieve, everything was meaningless, a chasing after the wind; nothing was gained under the sun.

The world measures success in how much we have materially. They admire those who have amassed great fortunes. They perceive them as people who have gained all that they need to be happy. It attracts people of little substance and pulls them in by a desire to be just like them. Money does not buy happiness or contentment. On the contrary, most of the tine it leads to a feeling of emptiness: An emptiness that can only be filled by Jesus.

Solomon was a wise man, a man of great wealth, but when all was said and done, he looked back and saw that it meant nothing at all. *What good is it for a man to gain the whole world, yet forfeit his soul? Or what can a man give in exchange for his soul? Matthew 16:26*

In my eyes those who are successful, are the ones who have put their love and energy in serving the Lord. It is a wealth that will last. Jesus said, *"Do not store up for yourselves treasures on earth, where moth and rust destroy, and where thieves break in and steal. But store up for yourselves treasures in heaven, where moth and rust do not destroy, and where thieves do not break in and steal. For where your treasure is, there your heart will be also." Matthew 6:19-21:* Where is your heart?

November 16

THANKS AND GRATITUDE

Luke 17:15-17 One of them, when he saw he was healed, came back, praising God in a loud voice. He threw himself at Jesus feet and thanked him—and he was a Samaritan. Jesus asked, "Were not all ten cleansed? Where are the other nine? Was no one found to return and give praise to God except this foreigner?"

As I was reading this passage of scripture about the 10 lepers who were healed, I thought how ungrateful the other nine were. They didn't even thank God for what He had done for them. Only one of them approached Jesus with gratitude and praise, and he was the foreigner.

How many times does God answer our prayers and we fail to thank Him for meeting our needs? I fear that the answer to that question is, far too many. We have something to praise God for everyday of our lives. Each night when we are ready to retire, we should give God thanks for the un-noticed miracles of the day. We should thank Him for every one of the blessings that He has given us.

Yes, our God is worthy to be praised, honored, loved and adored. Let's give Him thanks for all things.

November 17

WHO IS IN CONTROL?

Psalms 118:8-9 It is better to take refuge in the Lord than to trust in man. It is better to take refuge in the Lord than to trust in princes.

We have all had times when we needed direction, instruction, encouragement and wisdom about how to handle situations in our life. We have searched for ways to handle the raging battles that seem impossible to win; and the high mountains that seem too high to climb. We so often look for our own solutions, by seeking out other people.

Why do we try to control our lives? Is it because we don't trust God? Do we think that someone else is better qualified? Or could it be that we don't want God in control? Even in times that we are able to control certain situations; it might be detrimental to us if we haven't sought God's wisdom. I guarantee you that there will come a time in every ones life, when we will encounter a situation that is out of our control.

I read a statement the other day and I know that it is true: 'When you relinquish the desire to control your future, you obtain happiness.' Only God knows what is best for us and we can take refuge in Him. He is our refuge and our strength in all things. *Give thanks to the Lord, for he is good; his love endures forever. Psalms 118:29*

November 18

WEALTH OR WISDOM

Proverbs 17:16 Of what use is money in the hand of a fool, since he has no desire to get wisdom?

We live in a world where earthly wealth is esteemed. People are driven by their desire for money and the things that money can by. They admire those people who are rich by the world's standards. They falsely believe that if they obtain earthly wealth then they will be happy. But they are so wrong: I have known many people who are rich by the world's standard, and they are the most unhappy, miserable people in the world.

Whoever loves money never has money enough; whoever loves wealth is never satisfied with his income. This too is meaningless. Ecclesiastes 5:10. Some people spend their lives in the pursuit of money at the expense of their spiritual needs. They never seem to have the desire to gain the knowledge of God: The one and only one who can bring happiness and contentment.

"No one can serve two masters. Either he will hate the one and love the other, or he will be devoted to the one and despise the other. You cannot serve both God and Money. Matthew 6:24. Jesus himself spoke these words. If we are so consumed with the love of money, we cannot possibly give attention to the things of God.

Now I am not saying that it is a sin to have money, rather it is what we do with it and where we place it in our hearts that matters. Do we love money and what it can buy more than we love God and the things that He has to offer? *1 Timothy 6:10 For the love of money is the root of all kinds of evil.* When we put anything before God, they become our idol and our first commandment says that we shall have no other gods before Him.

Let's pursue the wisdom of God instead of money. In doing so we will gain wealth beyond measure—the wealth of God.

November 19-20

WATER FOR THE WEEKEND

THE SOWER
by William Cowper

Ye sons of earth prepare the plough,
　Break up your fallow ground;
The sower is gone forth to sow,
　And scatter blessings round.

The seed that finds a stony soil
　Shoots forth a hasty blade;
But ill repays the sower's toil,
Soon wither'd, scorch'd, and dead.

The thorny ground is sure to balk
　All hopes of harvest there;
We find a tall and sickly stalk,
　But not the fruitful ear.

The beaten path and highway side,
　Receive the trust in vain;
The watchful birds the spoil divide,
　And pick up all the grain.

But where the Lord of grace and power
　Has bless'd the happy field,
How plenteous is the golden store
The deep-wrought furrows yield!

Father of mercies, we have need
　Of thy preparing grace;
Let the same Hand that give me seed
　Provide a fruitful place!

November 21

GIVE THANKS IN ALL THINGS

1 Thessalonians 5:16-18 Be joyful always; pray continually; give thanks in all circumstances, for this is God's will for you in Christ Jesus

As we enter this week of Thanksgiving many of us are thinking about the preparations of the feast that we will enjoy together with our loved ones. It is a joyful time for most of us as we gather together in fellowship.

This is not necessarily true for everyone. There are many who are suffering in one way or another, and it will be difficult for them to offer up thanksgiving to the Lord. God's word says to be thankful 'in' all circumstances, not 'for' all circumstances. We surely know that God does not expect us to be thankful for tragedies in our life. But every Christian can give thanks to God for being our peace in the midst of every tragedy and storm. He is there for us, walking right beside us, carrying us through the storms. He will take every circumstance and use it for the good of those who love Him. And for that, we can give Him thanks.

As we gather together to offer thanks to God for all of our blessings, let's especially remember those who are going through difficult times in their life and lift them up in prayer.

November 22

THANKSGIVING

Psalm 100:4 Enter his gates with thanksgiving and his courts with praise; give thanks to him and praise his name.

In this season of Thanksgiving, let's just pause to thank the Lord for all of His blessings. He is our Heavenly Father, He has, and is, and always will be all that we need. As Christians, we can truly give thanks in all circumstances. Don't dwell on the circumstances around us that may look bad, but look to God and His glorious Grace that supplies all of our needs.

We have so much to be thankful for. We live in a country where we are still free to worship—-many don't. We have roofs over our heads—-many don't. We have clothes on our back—-many don't. We have beds to lay our heads on—-many don't. We have food to eat—-many don't. We have families to love—-many don't.

This Thanksgiving let's pray for others who are less fortunate than we are. Let's concentrate on our blessings and what God has given us, instead of the things we desire.

Let's just Praise the Lord and give Him Thanks for all things.

November 23

I GIVE YOU THANKS

1 Thessalonians 5:16-17 Be joyful always; pray continually; give thanks in all circumstances, for this is God's will for you in Christ Jesus.

Thanksgiving comes and goes every year, and we celebrate the day as we get together with family and friends. Some even verbalize what they are thankful for. It is a wonderful day to give thanks.

I wonder though if we give thanks to God everyday for all the things that He has done for us. Even in times when our circumstances would not seem like something to give thanks for. God's word says to give thanks in all circumstances. Sometimes it is the difficult times that God allows to come in our lives, which help us grow. I am reminded of a time a few years back that I was incapacitated for a period of time with a broken leg. It was one of the most precious times in my life. It allowed me time with the Lord that I may never have taken otherwise.

Most of all I give thanks to God for the salvation that is mine because of His death and resurrection. *Thanks be to God for His indescribable gift. 2 Corinthian 9:15.* O the amazing grace of God.

November 24

SHARING HIS LOVE IN MARRIAGE

2 Samuel 6: 16, 20, 21, 22. As the ark of the Lord was entering the City of David, Michal daughter of Saul watched from a window. And when she saw King David leaping and dancing before the Lord, she despised him in her heart. When David returned home to bless his household Michal daughter of Saul came out to meet him and said "How the king of Israel has distinguished himself today, disrobing in the sight of the slave girls of his servants as any vulgar fellow would." David said to Michal, "It was before the Lord, who chose me rather than your father or anyone from his house when he appointed me ruler over the Lord's people Israel—I will celebrate before the Lord. I will become even more undignified than this, and I will be humiliated in my own eyes. But by these slave girls you spoke of, I will be held in honor."

Can you just imagine this argument in the house of David after He had celebrated bringing the ark into the city? He came into his house to celebrate with joy and to bless his family. Instead he was met by a furious wife berating him and accusing him of being naked in front of all the people. In fact he wasn't naked at all; he had simply changed his kingly garments for those of the common man. He loved the Lord far and above his position as king. Obviously, Michal did not share in his love of the Lord. She was more concerned about their status of being the royal family. She was humiliated because of David's love for the Lord and his total abandonment to show that love to the world.

How said this story is. A marriage that started out with love, but because one of the partners did not love the Lord that marriage was destroyed. I wonder how many today are having that same problem. One partner loves the Lord while the other one shows contempt for that love. One will not compromise their love for the Lord and the other will not succumb to the love that God wants to pour out to them. One wants to be a blessing to their spouse through the love of Christ, but the other wants no part of it. This is a marriage that will never find contentment unless the rebellious one sees the error of their ways and turns to the Lord. There are loving relationships in the Lord's Church today that are destined for this same disaster because the love of Christ is not shared. One is in love with the Lord and the other is in love with the world.

How is it in your family? Do you serve the Lord? Are you prepared to humble yourself before the entire world in spite of where your mate is in their relationship with God? We must pray for our marriages. If you are a Christian and your mate isn't, pray that God will reveal Himself to them in such a way that they will surrender their hearts to Him. Every Christian must do all they can to win their mates to the Lord while never compromising their love of God.

November 25

WISE WORDS

Matthew 12:36-37 But I tell you that men will have to give account on the day of judgment for every careless word they have spoken. For by your words you will be acquitted, and by your words you will be condemned.

While walking into a retail store awhile back, I witnessed an enraged mother literally asking God to damn her child. I was struck by the enormity of what her words were saying and I was heart sick to think of what her child must be feeling. The child was around 3 years old; I pray that he was too young to remember what damaging words his mother said; I pray that he doesn't hear such things on a daily basis, for I suspect that if she has no control in public, she probably is worse in a private setting.

The bible has much to say about the tongue and how we use it. *James 3:6 The tongue also is a fire, a world of evil among the parts of the body. It corrupts the whole person, sets the whole course of his life on fire, and is itself set on fire by hell. Verse 8-9 No man can tame the tongue. It is a restless evil, full of deadly poison. With the tongue we praise our Lord and Father, and with it we curse men, who have been made in God's likeness.* This is a very serious matter considering that we will have to give an account for every word that we have spoken. We ought to be conscientious about how we use our tongue.. *For out of the overflow of the heart the mouth speaks. Matthew 12:34b* If our hearts are centered on God, we will certainly not purposely hurt someone with hateful and damning words. Do we seek the heart of God? Do we weigh the words that come from our mouth with what is in our heart? Do we understand that when we damn others, we are damning our Lord? We are made in the image of God; we must remember that and speak accordingly.

November 26-27

WATER FOR THE WEEKEND

THE WAITING SOUL
by William Cowper

Breathe from the gentle south, O Lord,
And cheer me from the north;
Blow on the treasures of thy word,
And call the spices forth!

I wish, Thou knowest, to be resign'd,
And wait with patient hope;
But hope delay'd fatigues the mind,
And drinks the spirits up.

Help me to reach the distant goal;
Confirm my feeble knee;
Pity the sickness of a soul
That faints for love of Thee!

Cold as I feel this heart of mine,
Yet, since I feel it so,
It yields some hope of life divine
Within, however low.

I seem forsaken and alone,
I hear the lion roar;
And every door is shut but one,
And that is Mercy's door.

There, till the dear Deliverer come,
I'll wait with humble prayer;
And when He calls His exile home,
The Lord shall find him there.

November 28

DON'T MISS YOUR CHANCE

Ecclesiastes 9:11 I have seen something else under the sun: The race is not to the swift or the battle to the strong nor does food come to the wise or wealth to the brilliant or favor to the learned; but time and chance happen to them all.

Each one of us is given the time, the chance and the opportunity to do the work that God has called us to do. We may not feel qualified but God does not call the equipped, He equips the called. He uses some of the most unlikely people, to do marvelous things. But His word says that time and chance happens to us all.

Let's not miss the opportunity to share the love of Christ. Let's take the time to minister to others. And by all means let's not miss the chance to do our job, because we may never have it again. No matter who we are, God has given us all that we need, through Christ Jesus, to carry out His commission to us.

November 29

ANGER AND REGRET

Esther 2:1 Later when the anger of King Xerses had subsided, he remembered Vashti and what she had done and what he had decreed about her.

King Xerses had summoned Vashti to come to the lavish banquet that he had thrown for all of his nobles and officials and other prominent people, in order to show off her beauty. She refused him and he was embarrassed and very angry. He allowed others to fuel the flame of anger and therefore abandoned her from ever entering his presence again. When his anger subsided he longed for her, but because of the decree, she could not come back. I believe that King Xerses regretted his decision to alienate Vashti, but it was too late.

Sometimes in our anger we make bad decisions and many times it causes permanent damage to relationships. Have you ever done things in your anger that you have regretted? I am sure that most of us have. I don't believe that anything done in anger is ever going to be productive. We need to put a lid on our anger. I have heard it said that you should count to ten before venting your anger. That may work for some, but I doubt that it would be very affective: I would think that the anger might just be suppressed. We need to let it go completely. I think praying for a sweet spirit would be a much better way of ridding oneself of the anger in our heart, don't you? *My dear brothers, take note of this: Everyone should be quick to listen, slow to speak and slow to become angry, for man's anger does not bring about the righteous life that God desires. James 1:19-20*

November 30

OUR PROTECTOR

Daniel 6:26-27 "I issue a decree that in every part of my kingdom people must fear and reverence the God of Daniel. "For he is the living God and he endures forever; his kingdom will not be destroyed, his dominion will never end. He rescues and he saves; he performs signs and wonders in the heavens and on the earth. He has rescued Daniel from the power of the lions."

Sometimes we become so familiar with the stories in the bible that we have heard from childhood, that we can miss the wonder of it all. Daniel is one such story. We remember the excitement of Daniel being rescued from the mouths of the lions, but have we missed the reality behind the miracle?

Darius had witnessed Daniel's love and obedience to God and he saw the results of that obedience. He recognized that it was because of God's protection over Daniel that he had survived the impossible odds that men had plotted to get rid of him. He not only recognized God's grace in protecting Daniel from the lions, but he declared to the world that He was Sovereign in all His ways.

Because of Daniel's witness to King Darius, he recognized the power of God. Does our life show the world around us that we are ready to stand up for our Lord through every trial and obstacle? Let's proclaim to the world, that we will stand firm in our faith and our trust in God. God will protect us in all things. He will never fail us. His grace is sufficient for all.

December 1

A HOMERUN

Jeremiah 33:3 Call to me and I will answer you and tell you great and unsearchable things you do not know.

Kyle is the son of a relative of my husband. He is in his last year of college. Kyle has spent his life playing baseball. As I recall he went to school on a baseball scholarship. As a result of complexities and advisement errors, he was ineligible to play this year. He relates that it was a frustrating time for him, but through it all he became friends with a young man who helped him grow in his walk with the Lord. As a result everything he has been studying, and all that he has been involved with since, has led him to a discipleship program. This group is trained to help students on college campuses to come to know Christ in a personal way, to establish them in their faith, and to help equip them to reach others. It is designed to help train them in the way to study the bible, share their faith with others, build strong relationships, and serve the churches in the area.

Kyle is excited about this path that the Lord is taking him on. As I was thinking about the circumstances surrounding all that has transpired in his life this year, I thought about how God had anointed him to do this thing that He has called him to do. I believe it will be something more wonderful than he could ever imagine. Had it not been for his circumstances he may never have been aware of this program. *And we know that in all things God works for the good of those who love him, who have been called according to his purpose. Romans 8:28*

It always amazes me how God uses other people in our lives to minister to us. God has every day of our lives planned out. What a wonderful life it would be if we could only recognize that fact and obey God's call on our lives. Kyle has heard and in obedience, answered the call. I truly believe that one of these days, if Kyle still desires to play baseball, God will see to it that he will. *You did not choose me but I chose you and appointed you to go and bear fruit — fruit that will last. Then the Father will give you whatever you ask in my name. John 15:16*

Kyle may not have been able to play baseball this year, but in my opinion he has hit the most amazing homerun that he could ever have hit on a baseball field.

December 2

A WIFE'S ENTICEMENT

Genesis 3:6 When the woman saw that the fruit of the tree was good for food and pleasing to the eye, and also desirable for gaining wisdom, she took some and ate it. She also gave some to her husband, who was with her, and he ate it.

Adam was warned about eating from the forbidden tree (Genesis 2:16-17). He seemingly was ok with that: That is until Eve came along. The serpent not only enticed Eve to partake of it, but he also, through his cunningness, and Eve's weakness, enticed Adam to also partake of it.

God gave Adam a wife as a helper. But instead of Eve helping him, she enticed him to take his eyes off of what God had warned him about. Are we helpers to our husbands? Or are we hindrances to them? Are we following God's direction for being a godly wife as the bible instructs us? Or are we so enticed by the things of this world that we cunningly convince our husbands to do things that God has not ordained?

Eve was so concerned about her own desires that she didn't care about the fact that God had forbidden Adam to partake of the fruit. Being a godly wife is a serious thing. We need to be reading God's word and searching for the things that make us Godly wives. If we aren't searching for the truth in this matter, we might be easily enticed to make bad choices and, entice our husbands to also.

December 3-4

WATER FOR THE WEEKEND

TRUE PLEASURES
by William Cowper

Lord, my soul with pleasure springs
When Jesus' name I hear:
And when God the Spirit brings
The word of promise near:
Beauties too, in holiness,
Still delighted I perceive;
Nor have words that can express
The joys Thy precepts give.

Clothed in sanctity and grace,
How sweet it is to see
Those who love Thee as they pass,
Or when they wait on Thee.
Pleasant too to sit and tell
What we owe to love Divine;
Till our bosoms grateful swell,
And eyes begin to shine.

Those the comforts I possess,
Which God shall still increase,
All His ways are pleasantness,
And all His paths are peace.
Nothing Jesus did or spoke,
Henceforth let me ever slight;
For I love His easy yoke,
And find His burden light.

December 5

WE MUST BE FED

Matthew 5:6 Blessed are those who hunger and thirst for righteousness, for they will be filled.

What do you do when you are hungry? Don't you look for something to satisfy that hunger? If we don't satisfy our craving for food, the gnawing hunger will become worse; it will not be satisfied until we have eaten. Without physical food we would become weak and unable to function; without food we would soon starve to death.

Our spiritual hunger is exactly the same. We will never satisfy the hunger for God's word until and unless we satisfy the craving. We hunger for the things of the world. Sometimes we get what we think we want, only to find out that they do not satisfy our longing. Without God's Word, we will surely starve to death spiritually. *"It is written; 'Man does not live on bread alone, but on every word that comes from the mouth of God.'" Matthew 4:4*

When we hunger for righteousness, we will be filled. God has promised us that and His promises are true. Are you hungry? Look into the Word of God and lean on Him for the things that will satisfy. His word will tell you that only through Christ can we attain satisfaction for our spiritual hunger. Even Christians need to eat at His table daily, or we will feel the gnawing hunger, and become weak or maybe even starve to death.

December 6

ASK—SEARCH—BELIEVE

Jeremiah 29:13 You will seek me and find me when you seek me with all your heart.

While studying on ways to be a Godly Woman, I ran across a formula for affective prayer. I believe the man that wrote it really hit the nail on the head. This is the formula that was suggested. He called it the ASB pattern. ASK-SEARCH-BELIEVE

Are we asking God for things with the right motive? So many times I think we use God as something like a 'Santa Clause'. We pray for our own selfish desires. Even when we are praying for something serious, we sometimes say a quick prayer and then expect God to just miraculously give us what we are asking for. We must ask everything according to His will.

God says to seek Him. How do we seek Him? His Word is where we find His instructions for everything that we need. If we are truly seeking for His answers, we will take the time to seek His face, not only in prayer but in His word. *Psalms 119:105 Your word is a lamp to my feet and a light for my path.* When we earnestly seek Him, He will be found. He will instruct us in the way that we should go. He will have the answer we are looking for. It may not be an immediate answer, but He will definitely answer in His time and in His way.

Then we must believe. If we pray without believing, we are not putting our trust in the Lord. We must pray for His will, and His timing. His plan for our lives will not be thwarted, if we allow Him to be in control. We must Ask, Search, and Believe.

Proverbs 8:17
1 Chronicles 28:9
Matthew 6:33
Psalms 34:10, 119:10,

December 7

BEWARE OF GOSSIP

Proverbs 16:2 A perverse man stirs up dissension and a gossip separates close friends.

Beware of those who continuously want to gossip. Have you ever had anyone spread vicious gossip about you? I have, and it is cause for tremendous hurt in one's life, especially when it comes from one that we have believed to be a friend. Gossip not only hurts, it destroys the confidence that we have in the one spreading it.

Why do people gossip? Is it because they think it makes them look better in another's eyes? Is it because of jealousy? Is it because of anger against another? Whatever the reason, it is destructive. We should not pass on stories about anyone. You can be assured that through gossip someone is going to be hurt. If anyone comes to us with vicious rumors, we should politely change the subject and not be a party to it as we might be pulled in to believing a lie.

There are people who gossip under the guise of prayer. We must pray for discernment about those things. It is certainly not pleasing to God when we use Him to spread rumors, it greatly dishonors Him. Let's be careful about passing on anything even in asking prayer for another. If it is something personal, or something that could hurt another, we should not pass it on to others without their permission to do so; simply give it to the Lord; He is the only one who can take care of any situation.

I have heard it said that if we can't say something nice about another person—don't say anything at all. We are supposed to build one another up. *1 Thessalonians 5:13a Therefore encourage one another and build each other up.* What possible good can come from gossip? Take everything to God in prayer. We can talk to Him about anyone or anything. He loves us all and it is our privilege to take our friends to God in prayer. Let's love one another and build one another up and STOP tearing them down.

December 8

CONTENTMENT

Philippians 4:11-12 "I am not saying this because I am in need, for I have learned to be content whatever the circumstances. I know what it is to be in need, and I know what it is to have plenty. I have learned the secret of being content in any and every situation, whether well fed or hungry, whether living in plenty or in want.

We are continually searching for things to make us happy. We make the mistake of thinking that something or someone will fill the emptiness that we have inside. Some think if I just had a new house, then I would be content. Others may think a new car would satisfy them; and others say if only I had a better job, then I would have everything I need. We barely attain one of the things that we think will satisfy us, before we start seeking the next. We will always be longing for more and more in the pursuit of satisfaction? The truth is, nothing in this world will give us the contentment that Paul is speaking of except our relationship with Jesus. He supplies all of our needs.

You may be a Christian still seeking contentment through things. God wants our mind to be centered on Him and not on the things of this world. Paul said that he had <u>learned</u> to be content. That indicates to me that He himself had struggled with this issue. But he had found the secret to contentment. The only thing that will satisfy completely is our total surrender to our Lord. When we put our full trust and faith in Him—-then we can be content and happy in all circumstances.

December 9

ULTIMATE SACRIFICE

Leviticus 16:20-22 "When Aaron has finished making atonement for the Most Holy Place, the Tent of Meeting and the altar, he shall bring forward the live goat. He is to lay both hands on the head of the live goat and confess over it all the wickedness and rebellion of the Israelites—all their sins—and put them on the goat's head. He shall send the goat away into the desert in the care of a man appointed for the task. The goat will carry on itself all their sins to a solitary place; and the man shall release it in the desert."

All through the Old Testament we read about the sacrifices offered for sins. Over and over again they had to make ceremonious blood offerings. The above scripture talks about the live goat that was used to carry the sins of the people on its head. It is a picture of what Jesus did for us. He became our scapegoat. The big difference is—Jesus made the ultimate sacrifice once and for all. He paid the price with His blood to offer us salvation for eternity.

I am so thankful for the Old Testament. I have heard so many people say they don't like to read it, but how could we possibly see the need for a Savior, if we didn't read God's word in its entirety? We no longer have to offer up blood sacrifices. Jesus died as atonement for our sins. The magnitude of that is awesome. Just think of it; He carried all of our sins to the Cross. And all we have to do is accept His offering. That is not the end of the story. He rose again and now because of His death and resurrection we never have to fear death, because just as Jesus promised, we will also rise again and live forever in His presence. Oh what peace we can attain from this knowledge.

December 10-11

WATER FOR THE WEEKEND

TRUE AND FALSE COMFORTS
by William Cowper

O God, whose favorable eye,
The sin-sick soul revives,
Holy and heavenly is the joy
Thy shining presence gives.

Not such as hypocrites suppose,
Who with a graceless heart
Taste not of Thee, but drink a dose,
Prepared by Satan's art.

Intoxicating joys are theirs,
Who while they boast their light,
And seem to soar above the stars,
Are plunging into night.

Lull'd in a soft and fatal sleep,
They sin and yet rejoice;
Were they indeed the Saviour's sheep,
Would they not hear His voice?

Be mine the comforts that reclaim
The soul from Satan's power;
That make me blush for what I am,
And hate my sin the more.

'Tis joy enough, my All in All,
At Thy dear feet to lie;
Thou wilt not let me lower fall,
And none can higher fly.

December 12

FIGHTING FOR FAMILY

Nehemiah 4:14 After I looked things over, I stood up and said to the nobles, the officials and the rest of the people, "Don't be afraid of them. Remember the Lord, who is great and awesome, and fight for your brothers, your sons and your daughters, your wives and your homes."

As the Jewish people were rebuilding the walls of Jerusalem, their enemies were threatening them and trying to discourage them. But all the time Nehemiah kept praying and encouraging them to remember how awesome God is. He told them to fight for all of their family and their homes.

Our enemy (Satan) tries to discourage us by throwing all kinds of obstacles in our path. He would have us look at our negative circumstances and tell us that there is no way we can overcome them. But our God is truly an awesome God. We need to turn to Him and allow Him to give us all the equipment we need to fight our battles. He wants us to fight for our families. He wants us to be victorious through every battle, and He will see to it that we are, if we rely on Him for our strength.

Satan would love to destroy our homes and our families by telling us that there is no hope. We must fight for them; we must remember where our strength and power comes from. If you are having difficulties in your family today in any area, I would encourage you to remember that God will give you all that you need to fight the battle. He didn't just fight for Nehemiah and his family and He doesn't just fight for your brother and sister. God fights the battle for all of His children, including you. Just remember our God is great and awesome and He will see you through when you put your eyes on Him and not the circumstances around you.

December 13

CHOOSING THE PERFECT GIFT

John 3:16 For God so loved the world that he gave his one and only Son, that whoever believes in him shall not perish but have eternal life.

Now is the time of year that we start thinking about the perfect gift to give each of our loved ones for Christmas. I remember one Christmas when I was around 10 years old; I went shopping with mother for the 'perfect gift' for my father. I was allowed to pick out whatever I wanted to buy, within our budget. I chose a tie that in my eyes was beautiful; it had very bright swirls of many colors. I was so anxious for daddy to open that gift. I will never forget his response — He exclaimed how pretty it was and I was so proud of what I had picked out. I know today that daddy was being very gracious because looking back I am sure it would not have been one that he would have chosen, but I understand that it was the perfect gift for him, not because it was so wonderful, but because it came from me and he loved me and I had chosen it for him.

God chose the perfect gift for us; the gift of His Son. In His love for us He sent his one and only Son to earth as a man: He died on the cross for our sins, so that we might have eternal life. It is truly the gift that keeps on giving. Not only is it a gift for me and for you, but for everyone who will accept it. It is a gift that we can share with others.

There is a wonderful song that our choir sang called 'The Gift Goes On' — It says 'The Father gave the Son, The Son gave the Spirit, The Spirit gives us life, so we can give the gift of love — and The Gift goes on.' *Thanks be to God for his indescribable gift. 2 Corinthians 9:15* Let's share that precious gift with the world.

December 14

CHRISTMAS MEMORIES

For by grace you have been saved through faith, and that not of yourselves; it is the gift of God. Ephesians 2:8

Every year at this time I become very nostalgic as I recall past Christmas's. I have precious memories of my family gathering together to celebrate the birth of Jesus. I remember the joy and fun we had as we shared that special time; the abundant table of food, the opening of gifts, and the games that we played. Just being together was such a blessing. I get a lonely feeling for my parents and others who have gone on to be with Jesus: But then I remember that one day I will see them again. We will once again celebrate Jesus together, and He will be right in the midst of us.

It is because of the birth of Jesus, His death on the Cross, and His resurrection that we have eternal life. It is a free choice for us who are left behind, as to whether or not; we will meet Jesus and our loved ones in heaven. I can't imagine anyone wanting to miss out on the joyous reunion in the presence of our Savior. This precious gift God has given us is free; all we have to do is receive it. We can choose life or we can choose death. We can choose to be with Jesus and our loved ones or we can choose to be separated from them for eternity. The choice is ours. *For the wages of sin is death, but the gift of God is eternal life in Christ Jesus our Lord. Romans 6:23*

If you have loved ones who are with the Lord and you don't have the assurance of seeing them again; you can. Just accept the gift of Jesus. Open your heart to Him, confess your sins and He will forgive you. Then you can be certain that you will spend eternity with Jesus and your loved ones. Our Christmas memories will pale in comparison to the joy that we will have when we enter the presence of Jesus. What a gift!

December 15

LET THAT LIGHT SHINE

Mark 4:21-22 He said to them, "Do you bring in a lamp to put it under a bowl or a bed? Instead, don't you put it on its stand? For whatever is hidden is meant to be disclosed, and whatever is concealed is meant to be brought out into the open.

Every time I read this passage of scripture, I can't help but think of a friend of mine. Boy does she let her light shine. Ginni has real charisma; she has never been ashamed or embarrassed about her love and excitement for the Lord. As a result of her enthusiasm, people are always drawn to her.

God wants His light to shine through us in this dark world. When we let His light shine, others will be attracted by it. We are always more attracted to light than dark. Why shouldn't we let His light shine through us? He is Our Lord and Savior. He is the Light of the world.

December 16

PERSEVERING IN TRIALS

Blessed is the man who perseveres under trial, because when he has stood the test, he will receive the crown of life that God has promised to those who love him. James 1:12

All of us go through trials in our life, some more difficult than others. I have a friend whose 4 year old nephew is battling cancer. This family is putting their faith and trust in God. It is amazing to see how strong they are because they have the Lord whom they are depending on. They are finding peace as they put their trust in God.

How many of us are trusting in the Lord through our struggles in life? Do we moan and rail at God because we are having some difficult times? Or are we turning to Him to help us through them. God sent His Son to die on the cross so that we might have eternal life and have it more abundantly. What greater love than this? Who could understand our hurts more than our Lord? When we are His children, He will walk beside us through the good times and the bad. He understands our hurts, troubles, trials and disappointments. He does not turn His back on us. Are we turning our backs on Him? Are we walking away from the peace that He offers us through our faith and trust in Him?

In this you greatly rejoice, though now for a little while, you may have to suffer grief in all kinds of trials. These have come so that your faith, of greater worth than gold, which perishes even though refined by fire, may be proved genuine and may result in praise, glory and honor when Jesus Christ is revealed. 1Peter 1:6-7

December 17-18

WATER FOR THE WEEKEND

VANITY OF THE WORLD
by William Cowper

God gives his mercies to be spent;
Your hoard will do your soul no good.
Gold is a blessing only lent,
Repaid by giving others food.

The world's esteem is but a bribe,
To buy their peace you sell your own;
The slave of a vainglorious tribe,
Who hate you while they make you known.

The joy that vain amusements give,
Oh! sad conclusion that it brings!
The honey of a crowded hive,
Defended by a thousand stings.

'Tis thus the world rewards the fools
That live upon her treacherous smiles:
She leads them blindfold by her rules,
And ruins all whom she beguiles.

God knows the thousands who go down
From pleasure into endless woe;
And with a long despairing groan
Blaspheme the Maker as they go.

Oh fearful thought! be timely wise;
Delight but in a Saviour's charms,
And God shall take you to the skies,
Embraced in everlasting arms.

December 19

REJOICE

I will extol the Lord at all times; his praise will always be on my lips. My soul will boast in the Lord; let the afflicted hear and rejoice. Glorify the Lord with me; let us exalt his name together. Psalms 34:1-3

These first three verses of Psalm 34 have never been more encouraging as they are today. As we face uncertain days, it would be easy to slip into a depression, but that would do us no good. God wants us to rejoice in all things. He promises that His people will not perish. He will be with them through all circumstances. *The eyes of the Lord are on the righteous and his ears are attentive to their cry; Psalm 34:15.*

We look at all of the evil in the world today and are terrified at what lies ahead. Things look bleak in our human eyes, but the Lord has it all under control. He will see that justice is done. *The face of the Lord is against those who do evil, to cut off the memory of them from the earth. Psalm 34:16*

You may be fearful because of something that is going on in your personal life right now. But God is with you and will never forsake you. *The righteous cry out, and the Lord hears them; he delivers them from all their troubles. The Lord is close to the brokenhearted and saves those who are crushed in spirit. Psalm 34:17-18*

If you are facing anything today that threatens your hope and faith, don't be discouraged. God is with you through it all. He loves you and will see you through every battle. Let's rejoice knowing that God is our HOPE, our STRENGTH, and our DELIVERER. *Rejoice in the Lord always, I will say it again; Rejoice! Philippians 4:4*

If you want to restore your peace, may I suggest that you take the time to read the entire chapter of Psalm 34? I believe that your spirit will be lifted high and you will <u>REJOICE.</u>

December 20

REBELLIOUS PEOPLE

Ezekiel 3:5-6 You are not being sent to a people of obscure speech and difficult language, but to the house of Israel—not to many people of obscure speech and difficult language, whose words you cannot understand. Surely if I had sent you to them, they would have listened to you. But the house of Israel is not willing to listen to you because they are not willing to listen to me, for the whole house of Israel is hardened and obstinate.

How is one to teach people who are not willing to listen? It seems like an impossible task doesn't it? That's what God called Ezekiel to do. He said go and speak to them, whether they listen or fail to listen. I wonder how many times God has called ministers to go and preach the word to congregations that have hard hearts and closed minds. What a task!

Has God ever asked you to speak to someone that has an obstinate spirit? It is a difficult thing to do. But God has a purpose for asking us to speak His word to another. He doesn't tell us that we will sway them one way or another. Our job is to obey Him. If we don't we will be held accountable. *When I say to a wicked man, 'You will surely die, and you do not warn him or speak out to dissuade him from his evil ways in order to save his life, that wicked man will die for his sin, and I will hold you accountable for his blood. Ezekiel 3:18* Wow, that's a very scary thought. Let's ponder that a minute or two. Do we want to be held accountable for someone missing out on heaven?

December 21

JOY TO THE WORLD

Isaiah 55:12 You will go out in joy and be led forth in peace; the mountains and hills will burst into song before you and all the trees of the field will clap their hands.

As I sit in the silence of the morning, I am reminded of the beautiful carols that are sung proclaiming the peace and joy of the birth of our Savior. I think about the day of His birth, the lowly manger, the stillness of the morning, the love that permeated around the lowly stable, the awesome feeling that Mary and Joseph must have felt as they looked upon their son, knowing that he was a Holy Child. I think about what this birth meant to the whole world. I think about the wonderful gift, this precious one, sent for one purpose—to be the Savior of the world.

What an amazing picture—the birth of our Savior. What an amazing love—the love of our Lord. What an amazing peace—the peace that our Lord provides. O what joy—the joy that is ours when we grasp the true meaning of Christmas. It should fill our heart to overflowing. It should make us want to shout to the world that—JESUS CHRIST HAS COME—HE IS OUR KING—HIS KINGDOM WILL LIVE ON THROUGHOUT ETERNITY—HE IS OUR GIFT FROM GOD.

Without Jesus, there is no Christmas: There is no peace; and there is no joy. When we sing Joy to the World, Our Lord has come; let's truly hear the words of the song, not just in our ears, but in our heart.

December 22

JOY IN CHRISTMAS

Luke 2:10-11 But the angel said to them, "Do not be afraid, I bring you good news of great joy that will be for all the people. Today in the town of David a Savior has been born to you; he is Christ the Lord.

Far too many times I have heard people say; "I will be so glad when Christmas is over." I would be less than truthful if I didn't admit that there have been times when I myself have either said it or thought it. Why do we have that attitude? It is because we are caught up in the human celebration of Christmas, rather than what the real celebration is for.

We celebrate CHRISTmas because it is the birth of our Lord and Savior. There would be no Christmas without Him. Yet we allow ourselves to get so busy and overwhelmed with the preparation and activities of the season, we don't even focus on why we are celebrating. In the rush of our busy schedules, we lose the joy of what it is all about.

The birth of Jesus is the most wonderful thing in the world to celebrate. Let's not get so consumed with the activities of preparation of the season that we lose the joy and message of why He came. He came to be our Lord and Savior. Now that is something to celebrate with Joy.

December 23

JUMPING FOR JOY

Luke 1:41 When Elizabeth heard Mary's greeting, the baby leaped in her womb, and Elizabeth was filled with the Holy Spirit.

Luke 1:57 When it was time for Elizabeth to have her baby, she gave birth to a son. Her neighbors and relatives heard that the Lord had shown her great mercy and they shared her joy.

One Sunday our minister preached on this passage of scripture. I have thought about it a great deal since then. This is a beautiful story about two women favored by God; Elizabeth the mother of John the Baptist, a prophet of the most high, and Mary the mother of Jesus, the Savior of the world. Scripture tells us that Mary spent three months with Elizabeth before she returned home.

As you read this story you can just feel the excitement of Elizabeth and Mary as they discuss the birth of their sons. The birth of any baby is exiting. I doubt that either mother knew the magnitude that their sons would be to the world. We now know the complete story, and should be jumping for joy as we realize the gift that was given to us. What more exciting story than the birth of the one who was sent to earth as a baby, raised as a man, sacrificed for our sins, so that we could have eternal life; King of Kings, Lord of Lords, Our Savior. Just like John in Elisabeth's womb, we should jump for joy at the sound of Jesus name. We should share our joy with the world around us. What a conversation topic—-the birth of Jesus.

This is Christmas Eve, one of the most exciting times of the year. But we don't have to be excited just this time of the year. Let's carry that excitement with us everyday—what is more exciting than talking about our Lord and Savior. Every other conversation is dull in comparison to talking about Jesus and what He has done for us. Let your inhibitions go and jump for joy at the name of Jesus

December 24-25

WATER FOR THE WEEKEND

WALKING WITH GOD
by William Cowper

Oh! for a closer walk with God,
A calm and heavenly frame;
A light to shine upon the road
That leads me to the Lamb!

Where is the blessedness I knew
When first I saw the Lord?
Where is the soul-refershing view
Of Jesus and his word?

What peaceful hours I once enjoyed!
How sweet their memory still!
But they have left an aching void,
The world can never fill.

Return, O holy Dove, return!
Sweet the messenger of rest!
I hate the sins that made thee mourn
And drove thee from my breast.

The dearest idol I have known,
Whate'er that idol be,
Help me to tear it from thy throne,
And worship only thee.

So shall my walk be close with God,
Calm and serene my frame;
So purer light shall mark the road
That leads me to the Lamb.

December 26

REPENTANCE & REST

Isaiah 30:15 This is what the Sovereign Lord, the Holy One of Israel says: "In repentance and rest is your salvation, in quietness and trust is your strength, but you would have none of it.

When we are promised that in repentance and rest, we will find strength and salvation, why would we not choose it? I believe that basically, the sinful man wants to be their own boss; they want to follow the desires of their own selfish ambitions. They don't want to put their faith and trust in one that they cannot see. They want to control their own destiny. It is such a tragedy when people go their own way, walking blindly in to a destruction zone. God will allow us to do that, and in so doing, we will never find rest and contentment. Only through Christ and His shed blood, will we ever find lasting peace. Only through Christ will we find completeness. Only through Christ will we have eternal life.

Isaiah 30:18 Yet the Lord longs to be gracious to you; he rises to show you compassion. For the Lord is a God of justice. Blessed are all who wait for him. What a wonderful God we serve; even after we have gone our own way ignoring Him, He is willing and desiring for us to come to Him. He is a just God. He is a compassionate God—who forgives our every sin.

Perhaps you have never given your life to Christ. If not, look to Him for your salvation. Perhaps you have received Christ at some time in your life, but have gotten off of the path that He wants you to travel. Return to Him with a willingness to surrender all and allow Him to lead you where He wants you to go. He is a loving, forgiving God ready to welcome us with open arms. Praise His Holy Name and rest in His arms.

December 27

SPEAK OUT

John 4:39 Many of the Samaritans from that town believed in him because of the woman's testimony, "He told me everything I ever did."

As I was reading this story about the woman at the well, the above scripture really popped out to me. I don't know how I read over it time and time again without seeing such an important message in this one verse. Suddenly I saw how very important it is to tell others about Jesus. What if this woman hadn't shared her experience of her encounter with Jesus? Some of them may never have become believers.

We have a responsibility to testify to others of what Jesus has done for us. Each one of us has a different account of what He has done in our lives. But the bottom line is the same. Jesus is the Savior of the world. People need to hear all about how He has saved us and forgiven us, and redeemed us. There may be people who are desperate to hear the salvation story and we may be just the ones that they are looking to hear from.

There have been times when I have struggled about whether or not to testify about what God has done for me; simply because I did not want to point to myself and be accused of being 'holier than thou'. I finally realized that I must tell my story because it is the only way to show God's Mercy and His Grace. Jesus said, *"I tell you,"* he *replied, "if they keep quiet, the stones will cry out." Luke 19:40*

Let's not be afraid to proclaim the word of God through our personal testimony. There may be those who need to hear from you. They may be experiencing the same things that you have experienced. They may be encouraged by your story and be saved.

December 28

WORKING FOR THE LORD

Colossians 3:23 Whatever you do, work at it with all your heart as working for the Lord, not for men, since you know that you will receive an inheritance from the Lord as a reward. It is the Lord Christ you are serving.

Wow, just think of that—are we doing everything as if we are doing it for the Lord? That's something to ponder. I wonder what would happen if we consciously consider that idea as we go about our daily tasks and activities. I think it would give us a brand new enthusiasm for doing the tasks before us. What an attitude adjustment we would make if we really stopped to consider the fact that we are doing it for the Lord.

I don't think that this scripture is talking just about our salary based tasks. It says whatever we do. It doesn't matter whether we are cooking, cleaning, ironing, playing with our children or grandchildren, or doing the Lord's work. If we think about doing them for the Lord, it would take on an eagerness and enthusiasm that we haven't had before.

If there is a task that you really don't enjoy, stop and think about whom you are doing it for. I think we all might have a change of attitude when we realize that we will be doing it to please God.

December 29

RIGHTEOUS

Romans 9:30 What then shall we say? That the Gentiles, who did not pursue righteousness, have obtained it, a righteousness that is by faith; but Israel, who pursued a law of righteousness, has not attained it. Why not? Because they pursued it not by faith but as if it were by works. They stumbled over the' stumbling stone."

There are many people who are turned off by the expression a 'righteous person'. I used to think that people, who believed themselves to be righteous, were people who were 'holier than thou'. That is until I met Jesus at the Cross.

What makes a person righteous? Self righteousness is not righteousness at all. There is no other way to attain righteousness outside of Jesus. No matter how good a person is and no matter how many good things one does, they will never attain righteousness. It is only because of the Cross and the price that Jesus paid for our sins, it is only because of God's grace and mercy; it is only when we accept His gift of salvation that we become righteous people

Jesus has given us so much through His righteousness granted to us through his sacrifice. If you have a concordance bible, I encourage you to take the time to look up the scriptures on righteousness to see what it means to us as children of God. We are truly blessed through the righteousness of our Lord and Savior.

December 30

HEAVEN OR HELL

Revelation 21:2 I saw the Holy City, the new Jerusalem, coming down out of heaven from God, prepared as a bride beautifully dressed for her husband. And I heard a loud voice from the throne saying, "Now the dwelling of God is with men, and he will live with them. They will be his people, and God himself will be with them and be their God. He will wipe every tear from their eyes. There will be no more death or mourning or crying or pain, for the old order of things has passed away.

I just can't imagine the beauty of heaven, not just the physical beauty but the tranquil beauty of our spirits. There will be no more sorrow, worry, death or destruction. We will live their in the presence of God. We will be reunited as His people; only then will we live in peace together without strife. We will be in one accord, we will all love one another as we should and their will be peace forever and forever. Who would not want to live for eternity in a place like that?

Compare Heaven with Hell. *Matthew 26:41 "Then he will say to those on his left, 'Depart from me, you who are cursed, into the eternal fire prepared for the devil and his angels." Luke 13:28 "There will be weeping there, and gnashing of teeth, when you see Abraham, Isaac and Jacob and all the prophets in the kingdom of God, but you yourselves thrown out.*

I heard someone say one day that she didn't care whether she went to Heaven or to hell as long as her friends were there. I was heart sick when she said that because I realized that she did not have a clue about the hereafter. Not only will those in hell be in physical torment but they will be in emotional torment forever and ever. Just imagine living in a place like that and looking up to see God and all of His loved ones living in absolute paradise while you are living for eternity in the fires of hell separated from them all.

God has prepared a place in Heaven for all those who have made covenant with Him through the blood of Jesus. How about you? Have you made a covenant with Him? Will your eternal home be in Heaven or in Hell?

December 31

WATER FOR THE WEEKEND

WELCOME TO THE TABLE
by William Cowper

This is the feast of heavenly wine,
And God invites to sup;
The juices of the living Vine
Were press'd to fill the cup.

Oh! Bless the Saviour, ye that eat,
With royal dainties fed;
Not heaven affords a costlier treat,
For Jesus is the bread.

The vile, the lost, He calls to them;
Ye trembling souls, appear!
The righteous in their own esteem
Have no acceptance here.

Approach, ye poor, nor dare refuse
The banquet spread for you;
Dear Saviour, this is welcome news,
Then I may venture too.

If guilt and sin afford a plea,
And may obtain a place,
Surely the Lord will welcome me,
And I shall see his face.

EPILOGUE

W e have spent 365 days together. Although we have never met, I pray that this time spent exploring His word has strengthened your faith and given you hope and encouragement. I trust that within this book there was something that spoke to your heart. God's word never returns to us void. It is truly the 'Bread of Life' and the 'Living Water' that quenches the thirst of those who are dying for lack of it.

If you have journeyed through days of dryness and found a soothing, cool drink within these pages, then you've discovered the well that never runs dry. His name is Jesus and He is the One you've been seeking. I'd love to introduce you to Him. Today, you can choose to make Jesus your personal Savior. I've provided a prayer for you to follow or you may want to use your own words. It doesn't matter how you say it as long as you pray sincerely from your heart to invite Jesus in.

Dear Jesus,

I believe that you are the Son of God and that you are the Savior of all who accept you. I am a sinner and I ask that you come into my heart and cleanse me from all sin. I desire to know you as my personal Savior. Forgive me for all of my transgressions and lead me to a full understanding of you and your will for my life.

In Jesus Name I pray,
Amen

9 781609 575496